Our Common Ground

Our Common Ground

Bruce Caines

Crown Publishers, Inc.
New York

I dedicate this book to Mom and Dad, my most positive role models;

to the children who I hope will learn the lesson of self-esteem;

and to the memory of my aunt Leona Edwards, who was like a second mother to me.

Published by Crown Publishers, Inc., 201 East 50th Street, New York, New York 10022.
Member of the Crown Publishing Group. Random House, Inc. New York, Toronto, London, Sydney, Auckland

CROWN is a trademark of Crown Publishers, Inc.

Manufactured in Singapore

Book design by Kay Schuckhart

Library of Congress Cataloging-in-Publication Data

Caines, Bruce, 1959–
Our common ground: portraits of Blacks changing the face of America / by Bruce Caines. -- 1st ed.
1. Afro-Americans--Biography. 2. Afro-Americans--Portraits.
I. Title.
E185.96.C12 1994   93-2355
920'.009296073--dc20   CIP

ISBN 0-517-59443-9
10 9 8 7 6 5 4 3 2 1
First Edition

Our Common Ground was sponsored by and photographed exclusively on Fuji Film.
Main photographs were taken with Hasselblad cameras.
Trans World Airlines is the official carrier of the Common Ground Project.
Additional photography created with cameras provided by Minolta Corporation.
Additional equipment provided by Calumet Photographic.

A portion of the proceeds from the sale of *Our Common Ground* will be donated to youth-oriented outreach programs.

Author's Note

On December 10, 1991, while returning home from a family gathering in South Africa, Headman Shabalala, a founding member of Ladysmith Black Mambazo, was killed in a baffling shooting. As Headman was driving home, his pickup truck was forced off the road by an off-duty white security guard working for a private firm. Twenty-six-year-old Sean Nicholas claimed he was attempting to make a citizen's arrest of Headman, who he alleged was driving recklessly. Nicholas claimed Headman grabbed for his gun and, in the struggle for control, it accidently went off.

The attorney for Headman's family was outraged when, after a hearing which lasted no more than two minutes, Nicholas was released on his own recognizance after posting a $360 bond. This was despite the

Lisa Bernad

fact that police reports stated Headman was found sitting in his truck, killed by one bullet through his mouth, something that seems improbable if Headman was struggling to get control of the gun.

Ultimately, though he felt that Sean Nicholas was lying about the course of events, the judge had to allow a conviction of a lesser charge—the equivalent of manslaughter as opposed to murder—because there was not enough evidence to prove Nicholas's intent.

Headman Shabalala was a gentle and loving man. It is a tragedy to see his or anyone else's life end needlessly, particularly under such violent circumstances. It appears a Black man's life in South Africa continues to be worth very little. My sincerest sympathies are extended to Headman's family and friends.

Contents

A c k n o w l e d g m e n t s

If there is one thing I learned while creating *Our Common Ground,* it's that you can't do anything by yourself. So many people, with little or nothing to gain, have helped make this book a reality. I cannot begin to thank them adequately, but I will try.

First, I must thank God for the gifts he gave me that allowed me to create something to share with the world and be proud of. Thank you to all of my family and friends who gave me encouragement, ideas, the names of people to check out, who loaned me money and understood why I became antisocial for two of the four years I worked on this project. Specifically, I want to thank my mother and father, David and Inez Caines, for all of the above, for their love, and even for their unabashed boasting to anyone who couldn't run away fast enough.

Thanks to my brother Dwight for his common sense, writing skills, and knowledge; my brother Vance and cousin Sandé Edwards for their artistic skills, which helped me to sell this thing; and to the world's best transcribers, my mom and my cousin Debbie McGee.

Special thanks to my best friend, Jack "Lin Ho" Lindholm, for his encouragement, his darkroom, and his creative assistance—I couldn't have done this without you; "The Great" Jim Barber, friend, mentor, and the only white guy I know with (almost) as much soul as James Brown; my good friend and favorite photo assistant, Sherry Knable, who from the beginning worked for no pay because she believed in the project; Janet Maya and Gavin Wilson, who also gave their time and talents as my second set of hands and extra brain; Ken "Kenzo" Fukae, who put me up, fed me, and played photo assistant on my West Coast swings; the late Steve Reilly, yet another victim of AIDS, who always had a place for me to stay, a kind word, and who

introduced me to the love of my life, Lisa Bernad. Thank you, Lisa, for supporting me (I mean that) and for putting up with me.

Without the efforts of the "Today" show's Mike Leonard and his crew, "The Famous" Alice, Jack, and Chuck, *Our Common Ground* might never have made it to a publisher. The same goes for Morry Alter of New York's WCBS-TV News, the man who first put me on TV. It's amazing what a little television can do for you.

To Crown Publishers' David Groff, who was determined to sell this idea to his colleagues, and to my editor, Carol "Deadline" Taylor, who with her colored pencils made my words much more intelligent—and as one of a handful of Black editors should be *in* this book—thank you. My agents, Linda Chester and Laurie Fox, who took me on mostly because they felt an emotional connection with the project, I thank you for *your* vision.

I particularly want to thank Fuji's Thomas Shay, and Nancy Madden, who twisted his arm; Marc Strachan and Deborah McDuffie for helping me look for money; special thanks to Bob Mann for his influence at TWA, and Wendy Rutkin for getting him interested.

There are several people, most of whom I have never met, who donated money, offered support, or gave me advice simply because they saw me on the "Today" show and were moved by my vision. I want to thank you all for your letters and phone calls; it means a lot to me that you went to the trouble to do that. Special thanks to Alan "Pete" Taylor, Michael and Marjorie Stern, Bill Moyers, Kelsey Kenfield, Kerry London Galloway, Diane Fitzgerald of the Marwen Foundation, Ellen Stewart, Dr. Ernest Rogers, DVM; and Ernest Pile.

Thanks to the people who may or may not realize that they did things to help me along the way: publicist Dawn Maniglia, who *never* takes no for an answer; Mary Anne Stewart, Normandy Hotel, Minneapolis, Minn.; Carroll Music, New York, N.Y.; Eclectic Encore, New York, N.Y.; Lens and Repro, New York, N.Y. (thanks, Sylvia); Tina "Tigger" Gauduin; Janet Bowblis; Allan Luftig; Dr. Lloyd Helper, University of Illinois, Urbana; Best Western Americano Beach Lodge, Daytona Beach, Fla.; Best Western Hotel Seville, Bloomington, Minn.; Best Western Hollywood, Hollywood, Calif.; Days Inns of America; Radisson Hotel, Duluth, Minn.; Saint Joseph Hospital, Omaha, Neb.; Ann LaCrosse; Annie O'Hayon; Gayle Fine; Colleen Slattery; Jolie "Jolster" Koblin; Rosaly Grunberg (makeup artist extraordinaire); Steve Rosenbaum; Jon Johnny; Jennifer Lauck; Trish Peters, for encouraging her boss, Bryant Gumbel, to do something he hates to do—talk about himself; Janet and David Haugan; the Leonard Family; Lyndon "Mr. Network" Barrois; Lester Lewis; Katie Daley; Paul Fleuranges; Jim Salzano; Melanie Penny; Adrienne Ingrum; Janet Lane; Night After Night—Mitch Goldstein and Mitch Goldman and "Sweaty."

And a very special thanks to all the people who turned their lives upside down and gave their time to be photographed and interviewed, especially those who are not included on these pages. You have my undying gratitude.

Preface

I have to admit, this is the part of the book I usually skip. I always want to get to the good part—the part I bought the book for. However, I *do* hope you will bear with me for a few moments before you move on to "the good part." If you decide to jump ahead, fine. I only ask that you eventually come back, because what I have to say to you will help you understand what *Our Common Ground* is truly about.

The idea for this project evolved initially from a completely selfish idea: I wanted to strengthen my portfolio of photographic portraits. As I began doing more and more portrait work for magazines, I was doing less and less fashion work, which was fine with me. Because, as much as I enjoy creating fashion pictures, I had grown weary of all the "fabulousness" that seemed inevitable with anything relating to the fashion business. I don't like fabulous.

The reason I thought Black celebrities would be interested in working with me—because there are relatively few photographers of color in our country—also made me stop and think about exactly what it was I was doing. How many young Black people would even think of considering photography as a career? *I* didn't. As a kid, I just liked to take pictures. For that matter, how many Black kids would think of becoming an engineer or a stonemason? And how many even know what a natural-resource biologist is, let alone that they could *be* one? What was it that allowed me to think that I could be the photographer I am now? Opportunity, exposure, and options.

My initial exposure to all the different options available to me was through my parents. Though by no means well-off, they found a way to be sure my brothers, Vance and Dwight, and I had the best that they could afford. I was well aware that not all young people of color were as fortunate as my brothers and I were when we were growing up. And this lack of exposure to opportunities and options is a disadvantage that may later prove to be insurmountable for Black children in our competitive society.

I also knew that if Black people didn't know much about themselves as a community, it stood to reason people who were *not* Black would know even less. There are countless numbers of people whose only contact with a Black person has been through television. *Our Common Ground* is an invitation I extend to everyone to get to know some wonderful Black people.

This has been a very personal experience for me in many ways. Although I spent most of my youth in a New York City housing project, it was a much more integrated place than the image that is conjured up when people hear the term "the projects." In fact, there were probably more white families where I lived than Black, and though my parents had friends of many ethnic groups, I found most of my childhood friends were white.

As much as I've cherished the friendships and experiences I had with those kids, I always felt a strange sense of alienation from my own people. It was a disturbing feeling, especially since I took such pride in being a Black person and knowing my family origins. My parents would spend hours telling my brothers and me the stories of the Black people who came before us and strove to make a place for us here. My mother would tell us of her parents' native Jamaica and her experiences growing up on New York's Sugar Hill, and my dad told of his childhood in Harlem.

Yet even with all this knowledge giving me a sense of my ethnic heritage, something prevented me from completely relating to many of my Black schoolmates. I didn't listen to the right music, I didn't use the right slang, and I didn't wear the right clothes. It took a long time actually, until I was an adult, to realize that I was buying into the *myth* of how to be Black: the myth that there was a certain way to act, or speak, or walk to be Black. It wasn't until I became more aware of who *I* was as an individual and began to respect *that* person, that I began to respect and love the *Black* person I was and am. That's when I stopped caring about the world's perception of me because I knew who I was. A Black *man*.

Yet, I still didn't know that there was another step I had to take to truly know and love that Black person; I needed to embrace and love all my Black sisters and brothers in the fullest sense, and that meant understanding them. As I spent year after year trying to create this work, a collection which hardly scratches the surface of Black beauty, strength, pride, and adversity, I began that journey. The completion and publication of *Our Common Ground* became the most important thing in my life, and I knew in many respects that for the Black community, it would be an important and oftentimes controversial statement, one which had to be made.

I became steadfast in my efforts as publishers told me it was a nice idea but they didn't believe it would sell. The audience, they contended, was too narrow, and it would, simply put, not be a profitable venture. It didn't take an astrophysicist to read between the lines: "Black people are the only ones who would be interested in this, and frankly, we're not sure they can afford it." They were wrong.

Since the time I sat in my little office at home and formulated this idea, several notable books have been released, photographically chronicling the achievements of Black people and their contributions to our world. For me, however, something seemed to be missing. I wanted to see beyond what these people were doing; I wanted to know who these people *were*. I wanted to meet them, to know how they got to where they are today. And I wanted to introduce them to you. That was my goal. I wanted young Black persons to open a book and see someone who shared not only their complexion, but also their experiences.

It's fine for a celebrity to say, "Stay in school. Don't do drugs," but it's something else to see another fourteen-year-old say, "I pushed crack. I've cleaned up my life, and I *know* I'm going to college."

Several common themes came up in my discussions with the people you will meet on these pages, but none more salient than the concept of *self-esteem*. Everything always came back to that one issue, the issue of Black people loving and respecting themselves and each other.

How can we convince young people that they can be whatever they want to be when the negative image of Black people in America is constantly before them? We blame the media for concentrating on the fifteen-year-old Black youth being escorted through a gauntlet of television cameras and reporters as he hides his head with his jacket, but what have we done as role models to counter that image? What have we done to say to young people, "You are a good person. There are things that you can do that no one else can do in quite the same way"?

As Black people, we must remove *nigger* from our vocabulary. Nigger—and it hurts me to even write it—is not a term of endearment, despite what many Black people say. It is the embodiment of disrespect, debasement, and hatred. *Webster's New World Dictionary* tells us, "it is now generally regarded as virtually taboo because of the legacy of racial hatred that underlies the history of its use among whites. . . ." Yet we hear Black people throw the word around with alarming nonchalance: "You're my nigger," "That nigger said to me, . . ." "Hey, nigger!" But, if others who are not Black dare to use that word, even with the same inflections, they can expect to feel the wrath of any Black person within earshot. Why is that? It is simple—because deep down, we know it's wrong. *We know what it means to be called a nigger!* This speaks straight to the issue of self-hatred.

I am not a nigger. Plain and simple! As a race of people who know the pain and oppression of slavery, who can relate to the internment of American Asians in *American* detention camps, or the extermination of Jews in Germany during the Second World War, who feel the pain of ethnic "cleansing" of Moslems, we should not allow *anyone* to use that word, least of all our own. When our actions say we do not demand respect from our own people, how can we expect others to give us the respect that we so tirelessly argue Black people are denied? Why we are so willing to *still* accept and use a name given to us by those who would put shackles on our feet and a bullwhip to our backs? A word that doesn't even have parity with the word *dog*. Please don't advise your children that using this word is a sign of liberation or empowerment. Using it is a sign of stupidity. It is telling that the comedian Richard Pryor, who had used this word as easily as he used his own name, said after his return from a trip to Africa that he was so moved by seeing so many beautiful Black men, women, and children that he could never use that word again.

We are African-Americans. We are Caribbean-Americans. We are Black Americans. Our blood, sweat, and tears have farmed the fields of slave owners as if they were our own. Our experience has been the shame of a nation. Our strength, resilience, and dignity are the pride of a people. We are many things, but we are first and foremost a proud people.

This book of photographs and stories celebrates the lives, the dreams, and the achievements of Black people throughout the United States. I refrain from using the term *African-Americans* for two reasons; some of the people you will meet are not American—they are African. Secondly, like myself, many of the people I have met on this journey do not consider themselves *African*-Americans; I am Caribbean-American. My parents' families came from the islands of Jamaica and St. Kitts. I know there are people who will say that my relatives only ended up there because of the slave trade, that they are originally from Africa. That may be true, but if so, then we are *all* African-Americans.

Anthropologically speaking, we know man originated on the African continent, so Irish-Americans, French-Americans, Swedish-Americans are by all accounts African-Americans, too. Many Cubans are just as dark as Africans; why are they not *Afro-Cuban*? Why is it that Black Americans are just *Black*? We have to acknowledge, accept, and revel in our diversity, because it is that difference, that experience, which has allowed us to become the creative, intellectual force that we are. *Our* backgrounds and experiences are as valid as that of any European-American. It is time we understood that simple fact.

Most of the people on the following pages you have probably never heard of; some of them you will know. I hope the celebrities you recognize will appear different to you after you have read about them here. For all their fame, they are just like the fifteen-year-old who collects cereal boxes with Black people on them. You *will* recognize that here. By the time *Our Common Ground* is published, some of the people portrayed in its pages may have gone on to do other things, but that really isn't important. Even if you don't get to this book until five years from now, their contribution to the world and the example they have set will not have changed.

So many of these people couldn't understand why I wanted to include them in this work. "I'm so *normal*," they would say to me. That was exactly my point. After we were finished talking, and they'd expressed why they do what they do, almost everyone would suddenly say, "Wow, now I know why you asked me to do this." It is their wish that I share their lives with you.

I have had a privilege and an opportunity, to which I can only hope I have done justice. I have spent four years being invited into the lives of complete strangers who have made me laugh and occasionally brought me to tears. I have made friends who will be with me for the rest of my life, and met people whom I will remember just as long. It is my wish to share that with you.

Okay, now, on to the good part.

BRUCE S. CAINES

Foreword

It was only a dream . . .

. . . and we were in it together.

We peered out cautiously, crouching behind a dry clump of brush which lined a clearing leading to the ocean's shore. The thud of footsteps trudging in unison echoed loudly across the burning sand as a seemingly endless procession of young Black men and women followed one another in single file toward the water's edge. Each youth wore a tattered sash which draped from the shoulder and was dragged and trampled along the way. Woven into the fabric of each sash were large golden letters spelling out the hidden potential of its wearer: AUTHOR, PHYSICIST, TEACHER, SURGEON, ARCHITECT, BIOLOGIST, POET . . .

An endless trail of stone-faced youth filed by us, and we watched, paralyzed with horror, as one by one they disappeared into the pounding surf. . . . PSYCHIATRIST, MATHEMATICIAN, VETERINARIAN, CHOREOGRAPHER, ENGINEER, PIANIST.

We didn't speak. We thought certainly there would be hundreds of men brandishing guns, forcing these young people to hopelessly end their lives without resistance, but there was no sign of that. All that we could see was this procession of what must have been thousands of our children headed toward certain doom. . . . SCULPTOR, RESEARCH SCIENTIST, INVENTOR, FILMMAKER, PEDIATRICIAN, HISTORIAN . . . The dismal parade continued as we stood by, idly watching.

Angry and frustrated, we turned to face one another. Glaring into each other's eyes we shook pointed fingers, each blaming the other's inaction, distracting ourselves momentarily from the painful nightmare in the clearing.

And then we realized we were not alone. There was movement along the line of brush, and we watched as others who had been hidden rushed forward, grabbed as many of the young people as they could, and led them away from the procession of hopelessness.

Though the task seemed overwhelming, we were encouraged that there were others along the line, and though many of those precious youths would be lost, we knew we must join in the rescue.

I awakened then, relieved that it was only a dream . . .

. . . and that we were in it together.

Just as it has been the task of the writer to create arresting images which are able to impact and even affect change in the reader, so has it been the task of the photographer to capture striking images which do the same. This book is a collection of such images: illuminating images that capture the spirit of Blacks in America who, despite the sea of hopelessness which roars and surges in a racist society, not only have succeeded in developing their own talents and potential, but have reached out to rescue others from the doom of that surging ocean.

What Bruce Caines has created in *Our Common Ground* is a reminder that role models need not be larger-than-life athletes and entertainers who loom far above us on their unreachable pedestals. To the contrary, more often than not, the most powerful role model is standing on the ground—someone who is close enough to reach out and help us discover those hidden talents which, if left untapped, are lost to us all forever. In fact, a role model might even be someone who, by focusing a camera on those who lead others away from the procession of hopelessness, inspires us all to join the rescue.

KATHLEEN CROSS, COUNSELOR, TEACHER, AND WRITER

Introduction

If a certain kind of camera, yet to be invented, achieved the capacity to record the instantaneous give and take between two black people meeting in the street, looking at the artifact this "camera" produces, you would see the shared sense of identity, the bloody secrets linking us and setting us apart, the names flapping in the air—Black, Negro, African-American, colored, etc., etc.—we sometimes answer to but never internalize completely because they are inadequate to describe the sense of common ground we exchange at this moment. We acknowledge the miracle and disgrace of our history in the twinkling of an eye, many, many times a day, as we meet each other, nodding or speaking or touching or just passing by, seemingly without a glance. Our ancient styles of gliding through the air can say enough, say everything that needs to be said. We are linked. I know something about you and you know something about me. Personal, intimate, revealing knowledge, though we may never have set eyes on one another before nor will again. To our everlasting shame and glory, what we may recognize first is something we are not; then because of, or in spite of that, something we are, survivors, carrying on.

Always more to us than meets the eye. Our eyes or the eyes of others who don't want to know what the more might be, who expend a lot of energy pretending there isn't more, insisting there must not be more. We carry the burden, the responsibility, the challenge and joy of creating the little extra, the something more that keeps us not exactly what we're supposed to be. What the novelist Richard Wright called a battle between blacks and whites over the nature of reality begins here, where we make up ourselves, the imagined space we preserve for ourselves and share with those others who would love us.

If we're different, who decides the meaning of that difference? Who shall create its form and who shall benefit from it?

The person similar to me because we are both different is sharing the work of giving meaning to difference. The ones who appear like us, who we meet in the street, are other answers-in-progress coping for better or worse with the puzzle of our identity. Although we can pretend not to, we see ourselves in them. How do we sustain within ourselves the determination, the grit, the voice saying yes, we can do it, yes. Not only am I surviving, out here doing, as you see, my thing, but there's more, more to me, and I'm doing that work, too. Being *me*, not what difference makes of me.

Americans of African descent share a continent, a gene pool, a history. Who we are is partly determined by this triple heritage. The complexity of each of these factors—Africa's size and ecological diversity, the gene pool's constantly percolating stew of combinations and permutations, the countless individual stories constituting the grand fabric of history—such complexity within our collective past guarantees as much variety as unity among African descended peoples. Now consider the centuries of interaction as African peoples encountered the planet beyond their home place. Clearly the potential, indeed the necessity, of diversity among African descended people exponentially increases, so drastically that any attempt to define common ground is suspect.

What do we know about a person, what can we assume or predict about their behavior if they assign themselves or we assign them membership in a group whose biological, temporal, spacial origins are so ancient and have been so implacably modified, so problematically conceived and perceived, that the most substantial evidence that the group exists, either in their own minds or ours, resides in the dogged efforts to define it, name it, ask questions about it, make predictions about its members?

Common ground. How can we seek it, understand it without slipping into talk about race? And once race enters the discussion, doesn't a net settle over our heads, capturing nothing but destroying what passes through its deadly weave? Chaos looms because *race* can mean everything or nothing. A denial of diversity. A claim of profound, unalterable difference between kinds of human beings. An empty word. A word bristling with the power of religious dogma and faith. A word obsolete, anachronistic, dysfunctional in vocabularies which attempt to model a rational, holistic version of humanity here at the dawn of the twenty-first century. A word hovering like a toxic cloud, obscuring discourse at all levels, as much a problem as it was a hundred years ago when W.E.B. Du Bois predicted that the major challenge confronting Europe and America in the twentieth century would be the question of race.

The discovery of people unlike themselves did not spark in Europeans a doctrine of cultural relativity; it produced the invention of race. Of all the weapons devised to conquer and subjugate the lands beyond Europe, the most effective, pervasive, and enduring, the one that served to coordinate, harmonize, and intensify the effects of all other weapons, was the concept of race. Soldiers who wielded the broad sword, musket, gatling gun, rockets, and bombs could slaughter, free of conscience and remorse, because the enemy belonged to a race less than human. Priests could sanction and abet the slaughter and share the booty of empire while they debated in learned councils whether or not the lesser races possessed souls. How could a race closer to wild beasts than to men own the land they occupied, govern themselves, or enter the economic life of European colonies except as slaves? The paradigm of race located within its victims the causes and justification of the victim's plight. Thus the oppressed, to the degree they internalized the message of race, became active agents of their oppression.

Dissatisfaction with European societies did produce a strain of speculation toying with the idea that the "other," the savage—American Indian, Ashanti warrior, Hottentot—might be closer to nature and thus noble in some sense. The terms of this minor dissent did not alter the hierarchical paradigm of race, the Manichean, essentialist assumption of different kinds, different orders of men. The paradigm remained intact even though a Rousseau might switch labels, invert it.

European theories of race were elaborated, as they have been since, to rationalize prerogatives of self-interest. By postulating that in other, lower orders of beings were very damaging, incapacitating, innate defects, lacunas, or wholesale global inferiority, the application of various cures (baptism, slavery, colonization, integration, search and destroy, education) or containment in its many forms (apartheid, segregation, reservations, prisons, homelands, concentration camps, missions) were not only reasonable, but humane, divinely sanctioned duties.

In this connection, the history of how subject peoples or minorities were absorbed into dominant societies, no word has as yet emerged for people of color in America who embrace the mores of the dominant group and merged into the mainstream. *Conversos* is such a word describing Jews in fifteenth-century Spain who converted to Catholicism rather than emigrate during the enforced ethnic and religious cleansing after Isabel and Ferdinand expelled the Moors who'd ruled Spain for six hundred years. Plenty of nasty, vernacular, funny/bitter words for minority members who attempt either openly (integration) or clandestinely (passing) to convert, but no official term exists for those who have crossed over because such a word would acknowledge the possibility that racial categories are permeable, not permanent. Leopards can't change their spots, can they?

Mulatto, a word we did import from Hispanic-Luso culture with its rich vocabulary of racial designations, sounds a little like *converso* and maybe it's as close as we've ever come to adopting such a word. But *mulatto*, like *mule* or *miscegenation*, a word invented just prior to the Civil War as part of a campaign of dirty tricks to discredit the anti-slavery Abolitionists, suggests a compound of immutable elements. Appearing first in a pamphlet entitled "The Theory of the Blending of the Races, Applied to the American White Man and the Negro" (1863), *miscegenation* rather quickly replaced *amalgamation* as the preferred term for propagation between blacks and whites. *Amalgamation* implies white and black could "unite into one body or organization." The neologism *miscegenation* eradicates the potential of biological unification, explicitly preserves in its etymology the divisive paradigm of race (Latin: *miscere* = mix; *genus* = race).

Though most of us have been conditioned to confuse *race* with *culture*, they are not synonymous. Nor is *race* the systematic description, classification, and analysis of what distinguishes one human group from another. The concept of race, whose presence continues to poison our society, gradually evolved during the long European diaspora to every part of the globe. The word *race* evokes a paradigm, a systematic network or pattern of assumptions, relationships, a model of reality, of history and causation as complete, closed and pervasive as a religion. Race is not a set of qualities inhering in some "other"; it's the license to ascribe such qualities allied with the power to make them stick. Race functions like Humpty-Dumpty's disconcerting habit of stipulating definitions: to surprise, destabilize, take control. Race can mean something or nothing or whatever lies between, an essentialist concept or an existential one, depending on the moment, the serviceability of a definition, its usefulness to the stipulator. Race is the ultimate *carte blanche*.

It's impossible to pin down the definition of *race* because *race* is a wild card; it means whatever Humpty-Dumpty says it means. Think of a blank screen, then seat somebody at a keyboard controlling what appears on the screen. *Race* is whatever the operator decides to punch up. The meaning of *race* is open-ended, situational, functional, predictable to some extent, but a flexible repertoire of possibilities that follow from the ingenuity of the operator privileged to monopolize the controls.

On the other hand, race signifies something quite precise about power, how one group seizes and sustains an unbeatable edge over others. When the race wild card is played, beware, the fix is in. Particularly if the word appears in a setting where some competition is occurring—a bargain, contract, ball game, courtroom, treaty, romance. Race is a clue, a sign the outcome is being rigged. Various unsavory, unfair maneuvers can be expected. Race in its function as wild card is both a sign and an enabler of these shady transactions in a game only one player, the inventor of race, can win. He always holds the winning cards because he can choose when he plays them and names their value.

One symptom of our national confusion, our multiple personality disorder in regard to race, is how we have severed the relationship between the words *race* and *racism* or *racist*. Daily, we depend on the notion of race to rationalize differences between blacks and whites, reinforcing the fictions these categories represent, in spite of all the evidence to the contrary, including the evidence of our eyes, hearts, and sexual equipment. Consider our mania for statistics. If racial breakdowns deliver more substance to measurements we take of ourselves, the omnipresence of race as a category in our counts makes race seem to count too much. Race appears to cause crime rather than be caused by a crime. Do black newborns die at three times the rate of white babies because of some factor intrinsic to blackness or because being black means they're treated by society as only one third as valuable as white newborns? Race serves almost everybody as a primal means of identifying self and others, further ensuring distance between blacks and whites. Yet the words *racist* or *racism* are usually applied only to those who admit out loud they like the way race serves us, especially those who celebrate, praise God, even swear they'll fight to the death to keep race dividing us as it does. In nice peoples' mouths *race* is a descriptive, normative, neutral term, and they feel free to employ it freely. Racists by definition aren't nice people; they embarrass the rest of us by giving race a bad name. *Race* and *racism* are equally predatory, destructive; one just wears sheep's clothes.

Ironically, the paradigm of race both insists on white supremacy and renders white people curiously innocent of their race. Beginning in the middle of the nineteenth-century whites sat, or were told they sat by other whites, at the pinnacle of power and privilege in the most privileged and powerful nation on earth. Reinforced every minute of every day to every citizen by the nation's mainstream institutions, culture, language, religion, economy, white superiority was supremely secure. White people were standard issue, nearest to God, the measuring rod for comparing other kinds of people. White might be imitated but never duplicated. Race was a difference, a deficiency stigmatizing others because they weren't, never could be white. Thus, for all intents and purposes, whites viewed themselves as raceless. Except for the occasional Fourth of July oration, Klan parade, or lynching, the paradigm of race was so effectively internalized, it seldom required explicit assertion.

The recent advent of public demonstrations of white power, neo-Nazi tribalism, the adoption of the language and techniques of civil rights protests of the sixties by white supremacist hate groups are signs of radical displacement. Unquestioned centrality and preeminence of white Americans at home and abroad are no longer secure. Barbarians are at the gates, in the adjacent neighborhood, the backyard. What once could be assumed as a birthright must now be negotiated. Others are laying claim to prerogatives that heretofore belonged exclusively to those who were "free, white and twenty-one."

In a legal system claiming to be colorblind, white immunity to race had been no disadvantage. In fact exactly the opposite. Since whites didn't need to go public about their race, all those court rulings favoring the majority could be perceived not as racist but simple justice. These intertwined fictions were unraveled simultaneously as courts were confronted with evidence of how race had affected their decisions. The majority's interest could no longer be treated as synonymous with everybody's interest. Or could it? If race was the basis of challenges to the legal system, why not race as the basis of a response to the challenge? The contradictions, paradoxes, fault lines in the paradigm of race were already in place. Consider the Bakke decision.

Bakke is like white minstrels who cork their skin, dance Jim Crow. His performance makes blacks blacker, whites whiter. Pretending he belongs to an oppressed race, preserves the oppressor's power.

When Africans who had been ripped away from the continent by the international trade in slaves learned the languages of Europe and entered the conversation about race, what they said about themselves, or attempted to prove about themselves, affected the theorizing about race minimally because the relationship signified by the paradigm of race devalued African contributions. Conversations inevitably were one-sided, circular. Sooner or later, often with stunning, bloody impact, the exchanges, such as they were, ended with this question: Who's in charge here? Listen to the anguished voices of the Xhosa in nineteenth-century South Africa or the Sioux in South Dakota during the same epoch. Consult the historical record for the responses of the European invaders of their lands. Race contained the answer, was answer, question, and end of discussion. Everything and nothing, depending on the message the technician operating the scoreboard chose to broadcast.

18

How can we talk about ourselves without falling into the trap of race, without perpetuating a debate we can't win because the terms of the debate already contain an understanding, a presumption of winner and loser?

Americans of African descent share a continent, a gene pool, a history, and everything else that has shaped us. Race authors one sad story, repeated far too often, that would reduce the complexity of our cultural heritage. Race preempts our right to situate our story where we choose. It casts us as minor characters in somebody else's self-elevating melodrama.

So race ain't it. Huh uh. The common ground is elsewhere; in the bonds we struggle to sever, discover, invent, sustain, celebrate. In the pages of this book we hear many stories of people trying to work out ways of living on the earth. Taken together the voices sing out a chorus of achievement. Whether the speaker is a photographer, dancer, stonemason, fashion designer, teacher, or train engineer, there is a moment of freedom, of self-revelation in their accounts when self merges with something greater than self. Strangely, miraculously, this detachment, this blending is also the surest sign of individuation. The power to let go, to become. To take a chance and—through hard work, luck, determination, fate, joy, pride, greed, hunger, whatever—push yourself past yourself to another, higher level.

Our power lies in our capacity to imagine ourselves as other than what we are. Common ground is the higher ground, spiritual and material we strive to gain.

African-American descent plays a part in each story here, a powerful role in many. Racism appears as a factor just as often. On the other hand, *race*—the doctrine of immutable difference and inferiority, the eternal strategic positioning of white over black—is given the lie by these life stories. Racism can stunt or sully or deny achievement, but the folks in this book are on the move, beyond the power of race to pigeonhole and cage. They are supplying for themselves, for us, for the future, terms of achievement not racially determined.

We don't have to lose to win. Don't need to prove ourselves in the no-win race game. Anybody who needs permission to be free isn't prepared for freedom. Anybody who understands how race works in this country—to confuse and cripple people, black and white and every color in the rainbow—will be happy to discover by looking at the faces and attending to the words in *Our Common Ground* that things don't have to work the old way.

The struggle continues. Never ends. That's one sure enough Common Ground worth sharing.

JOHN EDGAR WIDEMAN

Jim Goins and Fred Williams

At two o'clock the bell rings. It's an early bell and Mr. Fred and Mr. Jim are caught off guard. "Nobody tells us nothin' around here," says Fred as he and Jim hustle out of their office in the small building behind Markham Junior High in Compton, California. They are on their way to keep an eye on the throngs of children leaving school. "Get out of here you rug rats," Fred yells to the detainees in the office, kids who have been rounded up for cutting class or causing trouble.

The two quickly move across the street to a long stretch of railroad tracks that runs parallel to the road. A horde of children swarm across the tracks toward an opening in the fence on the other side. "Pretty quiet today," Jim observes.

"*Real* quiet," adds Fred. "That's good."

Jim explains, "These tracks separate the turfs. The kids on this side are the Bloods, and the kids on the other side are the Crips. Sometimes

things get a little heated here, so we have to keep our eyes open."

"*Damn!*" Fred vanishes. Coming around the bend, the headlight of a freight train cuts through the dust stirred up by the feet of the children. Fred is sprinting across the tracks, deftly keeping his footing on the gravel and hurrying kids to safety. He takes a position near the one opening in the fence, as he has obviously done a hundred times before.

Meanwhile, Jim is on the other side of the tracks, racing up and down directing children to hurry across. An earsplitting horn blast erupts from the train, and in a matter of seconds it is virtually on top of the mass of children. Jim has managed to stop most of the kids, but a few daredevils insist on playing chicken with the train—dancing in front of it.

The train does not slow down and the horn shrieks a long steady blast—tearing through the air. On the other side of the tracks Fred and the children hunch over and hold their ears just as the train roars by, blocking them from view.

Jim, holding his ears, looks down the tracks one last time. A boy is on his back in the middle of the tracks, legs flailing. Without hesitation, Jim runs toward the boy as the freight train blasts its horn with no intention of slowing down. In an instant, the flailing boy leaps up and darts to safety on the other side. Jim angrily punches the air and yells something that is smothered by the continuous horn blast and the sound of rolling steel.

Jim is visibly upset. "Jesus!" he exclaims as the roar moves into the dis-

tance. "We have been trying to get them to do something about this for *years*. The city finally put up a fence after three years of fighting. At least with the one opening it means the kids have to head to *one* point.

"They promised us that they would build an overpass this year, but they promised that *last* year. Every year there is at least one amputation and one death. That's when they make their promises."

In 1985, Jim Goins and Fred Williams did not know each other. They each knew, however, that they needed work. The two took jobs as campus aides at the 102nd Street Elementary School in Watts, a part of Los Angeles that has suffered from the pain of poverty, gang violence, and drugs. Fred is a homeboy. Someone from the neighborhood. Jim, on the other hand, is from Riverside, a suburb of Los Angeles County.

The two hit it off immediately. Although they had different backgrounds, ideologically they came from the same place. They wanted to make a difference. And so marked the beginning of the Common Ground Foundation.

On a starting salary of eight dollars an hour, five days a week, Fred, a former gangbanger, and Jim, a graduate theater student, worked together. Their job was to make sure kids went to school.

Physically they are two of a kind. *BIG!* Jim sports smart black-frame glasses and a goatee. Fred sports the "Mr. Fred haircut." Very short and *very* low maintenance. The two personalities are like night and day.

Fred is generally the catalyst. He likes to stir things up, calling out to anyone he sees that he knows, talking to people he

thinks he should know. He has a high level of intensity and he loves to talk about "his" kids. In his teens, Fred Williams was the leader of a "set" in south central Los Angeles called the Harlem 30s, a branch of the notorious Crips gang.

At nineteen, Fred chose to use his ability to influence people in a different way. He created the Youth Outreach Organization, a grass-roots group that acted as an intermediary between rival gangs. "I wanted people to recognize me as someone positive."

Jim Goins is the perfect counterpart. Jim's quiet approach should not be confused with disinterest. His intensity shows in the way he listens to every word the children say.

For Jim the job was a culture shock. He grew up in a middle-class community and was pushed to get an education. As he walked through the Jordan Downs housing project in Watts, he could not believe the apathetic attitude that accompanied the children's absence from school. "My mother used to pick cotton. She would tell me horror stories of life without an education—these are the images of her stories."

Fred relates, "There's a lack of parenting skills. School is not a priority. A lot of potential dropouts don't come because school is not sensible to them. They see their homeboys hustling and they'd rather be doing that."

It did not take long for Mr. Fred and Mr. Jim, as everyone calls them, to realize that getting someone to school involved more than keeping statistics for the school district's dropout-prevention program.

Every day they go out into the neighborhood to talk to parents, trying to find kids who have not been in school for years at a time. "Self-esteem," says Mr. Fred. "That's what it's all about."

One day the two went to the home of a young student to find out why he wasn't in school. He had been absent for a week and a half. There was no father in the house, and his mother was off to work before he had to leave for school, so she had no idea where he was.

Fred remembers, "This boy was missing school because he needed a *haircut!* He was too embarrassed to go to school because the other kids were making fun of him and he was getting into fights. He hadn't had a *real* haircut for years. For some of these kids, a haircut is a luxury."

"It's either that or a meal," adds Jim. "Take your pick."

The next day the two were back with hair clippers they had just bought, giving a haircut to the young man. He was in class that morning. That was the beginning of Mr. Fred and Mr. Jim's free haircuts. Anybody who wants a haircut gets one. "Most people who do those wonderful studies of urban problems never hit the streets or talk to the parents of the children," says Fred. "We're there for them."

In three years, working alone, Jim and Fred brought over 350 kids back into school. Until September of 1988 they were responsible for the 102nd Street Elementary School and Jordan Downs. They just about had Jordan Downs licked. It was much easier then. Now they cover four elementary schools, a junior high school, and five housing projects.

"If you broke down Watts into sections, me and Jim and six more—we could handle the projects," says Mr. Fred. Fund-raising, however, is difficut, and the two have to use all their skills to develop sources for financing. Although they are paid by the Los Angeles public-school system, their salaries come from "discretionary funds" of the regional superintendent. There is no specific money set aside for Common Ground. Thus, much of the funding shortfall must be made up through corporate and private donations.

They try every creative approach they can think of to remove the obstacles that keep kids from going to school. This includes giving away free clothing and backpacks, and going on field trips. One event was a baby shower for over 150 unwed teenage mothers. Formula and diapers were among the things given out. Among the newest strategies is the Celebrity Walk Week, where well-known Black celebrities accompany Jim and Fred on their rounds.

According to Fred, "Being visible and consistent is the key to a *real* dropout-prevention program. These kids need to know that they can do *anything*. But the key to *doing* anything is getting an education. If Mr. Jim and Mr. Fred have to come to your house and drag you out to get you to school, we will." He smiles slyly. Fred's broad shoulders shake with laughter. "Maybe we won't *drag* you. . . ."

Ron Whitmore

Ron Whitmore

When Ron Whitmore bursts into a room, you can't help but think that this is one happy man. At twenty-nine he has the smiling face and energy of an eighteen-year-old. A former high school and college star athlete competing at the highest levels in football, basketball, baseball, and hockey, he played with some of the best in the nation. Now Ron plays with a bunch of other great people—the students of his kindergarten class.

"I hang out in my classroom. I . . . hang . . . out," says Ron with a mischievous smile on his face. "I play with the kids. I'm down on the floor with the kids, I'm running around with the kids. That's the kind of personality I have and that's who I am. I love to play."

Ron taught for several years at a Head Start program and then at a preschool. After going back to school to earn his master's degree in education, he landed his current job at Orrington Public School in Evanston, Illinois. But being a kindergarten teacher was not the

original plan. Ron was hoping to become a podiatrist. "I was caught up in making money," he says with an embarrassed smile. "Then, during my last quarter in high school, I took an early-childhood education course where we got a chance to work in the day-care program. My teacher said, 'Ron, you're great with kids, why don't you think of becoming an educator as a career?' I guess that was my start, and I've been working with children ever since."

In his fourth year at Orrington, it's pretty obvious that Ron has made a strong impression. His renown has little to do with the fact that one percent of all kindergarten teachers are male, or that an even smaller percentage are Black males; it's because he's Mr. Whitmore.

Walking down the hallway where the lunch tables are set up for the first-grade classes, kids are practically jumping out of their skin to say hi to Mr. Whitmore. Handshakes, hugs, high fives, low fives, giggles from shy kids, and shouts about the latest thing happening in their young lives—all greet Ron as he runs the gauntlet of kids. Some of them are not even his former students.

"Mr. Whitmore, I still eat a hot lunch every day!" proudly reports one young boy as Ron returns another child's hug. "That's *great!*" he responds earnestly, paying attention to three kids at once. There's a din in the hall that's hard to believe.

"I never wanted to be that authoritative person standing in front of the classroom at a blackboard writing stuff on the wall. I wanted to be able to play with and nurture the kids, to work with them. I never want-

ed to create an academic boot camp, I wanted learning to be fun. So here I am in kindergarten."

A typical day in Ron Whitmore's class starts with getting together on the rug, singing songs, and handling the morning's business. This includes taking attendance, reciting the Pledge of Allegiance, planning the lunch chart, and naming happy helpers. Happy helpers have chores like watering the plants, taking care of the animals, and being the pledge leader for the week.

Later, the kids break up into smaller groups for activities at various tables. These activities help develop fine motor skills, language, and cognitive skills. At their discretion the children can move to the doll areas, a block area, a science area, or a reading area. There's a break for special things like music class, drama, and physical education. Ron's class is set up so the children have to take control of what they do and how they do it. He becomes a sort of invisible overseer, encouraging and intervening when appropriate, which fosters the development of the children's self-confidence and independence.

When one of the numerous "kid-tastrophies" occurs—something every parent or children's supervisor is familiar with—Ron is there. On the way out to the yard to play, one of his kids whirls around while putting on her coat and absentmindedly walks into a video cart, bumping her eye pretty hard. The tears don't take long to follow. Without even thinking about it, Ron quickly and without any fuss goes to the girl and wraps his arms around her.

"Hmmm ... no blood," he says, finally

able to convince her to let him see her face. "That's good. What does what just happened tell us?" he asks as he strokes her hair.

"I want my mommy." It's hard not to laugh.

"Well," he continues without missing a beat, "when we rush around we can hurt ourselves because we aren't paying attention to what is going on around us."

"I want to see my mommy."

"Sometimes when I get hurt, I want to see my mommy, but she's not always around. If we think good thoughts and about things we like, it can sometimes make us feel better."

"I want to look at my picture," says the little girl as her balled-up fists wipe her scrunched-up, tear-streaked face.

"Okay," says Ron as she goes to the box in her cubbyhole and pulls out a little photograph. She looks at it for a few seconds, puts it back, and is magically ready to go outside with her classmates.

Hugs are a big part of Ron Whitmore's teaching style. When the kids do something good, they get a hug. If they have a disagreement, they hug when they apologize. Ron laughs. "Teachers, we're thieves. We steal. I haven't reinvented the wheel in education. I don't have any new methods. The only thing that I bring to the classroom is my attitude, my personality, and my gift for life. No one can re-create that. That has to be *you*. That has to be *me* as an educator in this classroom.

"I bring in respect, love, and caring. I share their feelings, and I make the children aware that everyone has something to bring to the table. Whether you're Black, white, orange, rich, poor, have a mom, have a dad—no matter who you are and no matter where you come from. So we respect the differences in people because no two people are the same."

That philosophy is best expressed by recounting an experience Ron recalls occurring in his classroom. His usually exuberant demeanor becomes subdued as he tells the story: "I remember one year I had a child who was a burn victim. He was burned pretty badly—on eighty percent of his body—and was still healing. He was a couple days late for school.

"When he walked in . . . the kids were freakin' out," Ron's voice becomes a little softer. "I looked over at him and I guess he was used to dealing with it. I caught him up during our rug time, and I said, 'This is Dennis, boys and girls.' I said, 'You know . . . I love him. And he's a part of our classroom. So that means we *all* should love him, don't you think?'

"And they were like, 'Yeah! We should. But what happened to Dennis?' And I said, 'Dennis, they want to know what happened.' And he said, 'Well, I was burned.'

"From that moment on, the kids looked at his difference as a *difference*. Not as a deficit. It was like, 'Yo! Here's Dennis. He may have scar tissue all over his body, but he's a part of our class. So he's a part of us. We have to love him as we'd love ourselves.' I'm not trying to say that I don't feel uneasy about certain situations, we all do. But no matter what happens in this classroom, I can't afford to let children sense that I have a negative feeling about an issue, because they'll pick up on it. And I don't want that to happen."

Ron Whitmore's goal is to make a difference in the world. Here's a man whose family gave him support and love, and it's his opinion that he should return the favor. "Through children you can bring about change. I feel that I have something to give. I'm not saying I have the key to what education is, but I think that the world would be a better place if all people knew how to hug, or how to use words, or how to say, 'I like you but I don't want you to do that.' Teaching kindergarten gives me the opportunity to care about people.

"The kids get a chance to see a Black male in a positive light, and I think that's a big responsibility. What's my life worth if I can't make a difference somewhere?"

So what does Ron get in return?

"Love. I get, 'Mr. Whitmore, I want to be like you.' 'Mr. Whitmore, I love you.' 'Mr. Whitmore, I'm going to be a teacher.' 'Mr. Whitmore, can I come to your house?' 'Mr. Whitmore, can you come to *my* house?' Hugs. Money can't buy that. I feel honored that I'm lucky enough to create the kind of situation and atmosphere between me and the children that I deal with every day, one that allows them to be honest and lets them be who they are. Because the people can see it and say, 'Hey! This is something real happening here.'"

The big man you see rolling around on the floor, making goofy faces with the kids or telling stories, has won a Cole Award. With help from friends, he's written three teaching guides and has been on NBC's "Today" show. Not only does he enjoy sharing ideas with his coworkers, but he thinks that he has the best job in the world.

"You know, I can't wait until twenty years from now when I see one of my students and they're like, 'Man! I remember you. You're Mr. Whitmore!' And see if they give me a hug or not when they're as big as I am. That's what I'm looking forward to, because I'm still getting hugs from former students that are now in third grade.

"It makes me feel like I'm doing my job. I look at the big picture and I say, 'Man, I'm doing something right. Because these kids still love me!' It's not *my* gratification here. My mission is to make a better world, and in the years that I've taught, these kids still remember me. They still remember what I taught them, and I hope they remember that throughout life."

At age thirty-four, Benilde Little-Virgin (pronounced *ben-ILL-dee*) has quit her job as senior arts and entertainment editor at *Essence* magazine, the first life-style magazine for and about Black women. With a career that took her from the *Star-Ledger* to *People* magazine, Benilde has little to prove to anyone about her skills or her experience. Even so, she says complete strangers still chastise her for "leaving that good job!"

Benilde was born and raised in Newark, New Jersey, where she got her first real job in journalism. Growing up working-class in a city still reeling from the riots of 1967 was not always easy. Her father worked at General Motors and her mother was a nurse's aide, but sometimes Benilde's family didn't seem to fit in. While they certainly were not rich, Benilde's parents made it a point to provide their children with the very best they could afford. The Brooks Brothers–type clothes Benilde's mother bought her provoked taunts from kids in her neigh-

borhood, but her mother felt they were sturdy and practical.

"We were nowhere near rich, but my mother believed in taking us to the theater and the museum just to show us that life was bigger than our environment," she explains. "We always knew we were going to go to college. My mother showed us that there's a big world out there to pick and choose from. You don't have to be poor, live in a bad neighborhood, eat horrible food, and die at fifty. That doesn't *have* to be your life."

When Benilde's mother told Benilde of her plans to send her to a private high school outside of the neighborhood, "I screamed! I told her, 'You can't do this!'" Her mother relented. Though there were times Benilde says she was chased home and had to physically defend herself, she's glad she stayed in her neighborhood. "I needed that connection. Leaving would have changed my perspective as well as my life. I probably wouldn't have gone to a Black college. And I wouldn't have worked at *Essence*, because I don't think I would have had the awareness and the appreciation of Black folks that I have now.

"I did think I was going to be like Barbara Walters," she says of her original decision to go into broadcast journalism. She took a year off after high school and lived with her brother, a radio broadcaster, in Florida. She eventually went to Howard University, where she earned a degree in journalism. She followed that up with a stint at Northwestern University in Chicago for graduate work in broadcast journalism, but decided it wasn't for her.

"When I went to Northwestern," she says, "race was always an issue. I actually had a professor tell me not to do any more Black stories. My beat was the South Side of Chicago!" (a predominantly Black neighborhood). Howard, she insists, was different. "There is this commonality in being Black, so race became a nonissue. I didn't feel at all insecure about asking for help, guidance, or whatever. Funny enough, my mentor at Howard happened to be white."

During her college years Benilde did several different internships. She worked for the *Cleveland Plain Dealer* and interned for columnist and radio personality Carl Rowan. "With Rowan I researched his columns and his broadcasts, which meant reading five newspapers a day. His assistant would give me topics that Carl would be interested in, and I would clip everything related to that particular topic. If he was going on a trip out of the country, I'd go to the State Department and research the country he was going to."

Her intern experiences helped Benilde get a post at the *Star-Ledger*. "Years ago it was the *Newark Star-Ledger*, but after the riots, nobody wanted to be called the 'Newark' anything," she says with a laugh.

"The *Star-Ledger* job actually came pretty easily," she says, somewhat embarrassed. "It *is* hard getting jobs in journalism, but I had news clips and experience from my internships, so I just sent them to the *Star-Ledger* because I was at home and that was the hometown paper. And they hired me!

"I was at the *Star-Ledger* for three years. I was a general-assignment reporter, and I covered all kinds of stuff: fires, murders, city hall, whatever came across the city desk of the newsroom. For a while I was responsible for covering fourteen townships, which were small, primarily all-white towns. I was on call twenty-four hours a day. I used a beeper to stay on top of everything that happened.

"Getting the job at *People* magazine was embarrassingly simple," she says apologetically. "I was out covering a fire and something snapped. I just got tired of it. Two kids were killed—it was sad. I came into the newsroom smelling like smoke and I said to my friend Lucy, 'I'm gettin' out of here. I'm going to go work for *People* magazine or something,' not really *meaning* it; I had never even *read* a *People* magazine, but *People* represented the ultimate in 'fluff' journalism. I was tired of the hard stuff—it was really heavy burnout.

"Lucy, said, 'Oh! My stepmother knows the managing editor there. You can write her and use my stepmother's name.' I said, 'Great!' And that's what I did. It pays to open your mouth," she says with a broad smile. Her outstanding work at *People* easily qualified her for her position at *Essence*.

Essence gave Benilde the opportunity to discuss topics that she felt were significant, yet were overlooked. Benilde has often found that at other publications, when trying to push through ideas about so-called Black issues, "the response was no. Which translates into 'it's not within our experience, so it's not relevant.'"

Benilde has often been accused of being *too* honest. Not someone who speaks just to hear herself talk, she isn't afraid to voice her opinions, and she does so when she feels an important point should be made. Her position at *Essence* gave her the opportunity to help educate its readers by forcing them to take note of contemporary issues. *Essence* may be a women's magazine, but it is by no means a beauty journal.

As senior arts and entertainment editor, she has spoken out about how the entertainment industry fails to recognize Black performers. "After George Michael won for best R and B artist at the Grammy Awards in 1989 that was it for me. That's an insult to me as a Black person." There are so many talented Black artists performing rhythm and blues who are not getting recognition, she contends. When asked on the BET show "Our Voices" if the Grammys were racist, Benilde responded, "They were probably racist a couple of years ago. Now they're beyond that. They don't even *care* how we as Black people feel about it. N.W.A. and all those California rappers have gone platinum without any awards, or radio play, and I think that's significant and should be acknowledged."

She says about the message she tried to get across through *Essence:* There is racism that Blacks inflict on each other in our communities. Blacks who perceive other Blacks as "not Black enough." "I maintain that we don't have to talk a certain way, we don't have to look a certain way, or even dress a certain way. We've got to stop being so judg-

mental and bigoted amongst ourselves."

When she worked at *Essence*, if you looked around her office you would have seen evidence of someone who has her finger on the pulse of contemporary American interests. Photos of up-and-coming people, clippings about every topic imaginable. Stacks of books and magazines, all obviously read, evidenced by the dog-eared corners and bookmarked pages.

Working at *Essence* offered Benilde many things that simply don't come with being a free-lance writer. Her favor was constantly courted by people in entertainment and in publishing. That adulation, she says, is easy to buy into. "I knew I would be giving that up, but it wasn't a big deal. Sometimes the attention was too much," she admits. "It was like, 'Oh! Benilde Little is here!' I knew it wasn't because I was Benilde Little; it was because I worked at *Essence* and had some degree of influence. But that was always uncomfortable for me."

Leaving her job there was both a scary and a necessary move for Benilde. "In many ways it was a great job, but there was really nothing left in it for me. When I would go home, I would be completely exhausted. Once I left *People* and began working at *Essence*, I had no time to even wipe my nose! Besides, I always wanted to write this novel," she says of her current project.

"When I started writing the novel in the mid-eighties, I talked to a couple of people

in publishing, and they were like, 'If it's not about slavery and it's not about the ghetto, no publisher's going to buy it.'" She laughs. "So I put it away. Then when Terry McMillan published her *third* blockbuster and got $2.64 million for the paperback rights, I thought, there is a huge audience looking for contemporary Black fiction. It seemed like the right time to seize the opportunity."

Benilde is excited about the change she's made in her life. "I'm basically writing the book that *I* want to read, about characters who are like me and my friends—regular people who are succeeding *and* screwed up in the same way we are! There are some major snobs in it, and they are the most fun to write." She chuckles. "I'm having so much fun."

Her phone doesn't ring nearly as much as it used to, and she admits there are times she is staring at her blank computer screen wondering what she's done. "I've gone from speaking on this show and that, wearing fabulous clothes, and jetting all over the country, to being the Negro with nothing!" She laughs uproariously. "That's when my husband is there to assure me otherwise."

All of that's okay, she says. She likes things better this way for now. "It is important for me to make a name for myself—*by* myself. To define myself. It's something I think about every day." Meanwhile, she is busily writing at home, creating the people she hopes we will love to hate.

Anne Blair

When she would visit schools as the local film critic and talk to young Black kids about the Black characters they'd seen on the screen, Anne Blair would notice a lot of the children she spoke to were poorly dressed. Not that they didn't have style; they didn't have clothes—the kind of clothes that would keep them warm. She would ask the teachers about these kids and find out many of them did not have the money at home to buy better clothes, warmer clothes.

When she got back to her office, she talked to the other reporters and to friends she knew, and asked them if they would be willing to help buy some clothes for these young people. No one could turn her down. These were people who could easily reach into their closets and find something comfortable for themselves or their kids to wear. They decided to grant some simple wishes to kids who just wanted new shoes or a warm coat, and in the first year they tried it, Anne and her friends granted

fifty wishes. Pretty good for someone working out of her home in the late winter of 1979.

It quickly became obvious that there were a lot of young people and families who needed a helping hand, because Anne's home phone was flooded with calls from teachers who knew of kids who needed something. "After a while it required structure. There were just too many calls coming in," says Anne Blair, a woman with a quick smile and a sunny disposition.

Anne would take the calls at home and then pick up the donated items and transport them to her office downtown. The teachers would then come there and pick them up. In a short time, Anne, with the help of lots of friends, had started a program she named Grant-A-Wish.

"Grant-A-Wish provides for needy, handicapped, abandoned, and abused children, primarily through public schools," she explains. "We also work with agencies—almost any other social-service agency can contact us and tell us about a child that needs either shoes, eyeglasses, clothing, or simple medical or dental care.

"We do whatever we can do. We work a lot with children who have been involved with fires, or have been snatched from a home because they have been abused. We provide clothing as quickly as we can for those children. We also provide clothing for families who have lost everything; that's the only time we get involved with adults."

The Grant-A-Wish office is not a lavish place. In a small building in downtown Chicago, Grant-A-Wish occupies about six hundred square feet of space, and most of it is taken up by overflowing boxes of items donated by private citizens and large corporations. The back of the office is where you will find a few desks and the usual office equipment—a couple of typewriters, a few phones, and a computer. Anne's desk is by the window that looks out over the "el" train, which rumbles past the window every few minutes. The other desks, which should have staff members sitting at them, have been empty for many weeks because funding has been hard to come by, and Anne simply can't afford to pay for regular help. Even so, Anne cannot let Grant-A-Wish die.

"I'm very proud of it," she says with a smile. "Because Grant-A-Wish fills a void for children that I experienced when I was growing up.

"I tell people about the French teacher who bought me a sweater set. I was in a school with well-to-do girls during high school, and of course they had lots of clothing, you know. I had my two blouses, and two skirts.

"Well, they all had these matching sweater sets. They had the cardigan, then they had the matching sweater. My French teacher knew how desperately I wanted one, so she bought one for me. And it changed me—because it made me feel good. And this is exactly what Grant-A-Wish does, it makes you feel good about yourself, so you can get on with your life. And maybe even return the favor to someone one day."

Anne stresses that Grant-A-Wish is concerned with making young people feel good about themselves. She hopes that "when they go to school they feel that they are a part of their class." Grant-A-Wish is not for the people who donate things. It's not to make them feel as if they have done something wonderful or just.

"I try never to give a child something that I would not be proud of my own child wearing. When I tell a sponsor, yes, you can grant a wish, I also tell them, please make sure it's something the child wants. I don't care if you spend two million dollars for it at Neiman Marcus. If it's not what they want, it doesn't help. You haven't granted a wish.

Grant-A-Wish gives something *that* child wants, otherwise you have not done anything. If you're going to uplift the quality of life for children, they've got to be embraced in a way that works for *them*."

Each year a committee chooses ten schools or agencies to concentrate on. They make every effort to cover the state and to be as diverse as possible. The focus is on places where there are needy youngsters, and within that group, Anne and her friends concentrate on the neediest. In an average school year Grant-A-Wish will provide for thirty-seven hundred children. During the Christmas period there is an "emergency" program that targets about four thousand children.

"We started a program with teen moms, because I was concerned," Anne eagerly shares. She is anxious to let people know there is a lot of work to be done. "The infant mortality rate in Chicago is very high. And my concern, as I looked at young girls walking their babies down the streets, was that they hadn't covered the babies' heads. It is important that little ones keep a cap on their heads. So I started a campaign for caps. I used to keep caps in the trunk of my car all the time." She laughs. "When I'd see a mom with a little one that didn't have a cap, I'd make some excuse about, 'I'm a Grandma and you know my grandchild has so many things, and I just *happen* to have this cap in the back of my car. Would you accept it for your baby?' And most of the time they would, you know.

"But now, we work with the department of health and the various infant welfare stations. When they call and say, 'We've got fifty babies coming in,' we can provide for those babies and do a darn good job! Right now I've got a request for a three-week-old baby, and this mom just turned fifteen. So, I'm going to put a box of things together to carry the little one through at least a year. She'll have an adequate amount of clothing for the baby."

Sometimes help is not that easy to give. There are people who need help but are too proud to ask for it, or who are afraid to accept it because they fear there are strings attached. Anne remembers, "There was a young boy who was really something. I mean, he was a nine-year-old gangster! He came into the teacher's office; she wanted to just introduce me to him so that I could see who it was she was talking about. But we did not talk to him about what he needed. What he needed was a coat, and he had been braving the cold weather without one. I mean, this kid was tough."

He explained to them that he did not need any help because he was going to manage. He knew all about "managing"; he already took care of his younger siblings who were five, three, and two before he came to

school. His mother was an alcoholic. The teacher asked him if he would like to have a coat if they could arrange it. He told her, "I guess so, but it ain't no big thing."

A week later Anne returned to the school with a coat for the young man. She watched from another office as the teacher gave it to him. "At first he just stared at the box," Anne recalls. "This happens with so many of our children. They don't believe that it can happen. They have been disappointed so often.

"And this kid, when he got the coat, he didn't believe it was for real. It took him a while. He took the box and he kept looking back at the teacher and looking at the box." The teacher suggested he leave the box in the office and pick it up on the way home so the other kids wouldn't know he got a coat. He came back later and asked the teacher if he could open the box. She told him, 'Of course.'

"When he opened the box and saw the coat, he pulled it out slowly. He kept turning it around and around and around. Then he'd look at her and then back at the coat, as if to say, 'I wonder if she'll try to snatch this from me.'

"That young man stands out in my mind because he represents the child who has not had things. For these kids just being warm, and being warm wearing something that makes their peers look at them and say, 'Hey, man, you got a new coat. That's sharp!' is important."

The city of Chicago has helped Grant-A-Wish, too. Parking in downtown Chicago is next to impossible, and nearly every time the Grant-A-Wish van would pick up a donation, they had to park illegally. After

learning they had received over two thousand dollars in parking tickets on their van, the mayor decided to give Grant-A-Wish a break. Mayor Daley arranged to put several drop boxes in strategic locations on the street so sponsors could leave donations easily and the Grant-A-Wish van could pick them up without parking illegally. They still had to pay their outstanding tickets though!

Thank-yous are very important to Anne Blair, and it's not to satisfy her ego. It is a way to teach kids a simple lesson. "I grew up in a world where a thank-you was expected. It's no longer expected," she explains. "Some people get offended when I tell them to write me out a thank-you note. They look at me, and sorta say, 'Well, you know I don't have to do this.' I say, 'Wait a minute, someone had to provide these things for you. Surely you can give them a thank-you. That's all they're asking for.'

"So thank-yous became a big part of the program. It's simple—when these kids write thank-you notes, they don't go through life thinking somebody owes them something.

"If somebody's going to help me do something, I should thank them for helping me. There are so many steps in life and no one owes you the push up those steps. You're lucky if someone's there to push you at all.

Anne Blair is not going to get rich from Grant-A-Wish, if you are measuring richness in money. But if you talk about the happiness she sees on the faces of the kids whose wishes have been granted, and the knowledge that she is doing something every day to make someone's life better, well, then, Anne Blair is one of the richest women in America.

Neil Tyson

"A friend of mine had a pair of binoculars. He said, 'Neil, have you ever looked at the moon with binoculars before?' And I said, 'No, but why bother? It's so far away, why should binoculars help at all? I can understand if we're looking across the street to get a better view, but *the moon?* What are you saying?'

"I took a look, and the moon looked completely different in binoculars than with the naked eye. You could see mountains, craters, valleys, and hills. You could actually see these things and see the detail! From then on I was sold."

Neil Tyson was a sixth grader when his friend showed him the moon through binoculars, but the experience convinced him that he wanted to do something that involved studying the heavens. "The choice seemed so easy at the time that I didn't realize how fortunate I was to have such a clear life goal so early. When I went to college people were *still* trying

to figure out what to do with their lives."

Neil is an astrophysicist—a professional astronomer. "My first interest is studying the structure of the galaxy and star formation in other galaxies, to make a contribution to our understanding of the universe," he explains. "The best way to go about that is to obtain your own data by going to major observatories in the world, those that are best suited for the project that you have in mind, and then returning to your home institution with the data, reducing and analyzing it, and coming up with ideas about what the meaning is."

Far from being a "science geek," Neil Tyson is funny and interesting to talk to, and doesn't own a single pocket protector. For the most part, he prefers jeans and a comfortable shirt to suits and ties. He has also slowly built a collection of fine wines and has become somewhat of a vintage-wine expert.

At fourteen years old he decided to create his own business to pay for his first telescope. "I lived in a rather large apartment complex," he says of his childhood home in the Bronx, New York. "Five thousand people, and a lot of them owned dogs. Nobody wanted to walk the dog," he says with the robust laugh that is his trademark. "So I made a whole lot of money walking other people's dogs. I was soon able to get my first telescope. I think my parents chipped in a few dollars. They were pleased that I was being responsible and ambitious."

Neil spent hours in the library, reading everything he could get his hands on about astronomy. At the suggestion of his sixth-grade science teacher, he attended special junior-high-level classes at the Hayden Planetarium in Manhattan. By the eighth grade he was the only kid taking the planetarium's adult class. As a science project that year he built a spectroscope, an instrument for analyzing the composition of sunlight. It was the first time he had *built* a scientific instrument rather than buying it.

At the Bronx High School of Science, Neil remembers with a smile, "The whole school was filled with 'nerds.' Lunchtime conversations weren't about girls, or what you were gonna do Friday night. They were about discovering some new law of physics or Einstein's theory of relativity. This didn't mean there wasn't some time reserved for social life. But the time most other people spent talking just to pass the time, we spent talking about physical laws.

"Bronx Science is one of the few places where intelligence is rewarded by your peers." He was editor of the school science journal and went on two scientific expeditions after winning special scholarships that paid his way. One was to the coast of northwest Africa to observe one of the longest solar eclipses of the century. He was the youngest person on the trip, accompanied only by his telescope.

Taking physics early in high school was a huge influence on Neil. "It became clear that astrophysics was a career choice. I saw what the field of physics could do and why that's important." He began thinking about college. Each issue of *Scientific American*, which Neil read religiously, contained a section listing the credentials of the writers. Neil made a checklist compar-ing the colleges he was accepted to with where the writers had earned their degrees. When he finished, "the list for Harvard was four times longer than any other. I said to myself, if I want to aspire to what these scientists are doing, then the choice is already made."

Even as a physics major at Harvard, Neil spent a lot of time in the astrophysics department. His summer jobs at the Center for Astrophysics ended up lasting through the school year, and thus he was able to work alongside professional scientists during his college years.

"I'd say the most interesting aspect of my job is going to the telescope itself, because it involves not only flying to the nearest city, but then driving to the top of a mountain and adjusting yourself to living nocturnally. You'll never hear an astronomer complain about jet lag. The two or three hours that an airplane will do to you is nothing compared to what you have to do to yourself when you flip your schedule to use the telescopes!

Astronomers aren't rich. "People say, 'Why don't you just spend two years and go to business school and make a bundle? Or law school?' Even MDs are not in school as long as astronomers, considering what it takes to get the master's and Ph.D. As an astronomer you come out making an ordinary income. People have to be aware that true happiness in life comes from doing what you *want* to do. It's not from making a lot of money.

As a sideline, Neil has written a book taken from a column he wrote for the University of Texas magazine *Stardate*. As

"Merlin" he answered questions people had about space. "People would write in and ask, 'How big is the universe?' 'What happens if I fall into a black hole?' A lot of questions tended to be catastrophic in nature, like, 'What happens if the moon explodes?'"

He says his Merlin character "has been around since the beginning of time. So when people asked, 'Merlin, I don't quite understand gravity,' Merlin would recount conversations with Isaac Newton. And I'd construct a plausible conversation that Isaac Newton might have had, given Newton's personality and professional interests."

The Universe Down to Earth is a collection of essays based on lectures done while Neil was a teaching assistant at the University of Maryland. "This other stuff is fun. I like communicating my excitement about my research. If the research were removed, I'd have no food for the excitement and I'd get stale very quickly."

One of Neil's most treasured career memories is of an evening not long after he became a professional astronomer. "While I was growing up I was a member of the Amateur Astronomers Association of New York. Every month the association would invite a speaker from some academic institution to speak to us and convey the latest scientific findings. I would go every month to hear them. I'd think, 'Gee, I want to be one of those scientists.' About four years ago, I was invited to give one of those talks. There I was," he says with great pride as he recalls the evening, "giving a talk. And I remembered being in the audi-

ence, sitting on the other side. It was like, yes, dreams can come true. It was a remarkable feeling.

"The path is long and circuitous, though. You've got to major in physics, you've got to take the math courses, and you've got to do well. All this still has to happen before you get to where I am. But with perseverance, yes, you can get to this point. People see famous movie stars or famous basketball players, and they say, 'I want to be just like them.' They don't realize that you have to be one out of millions just to *be in* the NBA. What fraction of basketball players end up in the NBA at all, much less being a Michael Jordan?

"To be a scientist, even one who would be invited to speak before a group like the Amateur Astronomers Association, you don't have to be the one in millions. You could be the ordinary good scientist, and they will care about what you're doing because the public has a thirst for astronomy. Maybe I'm biased," Neil says, laughing, "but discoveries in astronomy have reached headline news."

Racism does not go away just because you are a professional, and Neil is constantly reminded of that, especially after being stopped by the police while going into his own office one night. Now, sitting under the big dome of the observatory, Neil remembers how guidance counselors told him to be a salesman. "Even astrophysicists have told me things they thought I should do. And I think it's because they could not picture me as their research colleague. Their equal. When I go to these astronomy conferences, there's

nothing overt. Still it's clear that when I get up there to talk, they're not used to having a Black person explain astrophysics to them. I'm not taken seriously until they hear what I have to say.

"Yes I was good at basketball, and yes, I could slam dunk in ninth grade. I was captain of the wrestling team. I was sort of your quintessential Black athlete. As expected. It was easy. And why was it easy? I'm convinced it was because all the forces in society *allowed* it to happen. When I was appointed the editor in chief of the physical science journal, people started murmuring, 'Well, how did *he* get to be . . . ?' 'What did *he* do . . . ?' All this sort of undercurrent. But no one questioned my athletic achievements. No one questioned that at all.

"Yeah, there are struggles. And to overcome them I had to say to myself, I'm running this race and I have more hurdles and my hurdles are higher. My whole profession is based on the challenge of problem solving. That challenge has had to be applied to my path in life. I'll just have to jump higher and faster to get to that finish line at the same time, or before anybody else."

To have his scientific contributions outlive him is Neil's ambition. As ideas and theories come and go, those that last often contribute an important link in the chain of human understanding. Just by being a highly respected astrophysicist, he has made a statement that will outlive him.

There are only 324 professional basketball players in the NBA. There are 5,000 professional astrophysicists. Right now, Neil Tyson is one of only 7 Black ones.

Judge Gloria Dabiri

A diminutive Hispanic woman in jeans and a colorful striped polo shirt enters and steps up to the table in the mahogany-walled courtroom. Although the courtroom is small and the table she stands by is unimpressive, she holds her bag close as if for protection and comfort.

The two uniformed court officers are imposing figures even if their attitude is somewhat relaxed. A couple of attorneys, one a man and the other a young woman, sit against the wall in two of the five well-worn chairs in the back of the room. They chat about other business. The court reporter gets comfortable before the hearing begins.

A young attorney, barely acknowledging the Hispanic woman, introduces himself to the judge—for the record—and speaks to her using legal terms that are hard to follow without a degree in law. Judge Gloria Dabiri looks up from her papers at the woman still standing by the desk. "Good afternoon," she says to her in a warm voice and with a friendly smile.

"Good afternoon," responds the woman, who suddenly looks a bit more comfortable.

"Please," says the judge, extending her hand, "have a seat." The woman sits, and although she is still nervous, out of her element, it looks as though she feels that she is dealing with a sympathetic person.

Gloria Dabiri (pronounced *DA-bree*) is a judge in family court in Brooklyn, New York. As a family court judge she deals with cases ranging from child abuse and neglect to custody and juvenile delinquency. Most of the people appear unrepresented, as they often do in landlord-tenant court or small-claims court. "People with money who have custody, visitation, or support issues end up in supreme court with an attorney," Gloria explains, then continues:

"Because family court is often considered a stepchild to the other courts, the litigants aren't always treated with the kind of dignity that I think they should be treated with. The waiting room is a disgrace, and the place needs a paint job. You have people sitting on the floor because it's so overcrowded; they have to wait for hours before their cases are called. They're shuttled into these tiny little courtrooms—some of the courtrooms are little more than offices."

Because judges have large caseloads and deal with the same kinds of issues every day, it's easy to do it by rote. "I just want to treat people with respect, because I don't think they get it out on the street,"she adds.

Gloria went to Catholic schools all the way through high school. "It was sort of difficult growing up back then because there weren't too many Black people in Catholic schools. I remember I was the only Black in high school. I think it gave me a lot of drive because I sort of felt I had to prove to white people that Blacks could be successful.

Grammar school was probably when Gloria first thought about being a lawyer. Doing research for a report about a prominent female judge got her interested. When she met her Nigerian uncle who was a judge in his homeland, she was thoroughly impressed. Yet she adds, "I don't think I really decided for sure about law until I was in college."

Gloria earned a scholarship to Merrimack College and majored in political science. By her own admission she wasn't a brilliant student, but she worked hard and earned another scholarship for law school, this time to Syracuse University.

"I spent a year doing legal services in Utica, New York, after graduating from law school beginning in 1976. There I had the dubious distinction of being the first Black woman to practice law in the county," she says with a smile. Gloria kept busy. "Work-wise it was interesting because it was a small office and you had to handle whatever came in"—everything from small claims to welfare rights to appeals. "Socially it was the pits. I was very, very lonely, so I only spent a year there. I hate to tell you how many dates I had. I decided after I got the bar results I was going to make a move."

After being notified that she had passed her state bar exam, a test all law students take to become certified lawyers, she was hired by the district attorney's office in Westchester County, New York. During her second year out of law school, she became a prosecutor. Gloria was stunned by how many cases of child abuse she saw. Being the only woman in the division that handled those cases, she was given many child-related cases and developed an expertise in the area. Family court seemed to her a place where she could do some good.

It takes ten years of membership in the bar to be considered for a judgeship in family court, and Gloria needed a few more years to qualify. In the meantime, New York's governor, Mario Cuomo, appointed her general counsel, the chief attorney, for the State Liquor Authority, which controls liquor licensing and other regulations. She spent six years there.

"I had a lot to learn; in terms of the law, I picked that up pretty quickly. The difficulty was having to manage attorneys, most of whom were white males who initially knew more than I did about the liquor law. There was a lot of resentment that this young woman was brought in from the outside." There was also little cooperation from coworkers when Gloria tried to make changes in the office.

"I was trying to increase the quality of the work," she says almost sarcastically and with a hearty laugh. "I had come from an office where people worked hard and took pride in their work. I had a certain standard. Just trying to get these people to come to work on *time* was a major problem. I had no management experience, so I must admit, my first approaches were probably not the best." One attorney who was forced out for not performing his duties told her "that he was going to do whatever he could to destroy me."

While general counsel at the SLA, Gloria had put in her application for family court judge. Her first application for the judgeship was turned down because she simply didn't have enough experience. Determined to get the position, she immediately worked on improving her credentials by teaching family law at Baruch College and working as a clerk for an appeals court judge. By writing opinions for the judge, she helped prepare herself for a job on the bench.

The second time around things got extremely complicated. "It's a really involved process that you go through," she explains with a furrowed brow. "First you go through the mayor's committee, then you go to see the mayor. Then you go before the bar association. I know a few people for whom it was just a matter of days or weeks, but for me it was months. So I sort of got the sense I wasn't going to get it."

The former coworker who had promised to ruin her was busily executing his plan. He systematically tried to ruin Gloria's chances by tainting her reputation. He contacted the review committee, "and he had some not-so-nice things to say about me," she says diplomatically.

The review process had gone extremely well up to this point. The committee was impressed with all she had done to improve her qualifications since her last appearance before them, and it seemed to Gloria that she finally had the approval. But this other information . . . "That," she says with all seriousness, "was probably the worst experience of my life.

"Their information was that I couldn't get along with people and that I was a bad administrator. Nothing about my work or anything like that. They didn't think I had the temperament to be a good judge. I said to myself, either I can stop here and say to hell with it, or I can really fight this thing. I decided I was going to fight it.

"I hired an attorney. I had done some legwork myself. I contacted people that I had worked for and judges whom I had appeared before, and I started a letter-writing campaign to the bar association. All of my bosses wrote letters. So did secretaries, investigators I had worked with, and other attorneys. As it turned out, over sixty letters were submitted. I had to fight to get this seat. Nobody gave it to me.

"It was a very difficult process for me because I felt my whole career and my reputation were on the line. I thought I had grown a lot at the SLA, but I really grew during this experience. I just realized no one was going to give me anything, and it made me really see how much I wanted this job, and that once I got it I really had to do something. I couldn't *just* be a judge. So I decided once I did get it, I would try to make a difference."

Nine months after her second application process started, the bar association approved her appointment. The ordeal she went through caused sweeping changes in the way a judge is confirmed for a post in New York State. *All* applicants who are turned down are allowed to ask for reconsideration and must be told why they were turned down. Before, an applicant only had this right if he or she lost by a certain number of votes. Now, any negative information the committee has about candidates must be revealed to

them in advance so they can prepare to defend themselves. "The chairman of the mayor's committee, Basil Patterson, said to me, 'You know, you are a heroine because you really took on city hall.'" Even so, Judge Dabiri adds, "I understand a lot of Black people who go to that committee, particularly Black women, have a lot of problems being approved. Even today."

Now a Family Court judge, Gloria had a promise to keep. Many of the young offenders who came before her were Black and Latino males. Punishing minor offenses with confinement was only going to give them an education in how to be better criminals. With the help of the Children's Aid Society, Gloria started a mentoring program for young men.

"We have twenty-three judges, lawyers, and professional Black men committed to being mentors to Black and Hispanic boys." During the school year, the mentors spend a few hours every other week with someone they are specially paired up with. The visits may just be hanging out and talking, playing ball, or checking out their mentor's place of business. "I know it's a drop in the bucket, but I figure it's a start. Twenty-three of these kids have a chance to be exposed to an alternative life-style, to build a relationship with a man who really is concerned about them, and to feel special as a result. You've got to do something, no matter how small.

"I think Black people need to have a sense of responsibility about forwarding our race. Certainly we experience injustices, but I don't think you have any basis for complaining if you don't fight."

Barry Martin and Aubrey Lynch

Over the last several years, Barry Martin has been asked a lot of questions about the 1983 accident in South Africa that put him in a wheelchair. He was left a quadriplegic after shoddy emergency treatment at the hands of doctors in a country ruled by apartheid. When Barry regained consciousness after surgery, the doctor assigned to his case inquired what his occupation was. When Barry told him he was a dancer, the doctor's matter-of-fact reply was, "Well, you won't be dancing anymore."

Barry has since faced an uphill battle to recover. Though his body is bound to a wheelchair, Barry's spirit did eventually recover from the shock of his new reality. That recovery was both painful and deeply spiritual.

Before 1983, Barry was a promising dancer. After completing his regular schooling as well as his dance education via scholarship at the

Alvin Ailey dance school, he signed on with the British multiracial dance company Hot Gossip. His future was promising and all was going well: He was embarking on his first world tour with the group, and garnering praise for his energetic, fluent, and technically flawless dancing. Their first stop was Sun City, South Africa.

Eight weeks into their stopover in the Transvaal, Barry and a white dancer from the company were involved in a car accident. An ambulance came almost immediately but took only his white colleague. "I remember seeing an ambulance take Peter away. I didn't realize at the time that it had left me behind because it was an ambulance for whites." Although Black bystanders drove him to a "white" hospital that would ultimately refuse to treat him, they left him at the door as soon as they got him there. "I was sitting on a bench for hours," he explains, after having walked in under his own power. "After hours of waiting, a political figure stepped into the situation and let them know who I was. They eventually transferred me to another hospital, seventy-five miles away." Despite what appeared to be a broken neck, Barry was given no neck brace and had no nurse travel with him to the second hospital. "At Paul Kruger Memorial in Pretoria, they sent me to the Black section of the hospital," he continues. "They were not equipped to treat me in the Black section, so they gave me honorary white status and allowed me to be admitted to the white section of that hospital.

"By the time I got to that hospital I was paralyzed. I'm convinced that all the things in between, combined with walking into the first hospital, caused the end result," he says with no visible emotion. As Barry relates the story he speaks with a certain hint of disbelief, as if he's telling the story of someone else's life.

"In order to get me out as quickly as they could," he explains, "they recommended that I have a spinal fusion done which would get me up quicker—into a wheelchair." It was a full month after the accident before Barry had an operation.

"I experienced a living hell in those two and half months in the hospital in South Africa. Some nurses and attendants were not very happy with my honorary white status or my suntanned skin," Barry says with a sarcastic chuckle. "One night my arm involuntarily contracted itself into a painful position. I yelled out for the nurse and an attendant came into the room. I asked her, 'Could you straighten my arm, please?' She looked down at me and said, 'I don't know who you think you are, but I'm not your bloody physiotherapist!' I yelled out, 'What?' She then took the sheet and threw it over my face. Being paralyzed, there was not much I could do except cry."

When asked if he had to pay for the medical services he received, a look of irony crosses his face. "No," he says quietly, taking a breath to continue, then thinking better of it. "No." When I remark on the obvious injustice of it all, Barry says, "It's in the past. I can't let bitterness keep me from living my life, I've realized that."

Barry was eventually transferred to a hospital in England, where he spent another ten months in therapy and recuperation before heading back to the States. "They always said that rehabilitation begins at home. I was so frustrated being in the hospital for a year. Imagine going to sleep at home one night, then never returning to your own bed and having a year's stay in a hospital. It gave me a lot of time to think. When I was discharged, I went right from the hospital to New York. I went back to my family home in Queens, where I stayed for ten months. Over those ten months, I dealt with the frustrations of trying to get help from the system and trying to get my life together.

"I saw my family change drastically, trying to cater to me. Their attitude, as well-meaning as it was, led to a lot of my frustration," Barry shares with me. "My room at home had been in the attic. I could no longer get to it. Our dining room was transformed into a bedroom for me. I had no privacy. My family was overconcerned and pampering me. I was very independent and active in high school and college; I didn't live at home during my four years of college. To get back into that situation of living at home was really having a negative impact on me, and I couldn't take it. Accepting the fact that I had to deal with other people taking care of me, and wanting them to understand that I still needed to be in control, was not easy," Barry explains. "I had to learn how to direct people to assist me to do the things that I could not do for myself." Barry had already begun handling basic tasks for himself, as well as learning how to maneuver an electric wheelchair. This increased his mobility and independence. "Keeping things in perspective and trying to stay in control of

46

my life, that was really the challenge of those first two or three years."

Barry was determined to live as independent and normal a life as possible, which included pursuing his desire to choreograph, something he had done before his accident. But obstacles were constantly placed in his path. "In dealing with the agencies created to aid people in situations similar to mine and trying to gather information as to how those agencies could help me, I ran into a lot of negativity, a lot of pessimism," says Barry. "When it came to me aspiring to be a choreographer, I was told that it was a farfetched and unrealistic goal. I was even told this by the Office of Education and Rehabilitation."

So, despite the naysayers, Barry began to work toward his dream. Wayne Rhone, an old friend from Barry's Alvin Ailey days, asked him to choreograph a solo piece for him after an emotional visit. "Barry called the dance 'Penance,'" Rhone recalled in a 1987 *Life* magazine article. "It had a lot of anger in it, and it was so strenuous I could hardly do it. But I understood why."

"Penance," which was choreographed in 1985, was a tool Barry used to release much of his frustration, as well as a great deal of pent-up anger. "'Penance' was my first piece of choreography following the accident. It also inspired me to form my dance company, Déjà Vu." His nine-member dance troupe, formed in 1986, features principal dancer Aubrey Lynch, whom Barry discovered while he was training with the Alvin Ailey company.

After his work with Rhone in 1985, Barry began to choreograph regularly. Something

seemed to take hold of him, something that helped redirect his anger and restlessness. "But it was not until I formed a relationship with the late Alvin Ailey that I found my true purpose as a choreographer. He became my mentor," he says, smiling fondly. "I am the last guest choreographer he used for his company, the Alvin Ailey American Dance Theater, before his death. Since its inception, my company has performed at Lincoln Center, the Brooklyn Academy of Music, and Carnegie Hall. And it came full circle for me when my company performed at City Center, which happened in 1991," Barry says with pride. "That circle started from the beginning of my training at Alvin Ailey and ended when I saw my company sell out performances at that same sacred dance space, City Center. That has, in terms of Déjà Vu, been the climax of my career."

"Oh God!" Barry exclaims with a laugh and a hint of embarrassment when I ask him how he explains the moves to his dancers, since he cannot physically demonstrate them. The explosive quality of his work would make any viewer wonder how a choreographer could get those ideas across without actually performing them. "I draw from my knowledge of dance terms to communicate to the dancers. My system is to use verbal and visual images. A lot of it has to do with my being able to talk the dancer through it and to attempt to be very clear about the feeling, or the shape, or the intentions that I'm looking for. Sometimes it's like trying to choreograph in a dark room where you can't see what is going on around you. The dancer has to be able to hear and feel to come to a conclusion of

what the step is supposed to be.

"It's not terribly unique," he says modestly. "But something that has to be developed over a period of time is the communication with your subjects, so they will be able to understand and convey what you want them to, and that's just being a good director. That's what I strive for."

Besides having a successful company, his aspirations are to go beyond choreography, and to convey his messages through other mediums, like film. The power of Barry's work can be no better communicated than through a story he told me of a recent experience of his. Someone from Japan was considering having him choreograph a piece for a performance. "I submitted my résumé and videos and all that stuff," he says. "When the man called me back he wanted me to schedule something the next week. As he was giving me the rehearsal schedule, I noticed the rehearsal studio was a location with lots of stairs, so I said, 'That particular place will be a problem for me because of my situation.' And he said, 'What do you mean?' So I said, 'Well, I'm in a wheelchair.' He says, 'No! Oh, I'm sorry to hear that.'

"I asked him, 'Didn't you read the material I sent you?' 'No,' he said, 'I just looked at the tapes and I *love* your work!'

"To me, *that's* what it's all about, and I wish it could always be that way. And some years down the road, that *will* give me a great amount of satisfaction. In the everyday struggle to do what I do, there are so many barriers that confront me, that's just the reality of the situation," he says. Then he smiles. "But that's pretty much the reality of the situation for everyone in life, isn't it?"

Aubrey Lynch

"I love being the center of attention—I'm just being honest—that's probably why I became a dancer in the first place. I was in tenth grade and no one really knew me. No one really *wanted* to know me. There was this dance contest that I entered and won. And suddenly I was the star of the school. I think that feeling of wanting to be watched and wanting to be the center of attention just stuck with me."

Becoming a featured dancer with the Alvin Ailey dance company and Barry Martin's Déjà Vu took a lot of work. Much of it had very little to do with dancing.

While Aubrey Lynch was spending his high school years in a small town called Brownstown, twenty miles south of Detroit, Michigan, he was going nuts. His family was living with his mother's sister. Tending the chickens his aunt kept in the backyard was Aubrey's job. "I collected eggs in the morning. I remember collecting those eggs and crying 'cause I didn't want to do it. 'I don't belong in this little town. I don't want to be here.' I needed to be in a big city. I wanted to travel and do all kinds of things."

Aubrey did well in school, earning himself a scholarship to the University of Michigan. He knew it would please his parents if he went there, as his father had. That was the plan—to earn a degree as a chemical physicist. But while he still was in high school, something caught his attention.

"My girlfriend got me to enter this dance contest, and we won! I started going to her dance studio and I just stuck with it, but it was more like a hobby. I wanted to do it, but I knew that dancers didn't make a lot of money, and I couldn't make a career out of it. My parents certainly didn't want me to make a career out of it. So I just thought I'd go to college and see what happened after that."

One weekend Aubrey came home from college to attend a special class being taught by choreographer Alvin Ailey. This rare privilege to study with a master was not to be missed. Compared to the ballet classes Aubrey had been taking, Ailey's style of dance was exciting, challenging, and different. It was an entirely new way of moving.

"There was an audition for the Ailey school the following day. One of the ladies running the auditions said I should go. I figured it would be a good way to see how I measured up compared with the other dancers, and to see if there was even a possibility that I could be a dancer later on. I figured I would get my degree first and dance afterward, not knowing you have to dance when you're young.

"I went to the audition and I got the scholarship to the school. Now what was I going to do? I just dropped everything and I went—of course, against my parents' wishes. I figured, if I'm good enough now, I might as well go and see what happens. I already had a year of college, and I had done really well, but my heart just wasn't in it. So I moved to New York; I was nineteen."

Aubrey worked three jobs simultaneously when he first arrived in New York. Not one paid much, but together it was enough to survive.

"Things started to fall into place after I went to New York. After a year and a half I got into the Ailey second company, and that's when I met [choreographer] Barry Martin. It was at the school gala. Every year the school has a gala: The students perform, the first company performs, and the second company performs—it's kind of a big to-do for the Ailey school. I got into the company in January of 1987, so it must have been June of '87.

"Barry had seen me perform as a scholarship student in the summer of '86. I do remember once this girl came up to me and said, 'You see that guy in the wheelchair? He's a choreographer, and he's very interested in you.' I was just so flattered because, again, I was just trying to make my mark here in the city with all these students, and I didn't think I was doing very well. I didn't think anyone had noticed. Barry had noticed, but I just kind of forgot all about it. I met him again at this reception, and he asked me to go to the audition for his company. I said, 'Great! Sure!'"

Although he was happy to be in the second company of the Alvin Ailey Dance Theater, Aubrey felt he wasn't being pushed to reach his full potential. Here was a chance to eventually become a featured dancer and challenge his abilities.

"I went to the audition and I got into Barry's company and started working with him one-on-one. And it's funny, people ask me a lot, 'What did you think when he asked you to join the company,' because Barry's in a wheelchair. And I never thought of that. He was there, and he asked me, and I thought, since he asked me he must be able to choreograph. So it never crossed my mind how he was going to do it. It never crossed my mind at all.

"There's definitely an energy there. He doesn't just say, 'Stand in second position with your arms facing the floor and do a turn.' He'll say, 'You're with this girl. You're in love with her but you've just had a fight. You're in second position, she slaps you—and that's why you turn.' Now there may not be a girl there at all, but he's giving you images, so it's more than just movement. When you're learning it you remember that; it's not necessarily the step. And by the time the piece is finished it's a totally different thing. It's not just a position."

Aubrey's fame has come from his ability to translate those images into gorgeous movements, powerful twists and leaps. "Look at that," says Barry Martin as he pulls out a photo of Aubrey in midflight. "Nobody leaps like that. *No one* gets the kind of height he does! The only reason he doesn't get the recognition he deserves is because he is a Black dancer."

Being pushed to his limits is what he wants, and working with Barry Martin does that for Aubrey. "I think Barry's been one of the most challenging choreographers I've worked with, and I've worked with a lot of them. One thing that makes his choreography technically difficult is that he's not up there doing it, so he doesn't know what feels natural. A lot of times he'll ask you to do things that are not really natural to do. You're fighting your body, you're fighting gravity." But then Aubrey finds a way to do that, to fight gravity. And it's beautiful.

"The emotional part of my dancing, I think, was the hardest part at first, because I was still a student. I had become intimidated by the city and by the school that I was in, so I lost a lot of my spark, a lot of my outgoingness. I had become very introverted and my dancing had become very quiet and timid. But apparently Barry saw *something*. It wasn't all gone.

"When I went into the first rehearsal with him, I was working on a piece called 'See the Hope,' in which there was a solo. Technically it was harder than anything I had ever done. But emotionally, he wanted me to be the lead in this ballet and represent a force and a power that could control everything. Everyone. He had to pull it out of me. He kept saying, 'More, more. I want more,' and it was very frustrating because I thought I was giving everything that I had, but it was never enough. It was like pulling teeth. By the time the performance went on, I was a different dancer.

"After that first concert I said I'd never work with him again because I was so humbled. I realized there was so much that I didn't have." But Aubrey knew he would stay. He felt as though he were Barry's legs. His job was to translate the ideas Barry couldn't physically perform.

"When we're in rehearsal, even when we're marking dancers' steps on the stage and doing it with less energy, he's got to see something. Some of the passion, or else it's not right. It's a very intense way of working, but I owe a lot of the way I dance to him. He'll deny that but it's true."

While the days of studying chemistry are behind him, Aubrey Lynch still has the notes he took in school. Too much hard work went into taking them to throw them away. Even though he may sometimes read a book about the sciences, most of the science he concentrates on these days is science fiction. "To keep my mind alive—in a scientific mode." He laughs.

Aubrey has avoided most of the vices many dancers fall prey to in order to cope with the high stress of trying to be perfect all the time, of knowing someone is waiting for you to slip up so he can take your place. No cigarettes, no alcohol, no drugs. "I've set an image for myself that sometimes I'm afraid I'm not going to be able to live up to. And that's part of it. No drugs. My true friends, they stick up for me. They respect me for not bending. It's almost like they want to see the other image of the dancer, that someone can still be straight.

"People think I'm weird. They think I act like a little kid—and I *do* feel very young. I hope I feel this young when I get older.

"I'd like to get into production and directing. I really don't want to choreograph. I'm taking acting lessons and singing lessons. I'd like to do a Broadway show and stay in the arts—because you can't dance forever. I want to do film and commercials and videos and . . . I want to do everything.

"I'm not really sure how it's going to work. But when I came here I really didn't know what I was going to do either. I think if I'm focused, disciplined, and try to get the best of my art together, more options will be available to me when I'm ready to leave the company."

Bryant Gumbel

PARADOX: a situation that seems to have contradictory or inconsistent qualities.

The word *paradox* seems to describe the condition of the American Black community, which at times is less of a community than it professes to be. Many times, we in the Black community hear the urging of other Blacks to "strive to be number one," "do us proud," and "aim high," only to hear those who have reached the top often ridiculed as "arrogant," a "sellout," or a "Tom." Few successful Black people have been tainted by this stain as often as Bryant Gumbel.

Since becoming the cohost of NBC television's national morning news program "Today" in 1982, he has been praised for his skillful, intelligent, and insightful interviews of personalities ranging from the Pope to Denzel Washington. He has made to appear simple what was considered by many to be a difficult transition, the switch from prominent sportscaster to respected "hard" news reporter. The awards for his achievements as

a broadcaster and humanitarian come in a never-ending wave, yet he is frequently the target of sharp-tongued attacks by both Blacks and whites, who label him an arrogant wanna-be.

"I've never really given it much credence," Bryant says, sitting in a small cozy room that looks more like his den than his office. "I think it's asinine and limiting to buy into an argument that a lot of racists would love to foster, which is that the minute you can articulate yourself or the minute you are a success, then you are selling out and trying to be white. Because the converse is, in order to be Black, you must be inarticulate and be a failure. If you buy into that, then you allow racists to win because you either consign yourself to failure, or you allow your own people to turn their backs against you. I think it's a ludicrous argument.

"I would hope by now we would have gotten past the idea that because somebody says 'ask' instead of 'aks,' they are somehow not Black enough. A lot of my friends, people who are in the public eye, have faced this same thing over and over. It's like too many of our people are being led around and led to think what racists would have them believe."

"He's arrogant," a friend tells me when I bring up Bryant Gumbel's name.

"Have you ever met the man?" I ask honestly, thinking he knows something I don't.

"No." The answer comes back in a tone of voice that says, "Do I need to?" I'd like to know why he thinks Bryant is arrogant. "I know some people who live in his neighborhood," the friend tells me. "They never see him. He just keeps to himself. He doesn't socialize with them."

My neighbors never see me, and I don't socialize with them. I guess when I become successful, I know what I can expect to hear about myself.

Despite Bryant's admittedly hermitlike life-style, he has made himself available to, and is active in, many organizations that further the opportunities of Blacks in America. He is a board member of the United Negro College Fund and is the recipient of three NAACP Image Awards. The Hundred Black Men Society has honored him, CORE has awarded him the Martin Luther King Award, and the National Urban League has given him top honors.

"I wish he would let people know about all the things he does for the Black community," says Chicago-based NBC reporter Mike Leonard, a colleague and longtime friend of Bryant's, who happens to be white. "Whenever you see unknown Black authors or controversial Black figures on the 'Today' show, he's the one who's usually pushed to get them there."

Bryant smiles but looks a bit embarrassed. He says in a subdued voice, "It's not my way. I don't feel compelled to run around saying, 'Oh look! Here I am and I do this.' Anybody whose opinions are going to be shaped by reading something about me, or hearing something secondhand about me—I've never felt their opinion was worth courting. So I'm not going to run around and make a big deal about whether I speak here, give money there, or raise money for this. That's my business, and I'm certainly not going to point it out so that they might like me. It's just not that big a deal."

Watching Bryant work, it is obvious that he has done his homework. It's very easy to ask a head of state or a controversial entertainer a passive question, one that they've had lots of practice answering. Those are not the questions Bryant is likely to ask. He asks the things the person at home is curious about. Or maybe not. Either way, when you hear his questions, you may say out loud to the TV, "Yeah! What *about* that?"

"Do I operate with a certain degree of confidence? Yes I do. I think my job asks me to. Am I rude to people? No I'm not. Do I respect them? Yes I do. But I do think, to some people, the minute a Black man turns to a white official and says 'Hey, wait a minute, two plus two is *not* three—two plus two is four, and you know it!' then that's arrogant! That's how they define arrogant."

Bryant sits back in his chair. Way back. Still in the suit from the show he and co-anchor Katie Couric finished only an hour ago, he seems very relaxed. He smiles warmly at a compliment given him but quickly tries to take the attention off himself. He listens with genuine interest to the questions asked him, then considers his answer with his feet up on the corner of the desk and his fingers folded together into a little steeple, thoughtfully tapping his mouth.

"I've always said that if you lined up Ted Koppel, Barbara Walters, and Bryant Gumbel together," he tells me, "and all three asked the same question of the

President, and followed it up with the same response, Ted Koppel would be viewed as confident, Barbara Walters would be viewed as bitchy, and Bryant Gumbel would be viewed as arrogant. And I think the characterizations speak much more to the accuser than they do the accused.

"Let's face it, I think there are some people who are uncomfortable with a Black man who is their emotional, intellectual, economic equal, if not their superior. That makes them uneasy. I think the fact that Black men in particular are threatening to a large portion of white America gives rise to an effort to tear those people down. Unfortunately, a lot of Blacks buy into that. That's sad, and it speaks volumes about mass media, but," he adds, "I also don't think it's an accident.

"I challenged a press conference some years ago," Bryant continues, "to name for me any Black man who had ever succeeded in television, really succeeded, whom they did not ultimately characterize as arrogant. Be it Flip Wilson, Bill Cosby, Bryant Gumbel, Ed Bradley, or Arsenio Hall. Any Black man who ever succeeds in television, ultimately, they come to accuse of being arrogant.

"It's the same mind-set that says kids that make good grades are trying to be white. Well, that's absurd. The Klan would love for you to believe that. I mean, honest to God! 'Show how Black you can be—get an F!'" I bring that up because ultimately the only way around the problem is education. Education would allow more Black people to move into areas where there are only a few Blacks. We would then not be viewed as something unusual. I think when a Black man is viewed as something unusual, then the next line of thought is, well, since he's the only one of that one hundred who's Black, he must be trying to be white. And I think that's kind of pathetic. It retards growth and it's self-destructive. A lot of kids are buying into this early on."

Women's magazines, he observes, will often go out of their way to applaud a woman they are writing about. Some of these women may not deserve the accolades they receive, and he disagrees with that kind of blind loyalty. But, he points out, "I wish Black folks would take a lesson from those magazines and not be so quick to jump on their own."

For six years Bryant worked diligently to sell NBC on a personal dream; at last, in November of 1992, the "Today" show broadcast an entire week from the continent of Africa. For five days the show came from different locations in the land that is the home of one-fifth of the world's population.

Convincing the people who count the money at NBC to pay for such a project wasn't easy. "The idea of doing the program from Africa is not a simple matter of just parking your stuff there and doing it. We had a number of problems, like how do you represent a continent of sixty nations and eight hundred million people in the course of one week and do it justice? How do you broadcast out of a continent that has very few broadcast facilities? How do you ensure the safety and credibility of your program when there's rampant insta- bility? How do you get from point A to point B when transportation in many instances is nonexistent?"

Bryant drew up several proposals and figured the cost of the production. NBC said no. Instead of just accepting their answer, he reworked the proposal, three and four times a year. Much of his time was spent going to the African embassies to get their cooperation—to coax them into doing anything they could do to make the job easier. "For example," says Bryant, "we want to do it from Zimbabwe, but Zimbabwe doesn't have the equipment we need. Okay, we'll fly in our equipment. Our equipment is worth thirty million dollars. Well, there's 20 percent duty on everything you send in, and that's sudden- ly six million dollars. It's like, *whoa!* Time out," he says, making a T with his hands. "I had to do a lot of elbow rubbing with our state department, with the African diplomats, and then deal with their lobby- ists in order to gain their support. That consumed an awful lot of my time, too. We then had to draw up some kind of a plan that we could live with editorially, and that NBC could live with economically."

After six years NBC's no became a yes.

"The trip meant a lot to me, it really did," Bryant says. "I took my whole family over. I thought it was important for Americans to see Africa as something other than a starving continent, something other than animals wandering around. I wanted Americans to discard this idea that every African lives in a thatched hut with a lion outside his front door and a jungle in the back. Life in Africa isn't like that."

NBC executives wanted to limit the locations to Wankie National Park and Victoria Falls. Bryant told them no. "It was of utmost importance to me that we have the city of Harare in the background. I thought a city behind us of skyscrapers and traffic jams and everything else would speak volumes."

The show featured engineers, artists, doctors, and businesspeople; it highlighted the traditions of Africans, as well as both the urban and rural Africans. Bryant took the viewers on a step-by-step trip following the tragic route of men and women imprisoned and sold for the slave trade. "I think what you realize is how inhuman some people can be toward others for the most asinine of reasons: because of their ethnicity, color, religion, race, or gender. It was difficult. Being painfully aware of the barbarity and the inhumanity of man toward man is something you don't get over.

"I had my fourteen-year-old son with me, and I was very concerned that he grasp the reality of it. When you consider that the slave trade removed from Africa twenty-five million of its best, brightest, strongest, and then left the continent to its own designs, you begin to realize what a crippling effect it had in a historical context. How much it retarded the continent's development. And we're talking about twenty-five million people from a continent of maybe eighty-five million, not today's eight hundred million."

As he and Katie wrapped up the last show from Africa, the voice of the usually controlled Bryant Gumbel cracked and his eyes glistened with tears. "It was emotional in a lot of ways," he tells me when I bring up that moment. "It's very hard to dedicate your life to trying to get something accomplished, and then see it accomplished. There's a great feeling of being spent when it's done. There's also a feeling of exhilaration."

I wanted to know if he had anything he wanted to share with young people. What would Bryant Gumbel want to tell them? He laughed at being put on the spot and looked around his office filled with sports memorabilia, hundreds of books, photos of friends and family, and tons of teddy bears. Bryant has a thing for teddy bears. "It seems a strange thing to say to young Black men who put such a premium on macho," he starts, searching for the right words, "but you gotta have guts. And not the kind of guts that says, 'Yeah, I can get away with something and the man won't catch me.' Not the kind of guts that says, 'Yeah, I'll fight you out in the street at three o'clock.' It's the kind of guts that says you've got to be willing to make A's while your friends laugh at you. You've got to be willing to study hard even though your friends say it's not cool. You've got to be willing to respect a woman when your friends may not. That to me is the definition of guts. You've got to be willing to take a chance, and to accept their ridicule if necessary, in order to do what you believe is right for yourself and for your family. And however you choose to define success, and you need not define it only in financial terms, *that's* what you should pursue. Don't chase after the popular opinions of people who choose to demean you because it makes *them* more comfortable."

Cree Summer and Kadeem Hardison

Cree Summer laughs. I can almost see her throwing her head back though she's three thousand miles away in sunny California. I'm stuck in cloudy New York in late winter and she's laughing. Despite my mood, I return her laugh, because it's contagious.

Cree Summer is famous for her character Freddie on the hit television series "A Different World." Although her role grew significantly from the brief screen appearances of the first few seasons, her thoughts on what her character should be doing while in the camera's view have always been ambitious. "I always asked that she wear a T-shirt saying Free South Africa or hand out flyers or be reading about our history. Anything, as long as she was doing something that could have an impact on the world around her," Cree explains.

The world around Cree is not always aware of social issues, other than what clothes someone wore to the Academy Awards ceremony or

who is sleeping with whom. Between shooting her series and taping her voice characterizations (Penny of "Inspector Gadget" is one among the many cartoon voices Cree has provided), this twenty-something actress has had little time to socialize. When she does, she avoids the party set, preferring her own company or spending time with friends. "With L.A., there's the ocean on the left and the mountains on the right and the pretense in the middle. I don't go where all the b.s. is. I've found that if you're secure enough in who you are, those kinds of people are not attracted to you."

There were certainly no plans for a life in Hollywood when Cree was growing up in Canada. Which is not to say her early years were uneventful. She has lived on the Plains Cree Indian reservation (she is named for the tribe) in Saskatchewan, in a church, and has traveled across Canada on a bus. School learning was not a priority, but *education* was. "My father would come and take me out of school for rides through the countryside if it was a nice day." He strongly believed there was much to be learned outdoors, she relates, in the open, *talking* to people, in a natural, unrestrictive setting.

After moving around a bit and seeing Canada, the Summer family settled in Toronto, where Cree began attending the city's Performing Arts High School. That lasted only a year. "It wasn't what I wanted," she says in retrospect and with no regret. "I was already aware of so many things," she continues, adding that she was distracted by outside interests.

Cree has just begun to have the chance to really shine on the screen, and she believes more chances will come. In the meantime, she does interviews and expresses her views about issues and social problems openly and with an ear for discussion, debate, education. In the early days of "A Different World" Cree didn't "get a chance to really say anything on the show. So I gave interviews." We met briefly in New York to continue our discussion of a few weeks earlier. Cree likes to speak her mind—no matter what. "The interview before this one," she says, laughing that Tasmanian devil laugh, "I'm sure the woman thought I was crazy!"

Misconceptions about who she is and what she may be about don't faze Cree. She is at peace with herself and with the world. "I'm very comfortable in my solitude," she explains quietly, with a hint of a smile. "I make myself laugh." To bring the point home, she guffaws joyously. Though Cree now has citizenship in both the United States and Canada, she does not believe in labels, ethnic or otherwise. "I'll be damned if I'm not just a human being. We're so busy putting labels on each other that we forget that we're human beings." The meaning of life, she says, is not all that mysterious. People need to think on what it is they *need*, not necessarily want.

"This may sound crazy," she starts, hesitating only a second before continuing, "but I think there should be segregation of the *individual* as opposed to segregation of races. I think that if each person said 'kiss off' to everyone else and just got their *own* selves together, then all the other stuff wouldn't be important anymore. When you sit by yourself for a while, you realize that we all have this thing called life in common."

Having spent the first years of her life with the Cree Indians on the Canadian plains, Cree strongly identifies with the Indian way of life and way of thinking, and the injustices they have suffered over the centuries. Kadeem Hardison, her series costar and good friend, opened the door to her awareness of the Black experience and history, and to her understanding of the injustices suffered by Blacks in America. Louis Farrakhan opened a few more doors. "He blew me away. I didn't agree with a lot of what he said, but the history, his knowledge made me think."

But Minister Farrakhan's visit to Los Angeles served also to strengthen Cree's personal philosophy. "There are five basic things—life, fire, air, earth and water; *they* are the most important things on this planet. We all share life, and that's a large enough common bond for us to try to live together."

Kadeem Hardison

Kadeem Hardison leans toward the tape recorder's mike and declares "Kadeem Hardison . . . take one." This young man seems to have no intention of taking just one of anything. He was cast in a small part in the television situation comedy "A Different World," originally a vehicle for Lisa Bonet of "The Cosby Show." It became obvious almost from the beginning that Kadeem's Dwayne Wayne was destined for better things. He stole scenes and teenage hearts and he got laughs.

"I had a lot of solo time," he says of his siblingless childhood. "It's the only way to get to know yourself, because you do stuff you wouldn't do around other people. And growing up surrounded by women . . ." A sly look creeps onto his face. "I won't say I know how to handle . . ." He waits for the laugh. Then more seriously, almost shyly, "I like women better, I feel more comfortable around them."

In a business notorious for turning heads away from more simple things, Kadeem has stayed reassuringly down-to-earth, a valuable asset for any talented up-and-coming actor. A new house is one of few indulgences—although it is quite a practical one. Kadeem breaks into a grin when I mention his home. "You should see what the designer is doing to the house," he says with a proprietorial air. "Wow!"

Acting was not part of anyone's master plan for Kadeem. "My mother asked me what I wanted to do. I had no idea," he recalls, shrugging his shoulders thoughtfully. "All the kids said, 'I want to be an astronaut,' or, 'I want to be a fireman.' I said I didn't know." When he finally found his answer, he began attending Eubie Blake's Amass Children's Theater in uptown Manhattan every Saturday, taking dance and drama classes. He went on to take commercial classes that trained students in front of the camera and encouraged criticism. At thirteen, he landed his first real acting job on an ABC "Afterschool Special." Other jobs and commercials followed. Now after several years on "A Different World," he has won an Emmy award, multiple NAACP Image Awards, and critical acclaim.

The exposure Kadeem has gotten through the hit series, he says, is positive in terms of more than just his career. "The *show*, I think, does more for Black people *everywhere* than is done by Black people simply finding success in the entertainment industry. When you see your own people up there doing something good, it makes you feel good. It gives you a different sense of yourself, something that you've possibly never seen before. It makes you proud to be Black."

The importance of the NAACP Image Award was not lost on the young actor. The positive images that were reinforced every week on "A Different World"—images promoting education, family, friendship, and social, sexual, and personal responsibility—made working with other Blacks all that much more important. He was oblivious to any racial tensions that may have been present while he was growing up and learning his craft. He was basically color-blind. He grew up secure about who he was, secure enough to believe that everyone was that lucky. But there began to be enough instances where he was the only Black person in given situations and surroundings that he noticed, but did not choose to comment. Then he worked in Spike Lee's *School Daze*.

"When I did *School Daze*, it was the first time I worked with an all-Black cast and crew, because in commercials I was always Boy Number One or the only Black guy in the cast. I've never been to college. That was my college experience. That was what woke me up." Shortly after that, "A Different World" offered Kadeem another chance to work with fellow Black actors, and with Bill Cosby and Debbie Allen.

"When Debbie came in, she showed us a lot of things. She laid down the law that when we read the script, we'd circle our lines, and make our notes, then when the reading was over, she'd open up the floor for discussion." The opportunity for that kind of input was instrumental in making the show accessible to the television audience.

"How do you change the way people think? You keep showing them that they can't believe everything they read. Everybody should hear Louis Farrakhan just once, to hear the dark side of what's going on. I went to see him. I wanted to hear him. I took Cree to hear Farrakhan because I wanted her to hear him, too. I was introduced to him by Larry Fishburne when I was working on *School Daze*. When it came time, I wanted to introduce someone to him.

"Farrakhan was talking about gang violence. The first twenty or thirty rows were given to high school kids. We were all blown away." He was most impressed with how the students absorbed what Farrakhan was saying, but he was a little concerned. He knew many did not have the knowledge or experience to balance what was said with other points of view. "Forty percent of what he was saying was a little off. But the rest was dead *on*. He asked for awareness."

The main message for everyone, Kadeem felt, was that "we have to open people up to what's going on." Everyone, Black and white, should pay some more attention, work on their awareness of themselves and others. "Everyone should just *listen* to each other."

Phadrea Ponds

"I look at things a little bit differently, because I look at things from a human perspective. So I'm often criticized by my colleagues because *they* don't do that. They'd rather sit in the lab or analyze something out in the field, staying away from people because 'people don't understand what we do.' So, if I try to bring in the human aspect, or ask them what kind of effects they think our work will have on the African-American community, they roll their eyes. I think I've started calling myself a natural-resource person instead of a wildlife biologist because I'm concerned with the environment as a whole and not only the little critters outside."

Natural-resource biologist Phadrea Ponds is finishing her graduate studies in Corvallis, Oregon, at Oregon State University. She has chosen a career in which there are very few people of color. This career move is a deliberate action on her part. Environmental studies has long been

thought of as strictly for European-Americans, many of whom became interested in the field in the 1960s, when people were communing with nature. Her decision to work with natural things would seem ludicrous to most who knew her when she was younger.

"I didn't grow up wanting to be a wildlife biologist," says Phadrea. "I can't even be outside that much because I'm allergic to *everything*. I didn't even like sitting on the grass! In fact, I *hated* being outside. Yet somehow the environment has turned into a really big concern for me.

"I don't consider myself an environmentalist—I don't think I would chain myself to a tree to save an owl. But if they were to take property away from a needy family in my community, then I would chain myself to that house. I wouldn't chain myself to an old broken tree to keep someone from chopping it down, because I think the tree's resources are just as important as the tree *itself*.

"I was a premed major when I started. But I decided I couldn't bear seeing people sick," she says, adding that her move into her current field was purely by chance. "I wondered what else I could do with all the biology knowledge I had. Schools were recruiting very heavily for wildlife biologists, and they wanted minorities. I figured, I'm pretty analytical, so I'll try it out. And I really enjoyed it."

While she found the work interesting and challenging, Phadrea began to question its value. Much of her time was spent doing research that seemed irrelevant to her world. "In undergraduate school I was studying mice and their homing abilities, how they were able to go from one place to the next, and then I tried to think, what in the hell does that mean to me? I'm not saying I *don't* care, but there are more important issues concerning my *community*."

Phadrea started looking into environmental issues that had an impact on people at home, with a particular emphasis on the Black community. There were things happening she felt no one was addressing directly, and the educating of the community about those things became *her* issue. "I confronted companies about toxic waste in the Black community. 'Do you realize you're dumping waste on the Black community?' 'Well we do,' they'd tell me, 'but we have to dump it *somewhere*.'"

It became more and more evident to her that someone had to be a voice for the Black community, "because I didn't see any other Black people doing it. In my department I was the only female, and there were five Black males. We felt very strongly about getting some type of message out, since we knew no one else would."

That message, she says, is that Blacks are just as concerned about the environment as Whites are. Phadrea knows that, as with anything, there are always voices of dissension: "There's an attitude of, 'Well, *we* didn't screw everything up. So why should we care?' There is a need for us to get the message to the community that the environment is here for everyone. We have to keep it clean. If we don't do our share to keep it clean, when it goes—it's gone for good. It doesn't matter who's responsible."

There can certainly be a balance between the needs of business and industry, and the need of the earth to have its resources protected. All too often, Phadrea explains, the disparate interests of the opposing groups win out; there is no compromise. "It's hard enough to get people to get out and vote for a president. If you can get them to get out and vote on environmental issues, that's definitely a step in the right direction. When they *do* vote, I hope they think to vote for the kind of person who will make changes."

Phadrea is employed as a technical writer for the U.S. Fish and Wildlife Service. "I translate all their technical literature into something the public can understand." A lot of her work in the community, with kids in schools and on field trips, is a direct offshoot of that job. She has gone out of her way to make herself available to young people—particularly Black youngsters. "If I were just in a lab, looking at parasites all day long for eight hours a day, I don't think I could do it. I have to be out with people I can make a difference with. I don't think I make a difference with the children who go camping all the time. I really don't." Phadrea brings nature and how it relates to us into the classroom and into young people's lives. "I talk to them. I don't just stand at the board and lecture."

Phadrea, who is normally very easygoing, becomes impassioned when she speaks of her self-appointed mission. "Before people can take pride in the surrounding environment," she says, "they have to have pride in their own community. So I work to get them involved with their community first. Once we've done that, we can move out and concern ourselves with more global issues."

Comparing community and global issues helps bring the information home in the classroom. Phadrea used the L.A. riots as an example for the students: "All that looting, rioting, and burning. What have they done? They've destroyed where they live. When someone goes into a forest and uses clear-cutting, which is a forest-management practice where foresters will clear up to six hundred acres of woods to even the growth and age of trees in an area, they're destroying the homes of animals. The animals don't see them coming; this isn't a normal thing that happens in nature. Although they often replant areas with saplings, or leave the debris thinking it will support smaller animals, the foresters don't check to see how many animals' homes are going to be lost or what type of habitat is subsequently going to be gained.

"In L.A.," she asks, "what type of habitat is going to be gained? How many new businesses are going to come out of the old businesses that were burned to the ground? What are the benefits of this destruction, and what are the disadvantages? We make a comparison. Once you can make it real, then kids will say, 'Oh, that makes sense!' Environmental and social issues go hand in hand. There has to be someone to make the link, and that's what I try to do."

Phadrea works with beautification projects. These projects employ students, making them entrepreneurs, and giving their lessons a connection to the real world. "You're not just going out and raking leaves. Students first learn how to do land-scape architecture. Then they provide that service, for which they are well paid."

The Black community needs to become more aware of environmental concerns in their own homes. These can be simple things like lead poisoning from paint, or how having plants in your home or even planting trees on your block can be beneficial to your surroundings because plants clean the air by creating fresh oxygen.

"Blacks were solely involved in civil rights during the environmental movement in the sixties. Although the social issues are just as important as the environmental issues, we're so busy fighting the day-to-day things, the daily needs, that we don't really have time to care if an owl becomes extinct or not. Parents are more concerned about their kids coming home at night or whether drug dealers are selling drugs to them. They don't care about that nearly extinct spotted owl thirty miles away.

"I'm not trying to convince you to *agree* that the spotted owl should not become extinct. I'm trying to explain the importance of community development. That's part of our natural resources—community upkeep, landscape architecture right around their own community.

"I had an experience with an outdoor school, which is basically a camp that stresses nature activities. I'll never forget it. I was the only Black counselor at this school. They wanted me there especially because they wanted these white kids to see a Black person in natural resources. The *adults* were just as amazed as the kids that I was there.

Then, I took some Black kids out, and the experience was so different because these were students who had never been outside of Portland. I took them only fifteen miles outside of Portland, but they thought we had gone deep into the boondocks."

There aren't many Blacks involved in environmental fields, Phadrea remarks. "Because of my thesis work I've met thirty over the last two months. And that's more than I ever expected to meet. If I were to look for another Black female wildlife biologist, I would go as far as to say there are maybe five of us in the entire United States. I know four Black female marine biologists, and that's pretty rare as well."

The environmental studies field is huge. You don't have to work in a lab to get involved in it. If you have an interest in law, you can be an environmental lawyer. If your interest is in business or economics, you can become an agricultural economist. Journalists can write about environmental issues. Phadrea has tied her studies into sociology. Many colleges give large, often full scholarships to students who major in environmental studies. Phadrea feels it's an excellent way to get a jump on a career you may have always wanted if you simply tie it into environmental studies.

"My friends are always asking me, 'Why are you an environmentalist?' I want everyone to know what *I* know, and I want everyone to recognize the world outside of their small world. Often, recognizing that world may simply mean seeing things a little bit differently."

Reginald K. Ceaser

As he moves through the hallways of the Swedish Institute of Massage Therapy in downtown Manhattan, it appears as though his feet are riding on a cushion of air. His legs hardly seem to move as he walks to his classroom; his steps are soundless. Students greet him warmly as they pass, each calling him "sensei," a Japanese term of respect for a teacher.

Reginald Keith Herb Dancer Ceaser has been teaching the art of shiatsu, a form of Japanese massage, at the Swedish Institute since 1986. Aside from being a practitioner of shiatsu, he is a herbologist and a massage therapist. The practice of herbology dates back to man's earliest appearance on the earth. It is the practice of using aromatic plants, roots, and other natural items to create medicines or for use as treatments on their own.

His foray into the field of Oriental medicine has been shaped by many things in his life, not the least of which is his family background.

Reggie's mother was Dutch and Matinnecock Indian; his father was of African and Blackfoot Indian descent. Reggie first saw his mother make use of liniments and natural healing methods to deal with family ailments.

Another thing that made an impression on Reggie occurred when he was studying martial arts in Chinatown at age eighteen. "I hurt my shoulder pretty bad in one of our practice sessions. It put me out of commission for a week. The teacher asked my practice partner why I hadn't been coming to class, and he told him. When I finally returned to class, the instructor put some liniments on my shoulder, moved it around, massaged it a couple of seconds, and told me to go out on the floor again.

"I was amazed. I was suddenly able to move my arm," he says, making big circles with his shoulder as he relives the moment. "I couldn't believe it! For a week I was at home, aching, and this guy fixes it in two minutes. That started my fascination with the Oriental culture. My buddy and I would go to Chinese movies, and we'd visit different Chinese doctors to learn about their practices. That evolved into my studying Oriental philosophy.

"Years later," says the soft-spoken Reggie, "I was teaching martial arts with a partner, and we thought, What happens if someone gets hurt? Besides just liability, we should know how to heal someone if we're teaching them, even if we can only treat them on a minor level. So, I took a class in shiatsu. I was curious because I knew these things *could* work. I had watched my mother use herbs and natural healing methods, *and* I'd experienced my shoulder being healed almost by itself."

Reggie enjoyed the shiatsu class and decided to take another. He quickly realized he was *taking* more shiatsu classes than he was *teaching* martial-arts classes. He decided that it would make sense for him to do something with all the knowledge he'd been accumulating. So he began to take on a few clients.

"After studying shiatsu, it was a natural move for me to go into liniments. Liniments and herbology, natural aids for injuries. My patients would come to me and say, '*You* know so much about the body, what can I take for a stomachache?' or, 'What can I do for *this* problem without using drugs?' So I started to research different herbs. I met several teachers whom I have to give credit for showing me different ways to look at various problems.

"After a while I thought, when you teach martial arts, people try to punch you, they try to kick you—and it's fun," he says with an ironic smile. "It's an exchange of energy. Then after your lessons, at the end of the month, some of your students will either give you the money willingly, or begrudgingly. If you do a shiatsu treatment, people *like* you," he says with a smile. "They give you hugs. You're not only paid with *money*, which is given gratefully, but they're making *gifts* for you, and you're in their presence as a positive force. So I figured it was better for me to do shiatsu on a professional basis than do martial arts!"

As Reggie was making this career move, the laws in New York State were changing. New York now requires all massage therapists, including those performing shiatsu, to be licensed in order to practice. Reggie enrolled in the Swedish Institute, which was and still is one of the few accredited schools that prepares its students for the state licensing exam. While at the school, he also became proficient in Swedish massage, which was a requirement to pass the test.

It seems that each step in his development has been tied to a particular event. During Reggie's studies, a guest lecturer gave a demonstration on the use of Swedish massage therapy in the treatment of Bell's Palsy, a condition that causes partial facial paralysis. Reggie was impressed for the first time by the use of the Swedish technique. The guest speaker told him that many people in her field did amazing things with massage, and that he should join the AMTA (American Massage Therapy Association). They had regular meetings, and it would give him a chance to network and learn.

"Eventually, the AMTA needed someone on the board that had an expertise in shiatsu, and they wanted to have minority balance," Reggie explains. "The person had to be an expert in shiatsu *and* licensed in Swedish massage. There weren't too many who fit the bill. Some of the teachers I met at the Swedish Institute remembered me and thought I would be a good person for the board." Within a short time Reggie was asked to become a board member of the AMTA.

The Swedish Institute wanted to add a shiatsu program to their curriculum, and Reggie Ceaser became the perfect choice to head the department. "It was one big circle," he says, with his gentle smile. "I see that happening many times—that I come full circle, and as I complete *one* circle, another one appears."

At one of the many conferences held by the AMTA, Reggie expanded his knowledge of herbalism. At that same conference he met a naturopath, someone who practices therapeutic methods that do not involve the use of drugs but employ the natural forces of light, air, heat, water, and massage. This practitioner took Reggie under his wing and taught him about Western herbalism. Another instructor, whom Reggie met later on, taught him about what Reggie likes to call "planetary herbalism": "It was Chinese medicine, but it used herbs from all over the world. He taught me how to understand and use the origins of each herb in my analyses. Then I formally studied Chinese herbalism in Philadelphia. So I was studying with different people; working on my patients, friends, and relatives; and reading whenever I had the chance."

Reggie explains the premise of the Japanese massage he practices, because it is more than just poking and prodding muscles. "Shiatsu is based on traditional Chinese medicine, with a recognition of muscles, nerves, bones, and Western pathology. The basic understanding of Chinese medicine involves the understanding of the yin and the yang, and the five phases. The five phases are fire, earth, metal, water, wood. Each of these phases relates to and tells us about something different. Each one of these phases relates to different aspects of similar things. The combination of these

relationships tells the practioner about the condition of the patient.

"What we do in shiatsu," Reggie continues, "is we try to balance the energy, or *move* the energy if it's stuck. Move it from one place to another using these basic concepts of Oriental medicine." Reggie emphasizes the importance of personal connection and involvement as a part of the shiatsu treatment. "These things are what make shiatsu an Oriental healing *art* as opposed to just a mechanical technique. It's the *spirit* that you put into your shiatsu and the *essence* that you get into, which is usually passed down from your teacher, that make it a healing art."

It seems Reggie has worked on everyone and everything, from babies a few weeks old to people in their eighties, even on animals.

Diagnosing patients, he points out, is much the same process as in any "traditional" Western discipline. "I also use the four methods of assessment: *bo shin*, *bun shin*, *mon shin*, and *setsu shin*. *Bo shin* is looking or listening; *bun shin* is listening or smelling; *mon shin* is questioning; and *setsu shin*, to touch or palpate. That's how I'd diagnose a client. The resulting therapy would either be shiatsu—or some type of touching modality—or herbology. To an extent, I use what I feel the most comfortable with, but in the end it's what the client would feel the most comfortable with that will make the difference. If I'm comfortable with Swedish massage, but the client is comfortable with shiatsu, then I realize I'll have to do shiatsu with them.

"It's not simply book learning. Because

anyone can read the books and buy the videos. There's a certain way the teacher works with the student," he says softly as he makes an imaginary circle in front of him with the sweep of his open hand. "As a teacher, the way that you move around the class, how you address your students, and how they interact with you gives you the *essence* of shiatsu. *That* makes all the difference.

"In all cultures, we'll see the yang aspects of things—the *visible* aspect. You don't realize that within each culture it's the yin aspect, the *spirit* and the *essence*, that is really the power for the yang." Reggie gives an example: "With the Native Americans, the thing that gave them the power to fight back, even against European oppression, was their essence of being connected with the earth. The thing that gave the Africans being brought to America the power to survive and not to die on the plantations, and helped make them a thriving part of the civilization, was that essence. It's now so diluted that you can easily forget about it. The thing that enabled the Jewish people to survive the Holocaust and gave them the power to be a thriving nation, the power simply to go on even though family members were dying around them in concentration camps, was that inner power."

The lessons and principles Reggie Ceaser has learned in shiatsu and in the healing arts have been invaluable to his daily life. "Find out about yourself, find out where your essence is coming from. When you know your center, nothing can shake you because you can always go *back* to that center and then take your life and move forward."

Reginique Green

Reginique Green is the first person to admit that she wasn't the person most likely to get into medical school, mainly because she didn't have the best grades. "I'm not like your typical did-everything-the-right-way-and-got-into-medical-school person. I always tell everybody that persistence overrides resistance."

Reg, as her friends call her, grew up in Memphis, Tennessee. Her dad worked in public education as a superintendent of schools. The family moved around quite a bit, because he would often be hired by different cities around the country to oversee their schools. His jobs took them to Louisville, Kentucky; Cleveland, Cincinnati, and even to Tuskegee for a couple of years.

Medicine seemed to be the right way to go for Reginique. "I always had a vague idea that I wanted to work with either people or animals, and I guess people are just animals." She stops and laughs. Reginique

laughs easily. "When I was a kid we had a poodle, and I would bandage it up—even though it wasn't sick. I'd usually find something to do like that. I've always been a very compassionate person and I've always wanted an intellectual challenge. Those two things together pointed me to medicine."

In high school Reg was taking lots of engineering classes. "There was a big push for Black people, men and women, to become engineers. I was actually vice-president of the math club and president of the engineering club in my high school."

During her junior year she got more involved in the program. "We did what you call 'shadowing,' where you spend time with an engineer, and I knew then that engineering wasn't for me. There wasn't enough people interaction.

"During my junior year I started doing volunteer work at the different hospitals in the community, and I realized I was really happy when I was doing that kind of stuff. And even though I wasn't helping those people medically, just getting to know them and finding out how people work, I began thinking maybe my calling was to be a counselor or to teach."

When Reggie went to Xavier University in New Orleans, she majored in chemistry but on a premed track. Now that she had an idea what she wanted to do, the rest would seem to be easy. But like so many students, there were a lot of things to sidetrack her. "My freshman year was kind of my transition year, so my grades weren't superb. It was my first time away from home and it was a Black college—I really got sidetracked.

"I started to get nervous when it was time to take the MCAT (Medical College Admission Test), and they're always asking you, what is your GPA? They view you along with everybody in the country, and that's one of the criteria they use to decide whether you're worthy of getting into medical school. Everyone says to get into medical school your grades have to be within the top ten percent of the country. When you get into med school you find out, hey! All these people can't be in the top ten percent!"

The number of applicants for dental school was lagging at the time. There was a big push to entice those students who didn't have the 3.5 GPA necessary to secure a shot at medical school into thinking about dental school. "I talked to my adviser at Xavier and he was like, 'Oh, you would be an excellent candidate for dental school.'" Reggie laughs unabashedly. "I said that would be a great option if I was interested in doing teeth all my life. But I'm not!" So Reg hit the books.

Aside from her new efforts at studying, all her volunteer work and her extracurricular activities made an impression. While her grade point average only rose to 3.0—about a B average—she earned a Dean's Scholarship at Creighton University in Omaha, Nebraska.

Now that she is on the path to her goal of becoming a doctor, she finds many new challenges. "It's a real humbling experience, and the only thing that helps you make it through it is just really wanting to do it. If you really want to do something, you can make it through no matter what the requirements are. You just do your best.

Your first medical school experiences are dramatic ones. You begin your studies with anatomy. "That's when you have the privilege of dissecting a human cadaver, which is a preserved body," Reginique says with reverence. She understands the importance of the gift these people have made. "People donate their bodies to science, and a lot of times, medical students are the ones who are receiving the bodies to learn the anatomy. Everybody always says that's the greatest teacher they ever had. At Creighton we give a memorial service for the donors."

Three days a week for four hours, Reginique would have lab. This involves dissecting cadavers to understand where things are and how they fit in the human body. Before lab, she has already spent about five hours in her biological chemistry lecture class. But she finds that many students, herself included, usually go back at night on their own time to work in the lab. "The first year you learn the body in its most perfect state, if the body was to never break down. Then the second year they introduce pathology to you.

"At this level you dissect a person who's been dead maybe two or three hours. Because you're working with pathology, that's what you call an autopsy. They say, 'Okay, we learned about the liver. Now let's throw ten gallons of alcohol in it and see what happens. And this is what happens when cancer affects it.'"

Cutting into the body of someone who was once somebody's sister or brother or friend is an experience most people will never know. It's something that stays with you. "I guess when you first look at someone when they're on the table, and they've only been dead about two hours, you're kind of saddened. You almost feel like you're violating the person—to cut them, open them up, and look inside." But, as Reginique explains, something keeps you focused. "You feel like it's such a privilege. You use someone's death as a learning experience to help another person. It's not an easily expressed feeling."

Many people decide, at that point, medicine is not for them. Some students realize they simply don't have the stomach or the interest to continue their studies. Some just pass out.

There are three major exams that medical students are required to take and pass in the course of their studies. They are the three parts of the licensing exam. The first part is taken after the second year in order to qualify to work in the hospital for your remaining two years of study. That first part is a test of your knowledge of the anatomy. The final two parts of the test are based on your experience after working at a hospital. "In your third and fourth year they put you in a clinical setting. That's what I'm doing now. They rotate you through all the different branches of medicine, and you actually work with the patients and apply all of your book knowledge. All of that is one hundred percent people skills. Just getting people to talk to you openly."

Being on call, like a regular doctor, means being available at all hours, when-ever extra help is needed at the hospital. Sometimes her beeper goes off when she sits down to dinner, sometimes when she just wants to have a peaceful afternoon with her cat. Reg figures she'll just have to get used to it.

"If you like people, medicine is the greatest field to go into. It's getting very regulated now and many people think you just have to be a book-oriented person to go into medicine. But people who want to work with people and enjoy being with people—those are the best physicians," she says with a smile.

This is a profession that tests your ability to work hard and get knocked on your butt a few times. Every mistake you make, every disappointment you run into, "you have to continuously pick yourself up, brush yourself off, and keep going," Reg says. "No matter what you do, you're going to run into obstacles and problems and you're going to feel like, is it worth it? The hardest part is keeping your morale high when it doesn't seem like there's any reason to do it."

The next step for Reginique is to apply for a residency at a hospital. That will give her the experience she needs to be a qualified doctor. After spending three years as a resident under the supervision of a major health-care facility, she will have fulfilled her requirements to practice medicine. There are a limited number of residency spots available at the various hospitals around the country, and you must impress the administration to be chosen. "It is a competitive thing," she says with a bit of amazement in her voice. "That's the weirdest thing about medical school. They want doctors to be humane and humanistic, but they make us compete against each other. Even if you don't want to be a competitive person, you're always being ranked against everybody in the country."

Reg is interested in preventive medicine. This is an area in the field of medicine that will save money for everyone in the long run. If you are taking time to keep healthy, you will have less frequent, less costly illnesses. At the same time, if you're sick less, you won't lose money because you can't go to work.

"I'm also interested in working with underprivileged people. Family practitioners would definitely fall within preventive medicine, she adds."

Reginique Green is someone not only who cares about people but who is committed to learning as much as she can about everything around her. Her passion for medicine is just one outlet. Reggie's main goal in life is to make a real difference. "No matter what it is that I do, I want to die a great person. I feel that all great people gave the world more than they took from it. And that's all I want to do. I want to help others. And I want to be my best, and to be your best you must continuously compete against yourself."

Becoming a doctor is not an easy thing to accomplish, and yet she is being realistic when she tells people they can be whatever they want to be—if they're willing to work for it. Reg is a good example of someone getting where she wanted without having the best chance. She's proved that anything can be attained.

Dr. Roderick Seamster

Before Dr. Roderick Seamster found himself at a community health facility in Watts, California, he had spent time working in a place many other doctors might avoid. After graduating from the University of California at Irvine and Harvard Medical School, he was provided a list of several places where he could fulfill the obligations of his National Health Service Corps scholarship, a program in which students work to pay back their scholarships with service. "I knew when I got out of medical school that I wanted to work in a place where I felt the people really needed the care that I could deliver. I looked at the choice of locations to work at and I said, 'That would be a good place.'" So, Rod spent eighteen months in San Carlos, Arizona, working with Native Americans.

His experiences working in a segregated society that has learned to be distrustful have been very useful in his current work at the Watts Health Foundation. "The Native American population has a history of people

coming and leaving, so they always have a feeling that you're not gonna stay for a very long time. There's no sense of trust, but there is definitely a need for clinicians on the reservation.

"After being there and living there, my whole approach to delivering the health care I felt that they needed shifted toward finding out what *they* felt their needs were and fulfilling those needs. But there was *always* the issue of trust.

"There was a high staff turnover before I got there. When I arrived, there was another physician who had arrived just two weeks prior. I was the second, and then two weeks later another physician arrived. So at that time we had roughly nine staff physicians there. Our group was going to be there for a while. I was there for eighteen months, while some of the other guys stayed there a lot longer."

Having a core group of people made it possible for Rod and his colleagues to create systems that would make their jobs easier *and* best serve their patients. "For example," he says, "diabetes is a major problem on the reservation. We were able to develop a diabetes program where the patients would come in on certain days for the diabetes care and we would have programs for them to watch on video. Teaching would then be done by the nurses. The patients would come in, get their lab work done, and then go and eat, because usually with diabetes testing you want to test the patients before they eat so it doesn't affect the results of the tests.

"Before we did this, it took so long for them to have their tests that they would be starving by the time we were ready for them. The patients were *very* unhappy," he says as he laughs. "So that was one of the problems that was solved."

There were many similarities between working on a reservation and working in an inner city. "I had a great time working on the reservation, but it also had its inherent frustrations. You can write a prescription, and give instructions, but whether or not they're carried out was always guesswork. Follow-up was also many times a problem—getting the patient to return to the clinic. We also had a deficit in terms of adequate staffing; there were not enough people there who could enhance what you were doing.

"When I first arrived at the hospital there was only an outpatient facility and an emergency room. The inpatient was closed. It was important and necessary that we bring the inpatient part of the hospital up to the standards of the accrediting organizations." By the time Rod left Arizona, he and his team had brought the hospital back to full-time, accredited status.

In the Indian community alcoholism is a serious problem. Rod felt compelled to get as involved as possible with seminars and other alcohol-awareness programs to help enlighten the community. He spoke at parades and rallies whenever he had the chance, because he knew the more visible he became, the more his patients would trust him on this issue. "I think I was very effective in that respect. The community thought of the people who came to work on the reservation as outsiders, that they didn't really want to deal with the community as a whole, so I attempted to get involved in the community. I think I did some positive things there."

When it was time for Rod to leave Arizona, it seemed natural for him to come back to the place where he had spent a good deal of his youth. At fifteen, he'd moved from Louisiana to California to live with his two sisters, who had headed West looking for greener pastures. Rod got in touch with the Watts Health Foundation, which seemed to have all the types of programs and systems that he and his partners had worked so hard to create in San Carlos. They seemed to understand the needs of the community.

"Follow-up is much easier for us than for most clinics. We have a system here where patients can call up and make appointments to be brought in for care. So there's no reason for a patient not to come in, especially if their complaint is, 'I don't have a way to get there.' It is true that some patients really *don't* have a way to get here, and we're sensitive to that. That's why we go out and bring them to the hospital."

Dr. Rod is proud of the care given by the Watts Health Foundation. And they are as sensitive to the needs of the homeless as to those of their other patients. "We have mobile units with hospital equipment," he explains. "We go out into the communities and deliver care in Los Angeles to anyone who needs it. And if we find that someone needs further care, then they're referred either here or to one of the other health facilities in Los Angeles.

"There are a number of physicians who

work here," says Rod of the complete medical services offered in this deceptively plain-looking building. A trip through the halls of the foundation reveals an extensive, modern, and inviting place. "In my department, which is adult medicine, there are six physicians who do internal medicine. We also have a referral system that consists of in-house specialists such as surgeons, including urologists. We have dermatologists, ophthalmologists, and a dental clinic here. By having all the different clinics here in the community, the patients can come right in and receive all of the services in one place, as opposed to being referred around the city. In that way, it's more likely they will get their problems taken care of because it's all in one place. No excuses."

Preventive medicine is one of Dr. Rod's biggest concerns. Too often he finds patients will not come in because they feel that they will not be able to pay for the medication. "They know that they have high blood pressure, but they won't come because they feel that they can't afford to pay, but high blood pressure can lead to a stroke. When the stroke arrives, then a patient will come in, but not for the *preventive* care. And *that*, in my mind, is the most crucial area that needs to be reworked. 'Cause there *are* a lot of patients out there

who can't pay. If they came here they'd see that we have a system that enables us to accommodate anyone who comes in. A lot of patients out there are not aware of that. We have attempted to set up a system which will help them to get medical care without them worrying about how they will pay for it.

"Preventive health, I think, is the health care of the future," Dr. Rod explains. "We'll only survive if primary care is the focus—and I think that's the most important issue we deal with here."

Rod sees this lack of focus on prevention as one of the biggest flaws of the insurance system, a system that seems to be happy to take people's money as long as they don't ask for anything in return. "And then when you need them, they may treat you, but then they will attempt to drop you from their services. So that *has* to change, and I think it will; something is coming down the pipe.

"I can remember back when I was growing up in Louisiana. I grew up in a poor family. I had three brothers and three sisters. My dad was a carpenter and my mom, she was a maid. I remember sometimes that my mom would take my brothers to the doctor and a lot of times things just didn't get done—they were told that nothing was wrong with them. *I* knew

there was something wrong with them, but nothing happened.

"I can vividly recall one night I had a problem and we went to the doctor. We waited and waited and waited, and when we finally got into the examining room, nothing was done. I was never *touched*. There were a few questions asked, which we answered, and then the doctor said, 'Oh, he'll be okay.' Today, I still can't understand how he could say I would be 'okay' without someone actually *examining* me. Since that time," Rod continues, "I knew that something needed to be done within the system itself. And I think that may have been a driving force in me way back then. The patients need someone who's sensitive to what their needs are, and that's very important.

"There's a need out there, and someone has to step forward and say, 'I'll take care of it.' And that's what I'm trying to do."

For Rod, understanding his patients' needs and being a real person, rather than that guy in the white coat, is very important to him. His work with Native Americans in San Carlos and at the Watts Health Foundation has certainly proven him to be a doctor who is not afraid to get involved with a community, or to help people see beyond the white lab coat to the man within.

Giancarlo Esposito

Although actors will seem to do just about anything to get work, Giancarlo Esposito feels he has a responsibility as an actor to choose his roles carefully. Not only because he wants to take roles that will elevate his standing as an actor, but because he feels he has a responsibility to his audience.

"I was walking down the street in Detroit," remembers Giancarlo, "on my way to a lecture, and I notice this car is following me. I was a little nervous about it. Eventually, the car pulls alongside me and I see these cats inside kind of arguing with each other. I realize when the window rolls down, they're arguing about me.

"One of the guys yells at me, 'Hey, man! You were on "Miami Vice."'" So I said, 'Yeah,' because I had been on a couple of episodes. We start talking and one of the guys in the car says, 'How much did you get for that kilo [of cocaine] you sold Don Johnson [the star of the television show]?'

"I just laughed, but the guy was serious. I said it was just a TV show, but he

kept at me. 'Come on, man, you can tell us. It's cool.' I said, 'That wasn't real, man. I don't really do that for a living. I'm an actor.' I could see that it wasn't really sinking in.

"As I'm talking to them a beeper goes off in the car. That's when I noticed that these are young guys in a *real* nice car. I asked them where they got the car. One told me it was a rental. I'm wondering how these guys could rent a car. One guy tells me his mother lets him use her credit card and he 'takes care of her.' These guys were selling dope and the mother is basically helping them do it. That hurt.

"That's what turned me around. I couldn't believe what I did on TV could affect somebody like that—that they thought it was for real. I started thinking that there are a lot of kids who can't tell the difference between reality and TV. TV *is* reality for a lot of them. I didn't want the work I did to affect them in that way.

"I made a decision to turn down roles that I feel portray people of color in a negative light. I don't do drug dealers, killers . . ." Giancarlo stops for a minute and laughs a hearty, robust laugh, breaking the serious mood. "I've turned down a lot of work!" But his principles have been rewarded. When he was offered the part of a drug dealer on a popular TV show, he turned it down. "I really wanted to work on that show, but I told them I wouldn't play that kind of part. They came back to me a month later and asked me to play the role of a Hispanic detective. Cool!" he says with a smile. "But," Giancarlo adds, "I *will* play a villian *if* he gets his just desserts in the end."

Giancarlo and his brother, Vincent, start-ed acting when they were kids to help their mom make ends meet when their parents divorced, "to help pay the rent because Mom was really struggling. She was sometimes doing eight shows a day at Radio City Music Hall." Their mom, a singer, and their father, a stage technician, met while both were working in Italy.

"My brother and I were sitting around watching cartoons one Saturday morning. When the commercials with kids in them came on, we said, 'Hey, why can't we do that?' So we asked my mother if we could do some commercials. We both thought it would be fun. She took us to an agent, and a couple of days later we had an audition for a Broadway show. We had to go down and sing 'Happy Birthday,' and we both got in the show."

While his brother eventually got out of acting, Giancarlo stayed with it, audition-ing for other Broadway shows. Most of the work he was doing was in musical come-dies. The work was good, but he felt to be a good actor he had to do dramatic work. "I never thought of a musical comedy as being drama—I never thought of it as act-ing. Nineteen eighty is when I decided I wanted to do something that would take me in a different direction.

"I remember there being an open call with the Negro Ensemble Company for a show called *Zoo-Man and the Sign*. I went to the audition and got a callback, and another callback, and another callback. Finally I landed the role. There were some great peo-ple who worked on that," he says, remem-bering the unique circumstance. "Charles Fuller wrote it, and Mary Alice was in it, and at the time her understudy was Phylicia Rashad. Doug Ward, who heads the Negro Ensemble Company, was directing it. So it was just a great opportunity and I had the lead, so I had to really stretch. It was my first legitimate acting role."

Obviously all the hard work paid off. For his performance, Giancarlo won the Off Broadway show award, the Obie, for outstanding lead actor.

Although his name is not as recognized as Denzel Washington's or Wesley Snipes's, Giancarlo's face is well-known to most television and movie audiences and to theatergoers. He has appeared in almost every Spike Lee film, playing a wide range of characters, from the arrogant fraternity leader, Julian, in *School Daze*, to the wild-haired "let's boycott Sal's Pizzeria" charac-ter, Buggin' Out, in *Do the Right Thing* and Malcolm X's assassin in *Malcolm X*.

His first major film role was in *Taps*, the story of a group of cadets who take over their military academy because they refuse to let it close down. Giancarlo had plenty of personal experiences to draw from, hav-ing attended a private military school in real life. "It was an interesting experience, being that I was the only Black officer in the movie, the only real Black character who had a little bit of screen time."

Giancarlo was the only major actor on the film other than George C. Scott who'd had formal theatrical training—most of it being on the stage. "It was very difficult for me to fit in with them," he says of his young costars. "They had all kinds of ways to get juiced up before the camera would roll. Tom [Cruise] would be banging his head against walls before he had to do a take. And I remember thinking that that's not really necessary.

"I have become one of those actors who does a lot of homework. I believe in a very thorough preparation. I put a lot of thought into the rehearsal period; I think that's the most important time." Preparation includes doing research to understand how a character would behave in a certain situation and why, what kind of experiences might they have had in life. How does history affect the person he is playing? It is also important to understand any physical things a character might go through.

"Afterward, my friend Evan Handler often wondered why, after *Taps* came out, certain people in the movie were hits right away, even though *a lot of them couldn't act!*

"I knew that I wasn't a great actor but I was pretty good, and I remember Evan looked at me one day and said, 'Why are all these guys making it, why are they all big household names and we're not?' I said to him, 'Evan, you're a minority too, man. For me, it's because I'm Black and it's going to take me a lot more time. You're Jewish, and that's still a minority in this business, whether you believe it or not. You might have an easier time of it than I do, but it's still going to be difficult for you.' He wondered why he wasn't a star, but I had never even thought like that. I'm not going to get many movie offers. These guys are making three, four million dollars a movie, and of course I don't make anything near that."

Giancarlo is far from being bitter or even jealous. In his eyes, discrimination is an unfortunate fact of life in America. Even so, he sees some very positive side effects. His extra work to reach the same level of recognition has probably made him a much better actor than his colleagues. "All those people have gone right to the top. Oftentimes I think, well, that wasn't for me, and I'm glad that it's taking time. I still have an uphill struggle to be recognized, but if it comes too fast, I don't think it's good. It's taken me time to really get comfortable on film and on screen."

With an African-American mother and an Italian father, Giancarlo only half-jokingly calls himself Afro-European. "When we are from America, we talk about Black people as just 'Black' people. But in Europe or in Haiti you'd say, 'This guy is African,' or, 'She's Haitian,' or, 'He's Guatemalan,' you know what I mean? And they could *all* be Black, but in the United States you're *Black*. You're not from a country. You don't have a culture. I think that's dangerous.

"It's great to be Black. *I dig it!*" Giancarlo says proudly. "It's what I am. I'm a Black Italian or I'm an Afro-European. Whatever way you want to put it. My mother has roots from the Cherokee Indian. We have to find out what a Black American is, what that means.

"I met a girl, I think her name is Andrea Dumas or something. She asked me, 'Did you ever hear of Alexandre Dumas?' And that was great to me—that she understood where her line of Blackness came from. That it was mixed with French, and she was proud of it. It was so interesting to hear that.

"We have Black Hispanics, and we have Black Filipinos. There are Dominicans who are as dark as Black people but are not regarded as Black, you know? We have a lot of different ethnic backgrounds just like white people have, and we need to understand that."

On the set of Jim Jarmuch's film *Night on Earth*, it is freezing. The scenes are being shot on Broadway at Forty-ninth Street in Manhattan, and the temperature is easily close to zero—the wind chill makes it feel like twenty below. It's eleven o'clock at night. Giancarlo, in character, is dressed in a funky Brooklyn homeboy outfit: big lambskin coat, big British Knights high-top sneakers with big fat laces (untied of course), and a big Elmer Fudd–type hat with a big brim and big fur-lined earflaps.

Even with all of this camouflage, three young men walking down the night street recognize Giancarlo. They nod their recognition at him and hesitate for a minute. They want to talk to him, but it's obvious he's on the job. Besides, he's a celebrity—why should he talk to them?

Giancarlo walks over to them and starts a friendly conversation. The three seem to take a few seconds to realize what is happening; they then have a casual chat with him. When Giancarlo is called back to the set, the three young men say good-bye and continue on their chilly late-night walk. Excited that they just got a chance to hang out with a real celebrity, they're high fiving each other down the street. To Giancarlo, this is no big deal. He doesn't consider himself special. He just happens to be lucky enough to do something that he loves for a living.

Sister

Sister is out on the lawn in front of her apartment at the Imperial Courts housing project in Watts, California. As she sits in her folding chair with a clipboard in her lap, every little kid in the neighborhood runs by, under, or around her. Half a dozen children are rolling around on the sun-dappled lawn while their young mothers, not much older then they are, sit and exchange the local dish. Neighbors walk by yelling greetings and bits of gossip to her from across the street. Sister's phone rings; she leans over and answers it. It's on the lawn, too.

"Hold on," she says as she looks through one of several huge folders on the grass.

"Sister!" A young man who's about fifteen years old jogs up to the open-air "office" and says, "I forgot—what else do I need for that job application? I got my Social Security number,

my mother's signature, and my school papers. . . ."

Sister answers, still thumbing through the folder. "You need your birth certificate, but your school papers are good enough."

"That's it?" he says with some surprise.

"That's all you need," she says with the phone cradled between her ear and shoulder. The boy smiles proudly at completing his task.

"Bet!" he exclaims as he turns on his heels. "Thanks, Sister," he says, jogging off. Cynthia Mendenhall-Cole, known to everyone in the neighborhood as Sister, looks warmly at the vanishing figure, another person put on the right track. She answers the caller's question and laughs at something said on the other end as she hangs up.

Sister knows everyone and everyone knows her. This might sound like the description of a neighborhood busybody, but it's just the description of a busy young woman. Cynthia is looking out for the kids in her community so that they can move on to brighter futures.

When she resigned from her job as an assistant to Assemblywoman Maxine Waters, the local media couldn't understand it. Why would someone with a powerful well-paying job resign to work as a freelancer? "I felt I wasn't getting what I wanted, I wasn't happy. I wanted to work with them," she says, pointing to the youngsters wrestling on the grass, "with the kids who need me. As long as I worked for her, I couldn't do what I wanted to do for them. I felt like I let them down. I quit, I didn't need the money. I just knew something wasn't right, so I went out on my own."

Sister's job with Assemblywoman Waters was developing programs and finding jobs for older members of the community. But at the same time kids weren't going to school because they were distracted by the craziness around them. School was boring because some teachers didn't care, and the imagined excitement of gangs was luring kids out of class and into trouble. Cynthia felt at the time Waters wasn't listening to the voice of the community, to what they really needed. "It was just getting swept under the rug. But I wasn't going to let that happen."

Most of the "problem" kids were suspended from school, which meant they had nothing to do but hang out on the streets. "There were kids missing entire semesters of school," she explains.

Rather than let these kids waste their time, Sister fought to have a small alternative school opened right at the edge of Imperial Courts. Opposition was fierce. The city council's attitude was: If these kids can't stay out of trouble, then they will just have to miss school. But Sister kept hammering the council and the school board until they gave in. A half-day program was started in a small school building that normally held adult-education classes, helping get the kids an education despite discipline problems.

"I'm finding out that the so-called bad kids are honor-roll students who just got lost in the crowd. The thing about out here, you're already marked because of where you live. If you're from Watts, you're told you can't go that far in life. You can't even go past this street right here,"

Cynthia says, pointing to the street in front of us. "You cannot cross 113th. You cannot cross Imperial. You're trapped. You're marked already."

Cynthia's schedule is always changing because she is personally involved with almost every person in the community. Besides attending the school and community board meetings to voice her opinions and see what the government is or isn't doing, she also helps many of the kids. "They tell me a lot of personal things they tell nobody else. I'm a counselor to them, a mother to them, a sister to them, a probation officer. I keep them on their feet. I go to the schools, and to their classes. I motivate them to keep going, keep going. I don't want them to be like we are, still stuck here."

It was obvious to Sister that most of the kids in the neighborhood wanted and needed jobs. Besides keeping them out of gang trouble, jobs would teach them self-respect and responsibility. She teamed up with Fred Williams and Jim Goins, who run the Common Ground Foundation in Compton, just across the tracks. She then approached the powers that be and asked for fifty summer jobs for the teenagers in her Imperial Courts Youth Outreach Program. Sorry, she was told, we can only give you ten. Ten was an insult.

Every day Cynthia would call, visit, or write someone she thought could make it happen. "I just kept on them. I prayed, I dreamed, and I prayed again that I got fifty slots. I had everybody in the neighborhood calling and writing letters. I dreamed that I had them. One day they called me and said, 'Cynthia, everything is done.'"

Sister's strong voice rises with pride. The jobs are on a first-come, first-served basis. The employers take anyone of age who is willing to work. There are no interviews. Everyone gets a shot.

"The kids nobody wants to be bothered with, those are the kids I'll be bothered with." Richard, a former gangbanger at fifteen, comes by and gives Cynthia some paperwork. "My card in there got the number on it," he says. She takes the information and quickly, instinctively, flips through it, checking for something. "I'll get back to you later," she says as he takes off again.

"People like this," she says about Richard, "nobody wanted to be bothered with him. He wasn't in school. He's one of those kids people call bad, but this is a good person. These kids make A's and B's but they made one mistake in their life. When you put them in jail and lock them up, you make them bad people. That's what they're doing to our kids.

"They're good kids but the environment they're growing up in today is turning them into bad kids. These days you'll rarely find a father at home. So you've got one parent in the home, and she's under pressure. She may be into drugs, that's pressure. She doesn't have money for clothes or food, so maybe she's gonna get out there and hustle. They don't have enough fingers to count how many strikes they got against them."

Cynthia looks at the small crowd that has assembled on her lawn. She's a magnet in this community. People look to her for the right thing to do and the right way to do it. Although she has her own family to raise, she makes time for everyone. Her business card, which includes her home phone number, reads: Imperial Courts Outreach Program. Call Any Time.

"The only thing the kids need is motivation. If we work with them and motivate them and make the politicians really get down and do what they're supposed to do, it'll start to feel good around here."

Lyndon Barrois

It's a Saturday afternoon in early February and the Mardi Gras celebration is just beginning in New Orleans. The city is getting fired up for the wildest street party in the country.

Marching bands from all the high schools and colleges parade down Canal Street, while men wearing dresses and too much makeup throw colorful plastic necklaces and fake gold coins into the cheering crowd. Lyndon Barrois and his friend Danny Wilson casually walk along the parade route. They ignore the tourists and people who have had too much to drink. This is old news to two young men who grew up here.

Green, gold, yellow, and red necklaces fly through the air, smack Danny and Lyndon on the chest, then spray out on the ground. Dozens of kids and adults dive to the ground, collecting them like crazed vultures.

"Hey!" Danny exclaims as he bends down and reaches through the sea of squirming kids at his feet. He picks up something flat, shiny, and silver that everyone else ignores. He hands it to Lyndon, who examines it and sees it's a perfect chewing gum wrapper.

"My *man!*" Lyndon says with a laugh in his typically cool New Orleans accent. Danny smiles. "Just feeding the creativity," he says. As they head up the street through the crowd, Lyndon carefully stashes the wrapper in his shirt pocket.

For Lyndon Barrois, finding a nice gum wrapper is much more exciting than Mardi Gras because it is what he uses to make his art. He builds miniature lifelike sculptures of sports scenes using twisted gum wrappers and paint: football fields frozen in time, dozens of players suspended in the air, tumbling; a runner sliding to safety just before the ball hits the glove of the waiting third baseman. Lyndon started making them at twelve years old; now they're making him famous.

"It was just a hobby. I just picked it up one day. I was always fooling with stuff—wire, clay, aluminum foil. I just made stuff with it," he explains.

Wires and foil were great to turn into little people, horses and motorcycles. Nice to work with, but they weren't perfect. Lyndon didn't realize the answer was right under his nose the whole time.

"*Gum* wrappers, man! Seen my mom chew tons of it! It occurred to me one day that it was foil on one side, and then paper. . . . I *drew*, so maybe I could paint on it. So I started putting stuff together."

Lyndon's sculptures are not at all like the Japanese art of paper folding called origami. Origami figures are fairly flat and angular; his creations, made from a single gum wrapper, are twisted and bent until the figure has the shape and curve of a real horse or basketball player. The twisted shapes of the wrapper give his tiny athletes a sense of animation. After he molds them, the figures are carefully painted with fine-point watercolor markers or regular paint and a brush.

"It never occurred to me that what I was doing was an art form. To me it was just a hobby. I'd pick up a wrapper, fold a man—and Lord knows how many of those things I made over the years. It's got to be in the thousands. I'd make some in the library at school and leave them on the shelf." People looking for a book would find a little man posing there.

Before he gained fame as "the man who made tiny people out of gum wrappers," Lyndon Barrois earned himself a reputation as one of New Orleans's hottest graphic artists. "I always aim for something. When I was in junior college, I aimed to have posters published, so I went to the biggest publisher in town, ProCreations, and I showed them my work. I said, 'I want to have posters published,' and they told me about some events that were coming up. That's how I got the Boston Marathon poster, with determination."

The official poster for the Boston Marathon is his favorite "because it's simple. What I wanted to focus on was the *legs*. All the other posters had the full figure on it, running. I just wanted the legs, because to me nothing says running like the *legs!*

It's as simple as that! I made it real hot with neon colors, then I sponged on the paint to make it textural.

"But that's the answer, man. You gotta be ambitious. You gotta be on top of your game. You can't just say, 'Well, I'm gonna design something.' I had all kinds of ideas. I had the gun going off, cats breaking the tape—everything. You got to research. You've got to know what you're trying to portray. No matter what you do, throw in a lot of ingredients at first, so you learn what to leave out. *Then* you show them the design you come up with, whether it's one or whether it's three. Regardless. But you got to work it like that.

"Then the next year I got the Jazz Festival poster, which is *the* biggest poster contract in town. To date I'm the youngest guy and the first Black guy to do that poster. I was twenty-one. That's just determination.

"That year I knew they were going for something totally different, so I took a lot of risks with it. You see, mine was the first horizontal poster. It was the first that had no people in it and no crescent moon." (New Orleans is known as the Crescent City.) "The only 'human' element we had in it was a carnation. It was all instruments done in multicolors."

Lyndon went to Xavier University to earn a degree in art. "I said, 'Before I graduate I'm going to have a show.' So when the Super Bowl came to town I said, 'This is my time. I'm a sports nut. Why not have a Super Bowl show?'"

After trying to decide how to create the show, he stuck with his gum wrappers. "I made two teams, the Steelers and the

Redskins. I took them to my professor and I said, 'I want to show you something. Over the years this is the kind of stuff I've been doing on the side as a little hobby.' He just fell out!

"He said, 'Man! I don't think you know what you're sitting on here!' I said, 'I'm just thinking about having a little exhibit with them for the Super Bowl.' He told me '*Do it!* Go for it. I don't think you realize what you've got.' I didn't. The more I worked on it, the more excited I became."

The scenes were laid out on fields made of green felt for Astroturf, grass mat for natural turf, and tan chalk dust for dirt areas. Each would be in a glass box with a wooden base. A small brass plaque attached to the base would describe each scene. Lyndon included mirrors in the boxes so the viewer could see the action from all sides without moving around the boxes.

"I had some elaborate designs. I even had boxes that were shaped like hexagons. Making the figures is nothing. To make the figures and paint the fields, everything is scaled out. But making the boxes . . . I'm just thinking to myself, 'How the heck am I gonna make these boxes?' I couldn't afford to have them made.

"So I did a little research, found out how they attach the pieces. I got the glue and bought the glass. I got a scriber, which is what you use to cut the glass, and put it together. So it was an education, man.

"Me and Dan hit the street trying to get press for all of this stuff and trying to find a gallery."

Finding someone to give up gallery space for an exhibit of football scenes made from gum wrappers was not easy. Danny worked in television, so he knew who to contact to get some publicity. He called the sports reporter at a local TV station, who thought the idea was just strange enough to make a good story.

The reporter came over with a cameraman, and a few days later Lyndon was on TV. Then a major paper did a story on Lyndon. In the middle of all this, Lyndon and Danny met Jana Napoli, a local patron of the arts, who told them they could hold the exhibit in her gallery. Before long all sorts of TV shows and newspapers were doing features about Lyndon Barrois and his sculptures.

Danny wrote to Mike Leonard, a reporter from the "Today" show, NBC's national morning news program, and told him what Lyndon was doing. A couple of months later Lyndon received a call, and the next thing he knew—he was on the "Today" show. This exposure got him calls from all over the country. One very important call came from the Ripley's Believe It or Not! Museum. They purchased fifteen sculptures from Lyndon that they've placed in different museums they own around the world.

"Danny's my right-hand man, my homeboy. We went to grammar school together and high school. We're stuck together in this brotherhood thing, man. We help each other out, says Lyndon."

When he's not working on his art projects, Lyndon volunteers time with inner-city kids who don't get much exposure to the creative arts. "Little kids ask, 'When you were our age, were there any people that could draw better than you?' I say,

'Sure! There's always somebody who can draw better than you. It's not a matter of who's better, but who stays with it. That's what makes the difference, man.'

"I get on myself sometimes for being lazy. I think I must be doing something wrong because I'm not rich. I'll see somebody on the TV or I'll read about somebody in the paper, and I've just got to slap myself and say, 'Wait a minute, dummy. *You've* been on TV!'"

Lyndon wishes more people of color would get into the arts. He feels parents suggest other careers because they think there is no future in the arts. "That's really tough, because people don't realize how much the arts affect our lives.

"When you get into a car—that car was on a drawing table before it was in your garage. Even houses, or you go to a library—all that stuff was designed before it was built. So there's no way you can say there's no money in the arts. The field is so vast, there are so many disciplines that relate to everything in life."

Sitting in his studio at home, Lyndon opens a desk drawer and pulls out a plastic sandwich bag filled with gum-wrapper jockeys and racehorses. They're paper gray, waiting for paint.

He says, "Keep driving yourself, but you've also got to stand back and realize, I *am* making these strides. It just may not be as quick as you'd like."

A clear candy jar at the back of his desk pops open and Lyndon adds the gum wrapper from the parade to the hundreds of wrappers in the jar. Before he can replace the lid, the scent of spearmint caresses the air.

Pierre and Karl Romain

Identical twins Pierre and Karl Romain look so much alike that their mother often could not tell them apart. Originally from Nyack, New York, they discovered early on the fun that could be had when there is someone in the world who looks and sounds exactly like you.

In school they were practical jokers, switching class several times during the same period on April Fools' Day and sometimes on other occasions. "I would take all the math tests, and he would take all the science tests," Pierre says, pointing at Karl. "He's good at that stuff."

The two started doing commercials together and appeared in the film *Breaking Away.* But, Pierre says, "we were in that syndrome where we were cast as twins. Nobody knew who Pierre and Karl were; it was always, 'There are the twins!'"

Toward the end of high school they both felt they needed to

create independent identities. Karl concentrated on his karate training, and Pierre got into weight lifting and basketball. But as they got older their interests split dramatically. While both were interested in fitness and athletics, Pierre openly admits that he wanted to make money. "*Lots* of money."

At seventeen he became a vice-president of a small computer firm, earning the position by designing programs while working there and selling them himself to graphics services, architects, and interior-design clients.

With the position came company cars and posh parties. Personal differences with his employer caused him to leave the company, but he "didn't know what else to do. There were no corporate positions I could get into. I was seventeen and had just graduated from high school." Pierre took a job at Jack LaLanne health spas as program director, the lowest position. Two and a half months later he became assistant manager. By the time Pierre was nineteen, he was the youngest manager in the company. He then reopened a floundering location and helped make it the most successful in the area.

His success at the health club afforded Pierre the chance to buy a BMW. However, this same rapid success soon caused friction and jealousy between Pierre and his coworkers. He left the company. Pierre eventually took a position at a pharmaceutical company for much less money. There he was accused by a coworker of being a drug dealer, because he was twenty years old and owned a very expensive car despite a modest salary. Hating that he needed to explain himself, Pierre realized that the job wasn't for him.

Combining his motivational, marketing, and managerial skills with those of several friends, he became a partner and vice-president of Foreman Construction and president of a venture-capital company, WAR Industries, which helped other companies find ways to finance their plans.

Unfortunately, a business associate stole money from the company's account, including Pierre's share of the profits, along with an idea Pierre had developed for a new kind of spa, which he then developed himself. "This was one of my closest friends," Pierre says. "He was there through a lot of tough personal stuff, and I confided in him. That's what really hurts." Pierre was left in a tough financial situation. Virtually all his money was gone. Next his car, which he had just replaced with insurance money after it was stolen, was totaled in an accident.

"I'm starting from scratch," he says, laughing at how weird things are. Pierre's attitude is that you have to keep moving forward even when things look bad. "I really believe if you feel good about yourself, you can achieve any goal that you want."

Admittedly, he likes material things. But not all of Pierre's dreams are self-indulgent. He says, "My eventual goal is to start a residence for the homeless, but not like the type currently available. I want to teach them a trade. I'll build apartments where they pay rent so they can return to society. I believe the system is holding back a lot of people."

Karl Romain

Like most kids, Karl Romain wanted to be like Bruce Lee. His martial-arts career began at age six, when he started studying karate at a local YMCA. But the training and exercises became too monotonous and repetitive to hold his interest, so he stopped practicing. At ten years old he picked it up again, studying with Ruben Pratt. Pratt made martial arts exciting.

"He practiced the Chinese martial art called Sho Lin kung fu," Karl explains. This included northern and southern styles and weapons. "Every time I came to class we had something new, different, and fun to do. At the same time he taught us philosophy, about muscles and the different systems in the body. It was a full education."

After graduating from high school, "I had my mind set. I worked all summer teaching at a day camp. I saved *every last penny*. Eleven hundred dollars." With the money he earned, he went to California to train with three-time national champion Keith Hirbiashi.

The regimen was a true test of Karl's will. They worked out every day from 9:30 A.M. until eleven at night. The day started with two miles of running, followed by sprinting up a staircase "until the point of exhaustion." That was followed by rigorous Chinese basic training. After lunch came weapons training; gymnastics and weight training followed dinner.

When Karl returned to Rockland County, he had skills his peers had only dreamed of attaining. He began coaching at a local health club and joined the tournament circuit with the sponsorship of the parents of one of his students. Karl's coaching had helped the fourteen-year-old student achieve the number-one rating in her region.

When she stopped training to concentrate on high school, Karl lost his sponsorship. He needed to work to raise money to pay for training and tournament expenses. He was soon working sixty hours a week, training three days a week while still teaching at Sport-a-Rama. Karl had promised himself he would be world champion before his twenty-third birthday.

On the morning of April 13, 1988, things changed. A reckless driver, weaving in and out of traffic on a crowded Tappan Zee Bridge, cut off Karl's car. Karl quickly moved into the next lane to avoid a collision, but the other driver swerved in front of him. Karl hit his brakes and his car went into a spin across two lanes of rush-hour traffic. "I don't know how *I* didn't get hit before I hit the divider," he marvels. "It was a good thing I had my seat belt on, because I would have been ejected from the car. God was with me that morning."

The pulled muscles, misaligned vertebrae, and nerve damage to his left side posed enough of a danger that his doctor told him he could never compete again. He was fortunate to be walking. If he was lucky, in a year he could do noncontact training to keep in shape, but he had to take it slow.

For months he went to tournaments as a spectator, watching former opponents he had beaten soundly leave the hall with tro-

phies. Without training or competition, he had very little to keep him satisfied. "I couldn't take going to work, coming home, and not having anything to do. I had to get back into my sport."

Rich Branden, a longtime friend in Boston, is nationally ranked by the North American Sport Karate Association and the Professional Karate League. He convinced Karl he could make a comeback. Rich had experienced many injuries in his career, but still "knew how to do a lot of difficult tricks without getting hurt." Karl worked with him, hoping to regain his abilities.

They worked nine hours a day almost every day for three months. "I learned the proper way to move my body, and that's been an important factor in my comeback."

Eight months after the accident, Karl returned to competition, taking first place in forms and first in weapons. Things continued on an upward spiral, bringing Karl to the national championships in Kentucky. Sponsored by his chiropractor, he was able to complete. He returned from the two-day competition as the World Amateur Karate Organization's U.S. National Champion.

The world championships were to be held in November of 1989 in Atlantic City, but wrangling by greedy promoters forced the postponement of the tournament three weeks prior to its scheduled start. Disenchanted by the unprofessional handling of the situation, Karl's sponsors pulled out. When the contest was rescheduled for January of 1990 in Venice, Italy, Karl had no money to get there. But his

brother Pierre and friends rallied around and collected enough money to pay for his trip to compete against representatives from thirty other countries.

Making the finals was not easy. "The Italians had been *practicing.*" Karl laughs. But he adds, "These people didn't know what I was made of. When the going got tough, the tough got going." At the end of Karl's routine, the crowd went wild. "It was amazing—three thousand people were cheering me on! It was breathtaking!"

Not only was Karl Romain the first American to receive a medal, he received the first gold medal of the tournament. His impossible dream had come true.

But Karl is not content to revel in his glory. Besides being chosen by New York Governor Mario Cuomo as a spokesperson for the New York State Safety Seat Belt Coalition, and being featured on billboards and in television ads, Karl wants to give back to the community that gave so much to him. In addition to opening his own martial-arts teaching facility, Karl regularly travels to schools to talk about alcohol and drug awareness. He stresses the need for people to strive for their dreams, no matter who says they cannot be achieved. It's a project he calls the Impossible Dream Program.

"Kids are our future. What better way to give them a future than to work with them now. I feel there's a lot of good that comes from the karate background. The discipline. It makes you know that you can't always take the easy way out. Sometimes you have to look a challenge head-on."

D. Ferg

Although he may be an artist, the skills Darrold Thompson wants to share are those of a successful businessman. D. Ferg, as he is known to just about anybody who's had the pleasure of meeting him, is the owner and founder of D. Ferg Mass Productions. His company makes and creates silk-screened T-shirts, something D. has been doing in some form or fashion since he was around sixteen years old.

"I used to hand-paint sweatshirts in my neighborhood," says the round-faced D. "Everybody loved 'em. I used to put whatever they wanted on shirts. However they wanted their name. I would go down and buy my shirts wholesale and print them up. Just stay in my house, have a blow drier drying it. I was into it! 'Cause I was making money! It was like I was onto something. I used to sit home and I was like, man, I got this talent, I've got to exercise it."

His work became so popular, it was soon very difficult to keep up

with the orders. Doing everything by hand meant he could only handle a certain amount of work at once. He decided to take his original designs to a printer to do large quantities, but he found he really couldn't make a profit. "I asked him how much it would cost me to have him print the shirts. He charged me an arm and a leg, and two thighs," D. says with a smile. "I put the work out on the market and everybody liked them. So I went home and brainstormed. I thought, I can't sit down and do everybody's personal shirt anymore. I have to do something that's creative, Afrocentric. I figured I've got to start saving my money because I need a machine that could mass-produce my merchandise. If I can't get something personal to them, then at least I'll give them something within their range they will like."

During this time, D. was a participant in the youth programs at The Valley, formerly the Manhattan Valley Youth Program. The Valley is available to kids who want counseling, job training, or simply someone who understands where they're coming from. He had known the founder, John Bess, since he was in ninth grade, and decided to ask him a favor. "After I received my equipment, I needed a place to put it, but I didn't have any money to rent a place. I just had this machine." D. leans back on his stool and laughs. "I didn't even have money to buy the shirts to print on, just the machine! So I spoke to John and said I needed a place to put my machine, and he said, 'Brother, you need a place to put your machine, bring it here.'"

With the help of another Manhattan Valley staff member, Ed Scott, D. learned all the technical aspects of making silk-screened prints. Silk-screen printing is a form of stencil printing. Paint or ink is applied to the back of an image carrier made of stretched silk attached to a frame. A rubber squeegee pushes the paint through the porous areas of the silk. Certain areas are blocked out and no paint goes through them. When more than one color is used, additional stencils are cut to let paint through for each separate color. Each screen is then printed individually.

"Slowly but surely I started doing business, doing things for John as well as things for myself. One person told two, two told four. It matched up well because I was a participant in the program. So when Valley participants come through the program now, and they see that I'm a member and how well I'm functioning as a businessman, it can be one of the best incentives to apply themselves I can think of."

D. Ferg Mass Productions has created work used on TV for "The Cosby Show" and "Here And Now" (the character played by Darryl Chill was modeled after D. Ferg). D.'s crew has made shirts for the celebration of the African National Congress's eightieth anniversary. One of his shirts was presented to Nelson Mandela. They have also made shirts for rapper Heavy D. His company cranks out sixty thousand shirts a year.

All of the people who work with him are part of the outreach program of Manhattan Valley, and that makes Darrold proud. "When you get a shirt from D. Ferg Mass Productions, you're getting a shirt made by young people who probably went through struggles in their lives. Who are going through problems right now. And despite all the problems in their lives, they're actually taking the time out to create this beautiful shirt. When people wear one, it's not just a regular shirt from any old company. This is a program where people are supporting people, and where everybody is somebody. It's not like going to a sporting-goods store and purchasing a shirt that's printed. This is a shirt that has more than just a cost on it, more than just a design."

In the early days, D. used to do everything. Now he has a small staff, including his brother Terry. They all work together to handle different aspects of the development of a shirt. "Say a person comes and wants to order some shirts. They'll see James. James will work out the pricing. When they okay it, they'll bring in the artwork and they'll pass it to Allen. Allen will sit down with Chris and they will have a discussion about the artwork, because it's better to have a few ideas.

"They invite the person back. They look at it, 'Oh! I love it! I love it!'" says a laughing D. Ferg. "Boom! That's when we take it to the printer, get the screens back, and Terry and James print up the work.

"Down here it's like a little family and we support each other. Working with young people, I find you run into problems, but they're not the same problems that you'd run into with adults. With adults, you run into more financial problems—they're not getting paid enough or sometimes they can't stick around until things get good. It has to be good in order for them to stay. But with young people, I find that if you're satisfying their needs by giving them the proper attention and being there for them, that's like a jewel to them, that's worth *more* than money. It makes them willing to do anything, 'cause we sit down here, and our chemistry is so good that we could have ten thousand shirts to do, and they may not be getting *anything*, like no money out of it, but it's the attitude, the focus. It's no problem. With adults it's like"—he rolls his eyes and throws up his hands imitating someone just asked to do something they don't want to do—"'Man, ten thousand! I ain't stayin' here. I got to go somewhere.' But young people are willing to give up their time."

D. knows that there's a lot to be learned from his experience with D. Ferg Mass Productions. He's already learned plenty. "The leadership training comes from me in a creative fashion rather than just verbally. They learn by example. You have a lot of creative brothers and sisters coming up in Harlem, but they don't exercise their talents. Not to say that silk-screening is one of the talents they have, but maybe they can use the marketing, the reading, the writing, or pricing skills. There are the mechanical and technical aspects as well. So there are different skills that they use in silk-screening. They could probably take one of those skills and build their own business, whether they want to bake cookies or be a carpenter."

D.'s studio, situated in the basement of The Valley, is filled with the smell of paint and stacked with boxes of T-shirts ready to go out to customers. His brother Terry, who maintains much of the equipment, is his right-hand man. He is another role model for the young people who go through the program. He spent several years in jail for a drug offense. Time, he says very seriously, he feels was like going to school. "I learned a lot about myself, 'cause I had lots of time on my hands," Terry tells me. When he got out, his intentions were to get his life back on track and pass on his experiences to others who might be tempted to go down the wrong path.

Terry had problems with people in a job he had taken after getting out. "There was no way I was going to do something that would send me back to the penitentiary, so I left that situation. That meant I had to find another job. D. kept asking me to work with him. You know how it is when family offers to help you out. Your pride gets in the way.

"John Bess finally convinced me that I should team up with my brother and help him out in the studio. I enjoy working with him. When other people find out I did time, they can't believe it. They always say, 'You don't act like you were in jail.' It's not something to be proud of, like some guys think. I try to let the young brothers know that. I'm proud of the positive example I'm setting by my behavior."

"A lot of our young Black brothers get so tied up in material things that they're not

really thinking about longevity," says D. "They don't think, five years from now what am I going to be doing? And I *always* think like that." D. and his brother share a desire to positively influence people's lives. "I want to make a difference. People see that I'm still young, aggressive, and still want a lot—they key in on that. The brothers who don't think workin' is cool, who think work is not for them, I think they could take a look at me and go, 'Damn, that brother over there is cool. He dresses cool, he's got a nice car.' I can't go and tell every brother how to do it, I just have to let 'em watch me and hopefully they'll pick up on it: 'If D. did it, I can do it.'"

John Bess

It seems appropriate that a place that helps develop, strengthen, and nurture young people is nestled safely under a church. In the basement of the Cathedral of Saint John the Divine in New York City is The Valley. The Valley, formerly the Manhattan Valley Youth Program, is a full-service project where kids can go for counseling, as well as job training, to learn social skills, and for motivation.

When John Bess first started the project in his community, it wasn't anything like the massive program it has become. John, who was working in Harlem as program director at a settlement house for seniors and young people, was asked to get involved with the new project. "Someone told me that the Cathedral wanted to do a youth program and asked me if I would come for an interview," John recalls. "They needed help and some direction.

"When Barbara Norris of the Harlem Commonwealth Council asked

me to come for the interview, I agreed. They had this proposal to do art therapy. Art therapy was in vogue that year, so the Cathedral received funding for a project using it. The concept was that if you got Black and Latino youths to do art projects, all their troubles would go away." John laughs. "I knew the proposal I'd read didn't make any sense. But I also knew that the Cathedral had the desire to do something for the community. We know that good intentions do not necessarily mean good ideas.

John continues. "The name Manhattan Valley is a community name, like Harlem or Crown Heights. Manhattan Valley runs from 100th Street and Central Park West to east of Broadway, and then up to 110th Street. That area had the most city-owned property *and* the most abandoned buildings. They also had a high concentration of cocaine and heroin sales taking place. There were Dominicans, Puerto Ricans, African-Americans, and whites—you know, it was multicultural."

John Bess has worked in all sorts of programs before this, from counseling in drug rehab programs to being a director of an Upward Bound program, but he'd never started a project from scratch. The challenge was just too good to pass up.

It wasn't easy going in the beginning, he recalls. "They had no place for me to work, so I had to work at home. The first few days I worked at home I slept instead of worked, so I knew it was not going to work. I came and found a space here in the Cathedral, but it was horrible. I remember tripping over all these old desks at first.

And there was barely room to work."

John knew the tiny space they were working from was not going to be able to handle the potential of his youth program, so he kept looking around the enormous grounds of the Cathedral of Saint John the Divine. "Then one day I saw the space that we are in now. At that time St. Luke's Psychiatric Program had two gyms and a kitchen, but they really were not using the space. So I made the director an offer I felt he could not refuse," he says slyly. "I politically, diplomatically, and aggressively got him to give up the space. We've since converted it into a youth center, and we've grown from a little program of a dozen people into a 2.5-million-dollar operation."

The Valley provides a diverse array of services for the youth of New York. It has become a part of the community as well as a part of the schools, so that kids can easily find their services. The employment-skills counseling, for example, teaches kids how to get a job, from applying for the job to how to handle an interview.

The Valley's Paul Robeson Leadership Training meetings create a weekly forum for members to discuss a wide variety of issues with each other on topics ranging from current world events to personal dilemmas. The kids develop the skills necessary to communicate effectively. "We have to try to strengthen young people's ability to do that. So that they in turn will be able to fend for themselves. We want them to be leaders and to not be persuaded by, or follow, others. They need to choose their own course of action—their own direction," John insists.

"We also have a dropout-prevention program. We are trying to work with young people who have already dropped out, are thinking of dropping out, or have the potential to drop out. We bring them back in school, help them to stay in school, help them to finish school. We help them deal with the atrocities that can take place in a school system that is basically antichild, antiyoung people; a system which is mostly proadult, in many cases exclusively sympathetic to teachers and administrators."

While many organizations offer teen mothers counseling, The Valley believes both parents need counseling. With so many teen fathers walking out on their responsibilities, and with many of the ones who don't feeling unable to deal with the reality of being a parent, there are too few places for these young parents to go for encouragement, information, or just a sympathetic ear. "None of my friends really understand what I deal with," says one young father. "They don't know what it's like when your baby gets sick and you get scared 'cause you're responsible now. They just say, 'Wow, man, that's rough,' then they change the subject or suddenly have to hook up with someone else. When I come to the group, the fellas are going through the same stuff as me, and we can give each other ideas about how to handle these things."

John Bess is very proud of what he's put together in his community. "Right now we are in the process of taking an even bigger space in the Cathedral in which we will develop a national comprehensive youth center. We will invite other agencies to help plan it and share their views. We hope to provide young people with every possible opportunity for success in whatever they do."

The Valley gives young people exposure to things they are often not exposed to. Architects, television writers, lawyers, and other professionals come to talk to the kids about their jobs, and often groups are organized to visit their workplaces.

Bill Cosby has been very involved in the work of The Valley and has used it as the model for the TV sitcom "Here and Now," starring Malcolm-Jamal Warner. Malcolm portrayed a counselor at a youth program much like The Valley. John was the technical consultant for the television show.

John grew up in the projects. Like many other kids, he found himself having to contribute to the family at an early age; his father died when he was only five. He's worked since he was thirteen years old. "I'm from Harlem, from the streets, so I know the difficulties. I've seen my community change from a place where all the doors used to be open. Where anybody in the community could send you to the store to run an errand. We watched the atomic bomb being dropped on our community—the atomic bomb being heroin—and we saw our community change overnight. We saw people ashamed to let neighbors go into their houses because of heroin addiction. Because someone might take television sets or the stereo system or money. People started locking their doors. Mothers were ashamed of what was happening to their children. Neighbors would say, 'You know your child is doing it,' and after a while that parent, who *did* know their child

was doing it, would tell those people to mind their own business. The community became very isolated.

"Like my young people, we all have our stories. We all knew someone who was brighter than us, more articulate, much more talented—but they just never made it. Whether they've gone to jail, been killed on the street, or are simply doing the wrong things. We've watched a lot of our young people fall by the wayside. Nowadays the act of killing someone is no big deal. It's almost as if it's a video game, or a cartoon. We've been so desensitized, killing someone, or hurting someone, doesn't seem to bother us."

The Valley works hard to change this attitude. No one is excluded. Anyone who needs help, no matter their income level, is welcomed into the bustling home beneath the Cathedral. Funding comes from many sources, but much of it is from private contributors. Like the programs John Bess feels the inner cities need most, little help comes from the government and surprisingly little money comes from corporations.

Are things getting better since The Valley came into being? "No! I have to report that things are far worse than they have ever been. We try to change the mentality of young men and young women. Young men especially, who are fathering babies they now call their trophies.

"Any commitment to limiting drugs is zero," says John, even more emphatic than usual. "'Just say no' means: '*No, the government ain't going to do nothing about it, no time soon and no time in the future.*' Young people are very aware that it's a billion-dollar indus-

try; they know that people are profiting on higher levels. People always have a rationale as to why they can use and sell drugs."

There are other facts which people seem to forget. "Young people put a lot of money into this economy!" John explains. "Anytime they go to the movies they spend about eighteen dollars. Six or seven of those dollars go to federal, state, and city taxes," he says, drawing an imaginary diagram on the table in the conference room. "I think we have to make government responsible for recycling—circulating resources of services *back* to those who need them.

"On the other hand, there seems to be an emerging quest for people to know more about their history, about our heroes and *she*roes, and I'm hoping that will be the new wave of hope and salvation. I think people are becoming more interested in who we are and beginning to recognize that we are dying as a people.

"The only signs of change," he continues, "are among those of us who have already joined the battle. We have to take on a greater mission. We have to do more than what we've been doing. We have to pull in more people to try to help save ourselves, to be responsible for ourselves, to preserve ourselves and change our destiny. I believe we can prosper as a people—if we can do what's necessary for us to live productively in the twenty-first century.

"Life is tough for everybody, but life is especially tough for those of us who are struggling up the ladder. Young people are destined to be great if given the right opportunities, the right directions, the right choices. *Then* they'll make it."

"I left Cleveland with the idea that only one of two things could happen in New York: they'd beat my ass and send me home, or I'd make it. I stayed almost twelve years. They beat my ass, but they didn't send me home." Rafala Green finishes her sentence with sultry laughter. "I always do everything differently—not the way that the manual says you're supposed to do things."

A large loom sits in the middle of Rafala Green's home. The renovated loft that used to be part of a molasses-processing plant in St. Paul, Minnesota, is currently where Rafala lives and works. "My commitment to be an artist was made when I was eleven years old. But I stopped for a big block—well, I didn't stop, but I moved to another commitment, and that was getting married at sixteen and having seven kids." Not to mention eleven grandchildren.

The loom itself looks like a piece of sculpture. Tall and narrow,

smooth and strong, it is a Navajo-based design and the tool Rafala uses to create her unique fabric-and-metallic sculptures.

Though she already had a degree in commercial art, Rafala found herself desiring training in fine art. "I had teachers in advertising class that would say of my work, 'This is not a Rembrandt, this is business. You've got to get it done.' And I'd say, 'Then I don't think I want to be here.' If I did it for money it would be okay, except I hated that garbage!" Again comes the smoky laughter. "I'm appreciative that I studied it because I learned a lot. Those teachers were the ones that helped me to move on to something else.

"When I decided to go to New York in 1979, I had resolved that there really wasn't any chance that I was not going to be an artist. And given that that was clear to me, my options were to either exist on a small scale in Ohio or go for the gold. So, since I didn't have a whole lot of time to be messing around, I figured I might as well just jump on in the water. I'd learn how to swim when I got in there."

The head of the art department where Rafala was studying suggested Parsons School of Design in New York, so Rafala immediately applied to the school. "I did not trust my application to proceed just as pieces of paper. Part of the requirement for application is the review of a portfolio. I already had four years of college, and rather than send my portfolio, I got on the bus and marched on to New York—'Take this bad boy!'"

The admissions board couldn't believe someone Rafala's age—she was not fresh out of high school—would be applying for admission to college. Rafala laughs at the recollection. She was accepted to the school but denied financial aid. "Being the nut that I am, I closed my house, gave away everything, and packed up. With three kids, a German shepherd dog, six cats, and a trailer, I went to New York. It took us six days and I lost everything!" She made it to New York with the help of Traveler's Aid. "The guy at Traveler's Aid said, 'Lady, why do you want to go to New York? New York doesn't need anybody else who doesn't have any money.' I told him, 'I'm not going back.'"

Completely broke, Rafala figured she deserved some financial assistance. "I marched into the Parsons office and said, 'Hey guys, I have left my family, closed my house, gone through hell to get here, and I have no intention of going back. I respectfully submit that you pull that application out again and take another look at it.' They did and one day before class started I got a full financial-aid package and I stayed until I graduated and got a bachelor of fine arts degree."

Rafala thought it best to put her plans to earn a master's degree on hold, since some of her kids still needed to complete their education. There was plenty of outstanding debt to deal with. While she was teaching art at a junior high school, a friend told her of the master's-degree program at City College. It was very inexpensive, but it meant she was going to have to quit her job and she only had enough money for one semester.

"The next day I called on the phone and said, 'I understand you've got a master's program there. I would like to find out more about it.' The man said, 'How long will it take you to get here?' I said, 'Twenty minutes.'

"I got there in twenty minutes. He looked at my résumé and the slides of my work. The interviewer took me over to the art building and introduced me to a distinguished visiting professor who had just come in from Brazil. He showed the professor my slides and said, 'She's interested in the master's program, what do you think about taking her on?' The professor said, 'Okay.' In an hour I had somehow gotten myself a full scholarship in a master's-degree program with a mentor from Brazil."

During the next two years, while she worked at her degree, Rafala became her children's child. With all of them working by this time, they helped support their mom. "I'd wake up in the morning," she remembers, "and they'd be out in the hallway saying, 'I gave her money *yesterday*, it's *your* turn.'"

Rafala completed her studies and got her degree. "For the first time I was realizing my dream: being a self-supporting artist, living off of my work." But Rafala was getting tired of the grind in New York—it's not an easy city to survive in.

During the summer of 1990 she decided to visit her brother, who was living in Minnesota. He took Rafala downtown to check out a building that was being renovated as part of an art-development project in St. Paul's manufacturing district. "This building was empty, they were just finishing it up. I stepped inside of it and started screaming! 'Ahhh! This is it! This is it! This is what I need!' It was wonderful."

The Lower Town Lofts/Artspace project was just beginning. Old manufacturing buildings were being gutted and refurbished to accommodate artists with limited financial resources who wanted large live/work spaces, much in the style of New York's SoHo and TriBeCa districts. Rafala's application was accepted and she began her career as a Minnesota-based artist, in a place that has a thirst for and desire to encourage artists.

Rafala has always been a community activist and participant in local affairs. She was chosen by neighborhood residents of Minneapolis's Phillips community to create a plaza at the corner of Chicago and Franklin avenues in to help replace a local eyesore for the Phillips Community Gateway Project. The corner was once the home of a notorious liquor store. Her entrance to the new plaza features three narrow oval pillars in its design, objects which seem to some observers almost too delicate. They wonder if they are sturdy enough. She assures them that the pillars will be fine. "I told them it was concrete with reinforced steel. It's *supposed* to look delicate."

Making metal look soft is a key to her creations. Rafala's work weaving materials on her loom, which she has had specially reinforced to handle the pressure of the metallic fibers that she uses, is her current focus. "Like any other artist, you go through periods where you explore materials, technique, and forms as part of your growth process to come into your own. I kept being increasingly frustrated with painting because it wouldn't move. I was constantly trying to make things be suspended in space on this flat surface and paint just wasn't doing it for me.

"While I was at Parsons I made the decision that sculpture was the thing that I really wanted to do. And like I said, I tried different kinds of techniques. By the time I had left Parsons, what was clear to me in terms of my own personal notebook of tools was that I had a thing for metals—I had a feeling for metals.

"My reaction and my fascination with metals was that it was just a charge to take this COLD, HARD, STIFF, RIGID, material and make it soft and *OOOZIE*. Make it flow. Put some heat on that bad boy and do anything you want. Then I started adding fibers. Then I got involved in hard and soft."

While Rafala Green works with metal, there is something interestingly different about her work. It *is* soft, yet at the same time strong. "I wasn't interested in mass. I never had any desire to do these great big, clunky, solid kinds of structures. And recognizing that I wasn't interested in them made me begin to look around. I paid more attention to my environment and began to see how much those kinds of forms *dominate* our environment.

"I became fascinated not in *this*," she says, holding a hand upright with fingers spread and rigid, "but *this*." Rafala's other hand gracefully weaves through the spaces created by her stiff fingers. "What was happening between, what was happening around. What was being created. How energy was being directed or how energy was *directing* this. It's also something of an ingredient that's involved in jazz. You know, it's like giving oneself up to it. Wherever it takes you, just go with it."

Rafala takes a long sip of her morning coffee. Her windows are open and the air is crisp in her loft. The weather is beginning to turn wintry in St. Paul, and it's just barely fall.

She is happy to have her work chosen by the community to help celebrate a new beginning and ethnic diversity. Artists, Rafala contends, should not be some sort of separate entity. In ancient and prehistoric times, they were very much part of the fabric of their community. They were simply regular people. Now she is hired to create *for* "the people." Ultimately, that doesn't really matter to her. "Who do I make my art for, or what is my concern in terms of audience? Initially I don't have one." She laughs heartily. "If there wasn't an audience and nobody looked at it, it wouldn't change a thing. I would still create it."

Ty Wilson

Several years ago, when I was making my way up the ladder toward becoming a "real" photographer, I worked as an assistant to a very successful fashion photographer. Bloomingdale's, the New York department store, was the client one day, and we were going to be photographing models in various designer wear for some newspaper ads. The art director, who was responsible for coming up with the artistic style of the shoot, had become tired of the same old white-paper background, known as a "seamless," which is seen in most studio fashion photos.

He decided to incorporate the photographic images of the models with the dramatic and stylized drawings of a fashion illustrator. Instead of the usual pristine background of white paper, an illustrator would create giant fashion sketches on the seamless background, featuring the same clothing the real-life models were wearing. Early that morning, after the other assistant and I had set up the studio, a young man came in with a few

assistants of his own. I remember how pleased I was to see this Black person working in a business where I was used to seeing mostly white faces.

He and his crew examined the ten-foot-high, eight-foot-wide paper that we'd rolled from the suspended crossbar down to the floor, and after some brief discussion, they whipped out several paintbrushes of various size, tins of paint, and he went to work.

Several minutes later, the photo crew was standing in a semicircle around the set. Our mouths were open, but in the fashion world, it's not cool to be impressed so everyone tried simply to look pleased. The other assistant and I were simply impressed. I was too afraid to tell the artist how good his painting was. I knew he had to be a big shot, and I was a nobody. He whipped off sketch after sketch as the models changed outfits and we put up fresh paper. The artist seemed confident as he went about his work. He'd start with a bold sweeping line, a curvy line at the top, fat and heavy with paint. But by the time it reached its destination at the bottom of the paper, it was a thin, graceful, sexy line, breaking up as it came to a crisp and delicate tip.

Years later, as I searched for people to include in *Our Common Ground*, a friend called to tell me about an artist she was representing. She thought I would find him interesting. A few days later a large envelope arrived containing some materials about the artist. His name was Ty Wilson. The name rang a bell. Then I pulled out the cards with the samples of his work. *This* was the guy who'd impressed me so much at that Bloomingdale's photo shoot more than five years ago.

"That was probably my first job in New York!" says Ty as we talk in his apartment/studio. "I was scared to *death*. I didn't have the slightest idea what I was doing. I had never worked on anything that big before. I never used brushes that size, so I wasn't even sure I could get it to work. I just kept praying that they wouldn't throw me out once they found out I was a fraud!"

One reason Ty may have been so nervous was that just a few weeks before he was living in Kansas City, had just quit a job at Hallmark, the greeting-card company, and was working as a free-lance artist. He was also making plans to try to make a go of it in "the big city."

Ty (which is not short for anything) grew up in suburban Maryland. His parents were divorced, so he and his older brother spent a lot of time entertaining themselves after school. "We were latchkey kids," he says. "We had to bring ourselves home from first and second grade and stay there until Mom got home. Since she worked all day and didn't have money for baby-sitters or anything, she tried to make indoors as inviting as possible.

"I didn't play any sports, and I didn't have much interest in playing with other kids. I was always drawing, watching movies, or reading books. I was a real introvert, so I got teased and picked on a lot."

Eventually, Ty found out that being able to draw made him popular. "First I was just 'the fat boy,' then I became 'the artist.' They stopped hassling me because I was 'the artist.' 'There's Ty Wilson, let's beat him up!' 'No, no. He's the one that draws.' So I was cool all of a sudden. Before they'd beat me up I'd say, 'Wait a minute. Let me do a sketch for you.' I'd do Captain America or something, and they would leave me alone. That was my passport."

Ty's Black Studies teacher got him interested in reading quality books. The first author he read was Maya Angelou, and her work changed his whole perception of reading. He found these new books had substance to them, and the recurring theme running though them was how people could change their lives by taking control of them. Ty resolved not to be stuck in the town he lived in, getting a job he would hate and working until he retired.

A guidance counselor scoffed at Ty when he said he wanted to be an artist. "She said, 'Get real! Take the civil-service test and get a government job.' I resented her for that. Somebody else trying to step on the dream. She didn't even say, 'Apply to this college,' or, 'Here's this option,' or, 'What about this?' *Nothing.* It was just, why don't you be realistic? She was trying to push me into a technical school. I don't know what her agenda was, but that just made me all the more determined to be an artist."

Encouragement from his high school art teacher pushed him to draw something other than comics, and to develop a portfolio. While Ty worked hard to earn enough credits to graduate a year early, his art teacher submitted his portfolio to Maryland College of Art and Design, hoping for a scholarship.

"I figured I'd try to get some money to go to a community college by working at a warehouse. Every day I was on that loading dock," he remembers. "My resolve grew stronger and stronger every day *not* to make that my life. There were other guys on the dock—not to say there's anything wrong with it—but they'd been there ten, fifteen years, making minimum wage to haul boxes.

"Then that call came, after I'd been there months and months, and months, it seemed. The voice on the other end said, 'Ty Wilson? You've been selected to get the scholarship.' I quit that day! I was jumping up and down and guys on the dock were saying, 'What's going on?' And I said. 'I got a scholarship to go to college!' They were like, 'You mean you're not staying here with us?'"

Ty was someone who never thought he'd go to college. "I don't know if that was because I felt I could never afford it, or because I thought as an artist you didn't need it. I started to realize that it's a wonderful vehicle because you get so much. Once you get in college, what you get out of it is what you put into it. It's not about a piece of paper; it's more about life experiences."

At Maryland Ty won a scholarship to go to Pratt Institute in New York, and got a job offer from Hallmark. "Hedging my bets, I accepted both. I went first to Pratt and it was a rude awakening; I saw that I was not the only talented person in the world, " Ty says, shaking his head. "It's like the football player who's a star in high school, goes to college, and finds that *everyone* in college had been captain of the football team. That's what it was like for me." So I tucked my tail between my legs and left for the job at Hallmark, out in Kansas City, because I thought that it would be easier to find out about myself there.

Although everyone told Ty to go to Pratt, he was happy with his decision to work at Hallmark. The opportunity was a learning experience. It was his first time out of a major metropolitan area, but he found that it made him more aware of being Black. Being turned away from clubs, and seeing people cross the street as he walked toward them, were new experiences for him.

"Once I found out that I wasn't going to go anywhere at Hallmark, I took the last promotion rejection letter that I got from the head of the creative department and framed it. I put it on my wall where I could see it while I was working at home on my portfolio at night. That was my motivation to get out of there and to be successful. I quit Hallmark and took a year to free-lance in Kansas City. I decided if I liked the free-lance life, *then* I would take my act to New York."

Ty's drawing style then was very realistic. He eventually talked a local magazine into giving him his own page in every issue. His current style evolved from that experience.

"I had a deadline," Ty remembers. "The magazine editors told me in no uncertain terms how dissatisfied they were with what I was doing. Month after month I was doing these tight, stiff drawings that looked like everybody else's. They wanted something different. I was awake, literally, for three days, finishing pad after pad and going through reams of paper. After drawing this same outfit over and over and over, it got looser and more uninhibited. It was due at ten o'clock in the morning and at eight that morning I finally had something

to show them. I came in and said, 'I'm sorry, this is all I could come up with,' when I showed it to them. They flipped for it."

His work has since graced the pages of *Vogue* and *Harper's Bazaar*, and the cover of an album by Chaka Khan. He's worked for Macy's and Bloomingdale's, and his T-shirt designs are sold at Nordstrom's. And he's recently started designing linens, dishes, and graphics for sportswear.

Ty works in India ink with brushes on paper, uses pastels for their soft quality, or uses vibrantly colored cut paper for the hard edges and strong shapes they can create.

The kindness of others is not lost on Ty. Had several people not extended a hand to him, he could still be on that loading dock today. For this reason, he has tried to make himself available to young people interested in his field. Speaking at schools or helping out strangers who call by critiquing their portfolio are not uncommon things for Ty to do.

"As a Black artist, or even a Black *person*, you've got to be this walking United Nations for all the rest of the Black community, and I feel that's not fair. Even in my art, people will say, 'Why don't you do more Black themes?' 'You're selling out!' is always the big thing. I wasn't selling out so much as I was doing what I wanted to do. I finally came to the conclusion, either you like it or you don't.

"I used to think I had goals," says the artist. "I don't really have any now because life just keeps presenting itself to me—I just try to be there."

Vernon Reid

Vernon Reid

"I heard you've been trying to get ahold of me, so I figured I would give you a call myself," said the voice on the other end of the telephone. I was caught off guard when I spoke to guitarist Vernon Reid for the first time. It's not every day that someone of his stature, a person whose work you enjoy and admire, just happens to give you a call.

My interest in speaking to Vernon was because of the work he has done to promote Black musicians in the music industry. As one of the founding members and the former president of the Black Rock Coalition, he has helped expand awareness of and opportunities for Black artists who were not strictly interested in playing R and B, funk, and hip-hop. As Vernon explains, the BRC was and still is, in many ways, about community.

"The roots of the BRC came from my neighborhood and the musicians I knew when I was coming up," he explains. "They were like

myself, into all different kinds of music. As we got older, we started bands. I started seeing a lot of my friends having real difficulties getting their music heard." Vernon noticed that certain clubs were not booking Black bands that played rock, and record companies were saying nobody was going to buy rock and roll played by Black bands. Rock is by white bands, they said. They seemed to have forgotten who'd invented rock and roll. It certainly wasn't Elvis.

There were too many solid Black bands struggling to get access to the same places white rock bands where hitting. Vernon decided to call a few people "and find out if it was just *me*, or if it was an exclusionary pattern in terms of where we could go with what we were doing. I was just looking at all this talent languishing.

"I called a bunch of people, and I didn't just call musicians. I called people who were involved in the other side the business as well. We just started getting together and talking about these issues and venting a lot of frustration as we started to identify the problems." There was no master plan, Vernon contends, it just evolved. When the group decided to choose a president for their organization, "everybody was pointing at me," Vernon says. "It was sorta like, 'Hey, you picked up the phone.'"

The Black Rock Coalition lived off membership dues and money raised at concerts. By including in their membership writers from various publications, and people who worked for record companies, they were able to start getting their message out. The BRC produced an album featuring the music of member bands and used it as a means of further educating the public and the industry.

But aside from educating the industry, the members knew they must educate themselves. They began disseminating information to their ranks about the music business. They discussed what various people and departments at a record company do. Simple nuts-and-bolts issues like management and taxes were covered, not just how to get on a label. As Vernon's band, Living Colour, became more successful, they were able to give lectures about their experiences.

"When Living Colour began touring, if we had a chance, we would put BRC bands on as opening acts, and we encouraged that sort of activity," Vernon mentions. "When you get to a point where you can do this, you've got to help to pull the other people along with you.

"I think one thing that the BRC does that's often overlooked," he adds, "is that it keeps the idea of *live, Black music* alive. On urban, or 'Black' radio, most of the records you hear are made by machines. No bands. There are a handful of exceptions to the rule, like Tony, Tonie, Toné, and Cameo. And Black music is *nothing* if it's not live music. That's why James Brown is so funky. Not to take away from programming and all that, but it has its place.

"There's nothing innate about a cultural thing like rhythms. If they're not passed down, they're lost. We don't know what kind of music was really played in ancient Egypt. We have things that approximate it, but we really don't know," Vernon asserts.

"Hip-hop people are thinking of actual prerecorded music as the instruments they're building on. One thing that's critical and crucial is that our musical heritage of live music is not lost.

"Our band goes out there and we take those chances. We may go out and maybe one night it's not good. But we have to deal with that because we're human. The idea of a consistently perfect performance is a trap."

But music is not what Vernon wants to talk about when he calls me. Vernon is picking my brain about photography. When he first picked up a camera around 1987, it became another way for him to express himself. Unlike the work of people who practice other professions and say, "Oh yes, I'm also a photographer," his work backs up and surpasses his modest claims to be "really into taking pictures."

His subjects vary, but the approach is always direct and instinctive. Vernon likes to "feel the picture, otherwise it's not really worth taking." The pictures he takes range from "arty" nudes that incorporate elements he describes as "industrial," to photo reportage—catching things as they happen.

One strong image shows the tightly cropped face of an elderly man looking intently into the camera as he holds an Arabic-language newspaper. His large and extended hand seems to say to the viewer, "Don't you understand?"

"This man was walking straight at me in this completely isolated area," recalls Vernon of the day he made the photo. "He was talking to himself and had no idea I was there. If he saw me, it didn't show. I could tell from his manner he was upset about *something* and somehow I could feel . . . I could relate to his pain. He just kept coming right at me and I just crouched down low with the camera and pointed it right at him. He practically walked through me. He turned and looked right through the camera as if I weren't there, and I took two quick exposures. The first one was *the* one."

The nudes that Vernon eventually showed me were in a completely different style. These were quiet images filled with energy. They all seemed to have a common thread. "There are two kinds of things I'm doing," he tells me. "Part of it is simply going out and finding things randomly. The other thing is taking certain *seemingly* random elements and pulling them together. Things that work thematically or compositionally. Like this clock," he says, showing me a series of nudes of a woman holding a very misshapen clock. "Time is sort of a theme.

"I went into a building that had burned in a fire. The fire was in the main room, but in an adjacent room where nothing had really been touched, the *heat* was so intense that everything in there melted. I found this clock in that room." In the photograph, the unclothed woman holds the clock in front of her face. It becomes a sort of mask.

When Vernon chooses a subject for his work, he looks for something special, something that makes that person the *right* person for his photograph. "The only thing I look for is a link between myself and the subject," he says. "I can't just shoot a beautiful woman because she's beautiful. If I don't feel a sort of empathy, it's not really going to work. And it's much more than a matter of us liking the same things.

"The few people I've worked with, I like to talk to them beforehand." Vernon arranges to get-together with potential models for dinner or coffee, so that he has a chance to get to know them. It is, he explains, a very important part of his photographic process. "I know it's an inefficient way of working, but for what I'm doing it's not . . . I'm not doing it as a fashion thing. I'm doing it in the hope that we'll strike a chord."

While his love for photography shows in his aesthetic, compositional, and technical abilities, Vernon never studied photography in the conventional sense of the word. "I didn't go to school. I just learned this by looking at books. Lots of photography books. What will ultimately tell the tale is what is in these pictures—what happens in the composition. Is it something that moves? I guess that's my criteria.

"I keep my options open because I look at photographers like Stieglitz, Man Ray, and Weegee. I have such respect for photographers who actually went out in the field and just *did* stuff. Like Weegee—he would listen to a citizens-band radio for police calls and go to murder and crime scenes for photographs. But at the same time he would also go out to dances and catch people when they were being intimate with one another."

Vernon has already exhibited his photographs in galleries and hopes to do more soon. He uses his downtime from touring and recording to work on his photography, often finding plenty to shoot while on the road. His one major setback was the theft of three years' worth of work from the trunk of his car. Not having a darkroom at home to do his black-and-white printing, Vernon was en route to a rental facility. When the thieves cleaned out his car trunk, they got the negatives and prints from his most productive time.

"It really kills you," he said to me, obviously still bothered by the theft, which had happened almost a year earlier. "It's like somebody came and took a piece of your life away. That is work I cannot replace. I really felt I was beginning to hit a certain kind of stride and find a true vision. I can only use that experience to make me go on and do new and better work."

As with his music, Vernon is already talking about taking chances. He thrives on the excitement of making mistakes on the way to doing something new. This sounds a lot like his musical philosophy: "the idea of a consistently perfect performance is a trap."

Branford Marsalis

Branford Marsalis is sitting in my living room on the couch, looking very relaxed. He is wearing one of his favorite multicolored, Bill Cosby–style sweaters, as I like to call them. He's got on a pair of well-broken-in jeans and equally lived-in sneakers.

"I'm moving to California," he says in an offhand manner. "I got a gig. I'm gonna be musical director on the 'Tonight' show." I think I was more excited about the job than he was. But that's Branford Marsalis; someone who is rarely impressed by his own accomplishments.

Branford Marsalis is one of the best-known (particularly after being seen five nights a week on the "Tonight" show), most sought-after and highly respected jazz saxophonists in the world. His family background has not hurt his musical development. Father Ellis is a brilliant jazz pianist. One younger brother, Delfeayo, plays trombone and has produced most

of Branford's albums. Wynton, who is Delfeayo's senior but younger than Branford (*looks* older, as Branford gleefully points out), has been the most familiar. People still confuse the two—if they can first get the names right: Winston . . . Whitney . . . Brandon . . . Branston . . . Margolis.

Aside from the legends of jazz and blues he has played with—John Lee Hooker, Herbie Hancock, Linda Hopkins, and Ron Carter—Branford also had a much-publicized stint with singer/songwriter/musician Sting. His foray into the world of "pop" or rock music caused a small and temporary rift between himself and his brother Wynton, who is a bit more of a traditionalist. But that didn't matter to Branford. To him, being an artist is not about satisfying other people; it is about making yourself happy, and if along the way others like what you do, that's a bonus.

At first he turned down the offer to put together and direct a band for the "Tonight" show, but he changed his mind after a couple of days. One of the things that might have caused his change of heart could be a story he told me about his father. "My dad used to travel on the road with Al Hirt's band, so there were years I don't remember seeing him. He'd come in and out of town, just like I do now. I remember when he quit; he had been away for three weeks and had grown a beard. When he came back I wouldn't let him in the house because I didn't recognize him. I was like, *'No!'* He said, 'Open the door. It's me!' 'You're not my dad! My dad doesn't have that stuff on his face.' I

was like . . . seven. It hurt him real bad, and right after that he quit the road. He got a teaching gig." Branford's own son Reese was close to that age when the call came from "Tonight" show host Jay Leno. When he accepted the job, many people accused Branford of selling out.

Taking chances and speaking his mind are two of the qualities that make people either respect or dislike Branford. Still, it's hard to imagine people not liking him. He is a young man with a terrific sense of humor, and he is both down-to-earth and respectful when he's with other people. Watching him meet fans backstage after a show, it's hard to believe he is the famous person people tell him he is. He is attentive and jovial, yet he has also been accused of being arrogant, and pessimistic.

Branford Marsalis would rather have a strong effect on people—love him or hate him—than leave them unchallenged. It seems that if he could, he would challenge every Black American to think about the world around them. Their enlightenment can only serve to open the eyes of others.

"The biggest problem with Black people and racism is Blacks and whites are more like each other than they would like to admit, and I know this just from studying European history," he says. "In the history books they teach us the Europeans came to America to escape religious persecution, and they turned against King George because they were against dictatorships. If you really study history, you know that's against human nature.

"The reason that the Americans resented the king was not because they objected

to having a king; they were upset because they *weren't* the king. So they wanted to get rid of the king so *they* could become kings. That's what human nature's all about. And when most Black people I know talk about racism, their philosophy is—instead of *Black* and *white* we'll use *oppressor* and *oppressed*—the oppressed are teed off at the oppressor not because the oppressor is *wrong*, but because they would prefer to *be* the oppressor. The one in charge."

These kinds of statements seem strong, but Branford backs them up with news events: "Take the situation in Los Angeles with the Martin Luther King Hospital in Watts, where the neighborhood is now seventy percent Latino, but the brothers don't want to let the Latinos get the jobs. If you look back twenty years, it's the same situation we [Black people] were in. And I hear the brothers sayin', 'Well they haven't paid the racial dues we have.' Then they have a march in the streets. Man, that has nothing to do with reality. If Black people said in 1965, we represent a large enough portion of the community and we want to see our own in positions of authority, then the same thing applies to Latinos or whoever!

"The brothers really aren't interested in that," he continues, "We're very angry people, and I'm not saying we don't have a right to be, but there comes a point at which you become consumed with the anger and the logic becomes flawed."

Like many Blacks, Branford has experienced firsthand the prejudice and small-minded comments toward people of color in America, or minorities in any country, face on a daily basis. His celebrity status doesn't exempt him from everyday life. Fortunately, even in situations that might warrant violence, he has instead been able to make people stop and think.

"I went to Yellowstone National Park, and I walked into one of those convenience stores on the side of the road. And these two dudes in lumberjack shirts, two white guys, said, 'Look what we have here! What the hell are you doin' here?'

"I said, 'I'm on vacation. That's still an American right, isn't it?'

"They said, 'Why don't you vacation your ass back to Africa!' Which I thought was very interesting," he says with the typical Branford smirk, "because, well—I can't even call it arrogance. It's more *ignorance* actually. It's very ignorant of the white people in this country who say that, to forget that they're not from here either.

"I have no tolerance for that kind of garbage at all, but I'm not going to resort to the usual, 'You white motherf——!' I said, 'Yeah, I'll take my Black ass back to Africa, if you take your Podunk ass back to Eastern Europe, where *you* came from!'"

Branford has to laugh. It sounds pretty funny to both of us after the fact. "So," I ask through my own laughter, "what was his reaction?" Branford throws up a hand with a casual "of course" gesture. "I could tell by the look on his face that he had never considered the fact that he wasn't from here, either. So it kind of threw him off guard. I bought my stuff and he stared at me. But he stared at me differently, because I don't think that Black people ever really use that as a response. Usually it's, 'You think you this,' 'You think you that. . . .'"

Certainly one of Branford's strongest assets is that he uses his brain. In a similar situation, someone else might have decided that he needed to prove manhood by assaulting the man, but Branford proved himself by outthinking someone who would have spoken before he thought.

The going-back-to-Africa concept is one of those things neither Black nor white people really understand, according to Branford. "Black Americans are like the omni-Americans. Albert Murray wrote a book called *The Omni-Americans*. Other than the Native Americans, Black people are the only people who truly have nowhere to go. We can't go back to Africa. We don't know nobody!

"We don't have a culture, man. Our culture is gone! You sit in class and they say, 'Who's your grandfather?' and all the little kids say, 'My grandfather's blah blah blah.' 'Who's your great-grandfather?' 'My great-grandfather is Great-Grandfather Oleg from Sweden.' 'What about your great-great-grandfather?' 'Oh that's Great-Great-Grandfather Bjorn from Sweden.'

"Me, my grandfather's name was Ellis, my great-grandfather's name was Simeon. 'Where's he from, Branford?' 'I don't know. Mississippi, I guess. He was a slave. Where's my great-grandfather's father from? *I do not know.*'

"'I don't know.' That's the story of our lives. That's why we have no self-esteem.

"Black people talk about Africa like it's a country," he tells me. "Like it's a state, like it's Maine. Rappers keep talking about Nubia, but Black Americans are from West Africa. They're talking about Nubia in the seventies when they were using Swahili. Swahili's not a language that was used in the section where we're from. They speak Ga, they speak Bo, they speak Wolof, they speak all these languages in West Africa. Nobody ever mentions that. They want to use Egypt, they want to use Nubia, Ethiopia—they want to use anything but the place where we came from.

"I was talking to some kids in high school, and they were talking about this Afrocentric stuff. I just asked a simple question. I said, 'What language do they speak in Africa?' One said he didn't know and another one said Swahili. I said, 'No man. Swahili has two thousand five hundred dialects. The thing you don't understand is there are tens of thousands of tribes in Africa. And every single tribe has its own language. It's the kind of stuff we know nothing about.'"

These are the kinds of things Branford will be sure to teach his son Reese. His life is about more than being a popular musician; it's about being an articulate and informed human being. Branford constantly challenges himself and his colleagues to think in different ways, whether it be musically or intellectually. As he told a writer for a jazz magazine, "Do you want to deal with the mediocre? I deal with the highest level of everything. I take the high road on everything that I do. I may not ever reach the high road, but that's what I shoot for."

Dawnn Lewis's concern for the future of young Americans has taken her places and shown her things she never imagined. What started out as a trip to her old high school, the High School of Music and Art in New York City, has become an important part of her life—and the lives of the many young people she meets.

Although she is an accomplished singer and dancer with a long list of acting and recording credits, which include costarring on the hit sitcom "Hangin' with Mr. Cooper," much of Dawnn's fame came from her starring role as Jaleesa Vinson on the television show "A Different World." Her character returns to college after a failed marriage to get control of her future. Although her character is older than the other students, she moves forward and gains the respect of everyone at the all-Black college she attends. That same respect is accorded Dawnn in real life.

Dawnn's effort to inspire young people was not planned. "It was a fluke," she says. "Talking at schools, that was a surprise to me because I don't consider myself a public speaker. I'm an actress, I'm a singer, I'm a dancer, I'm a writer—I'm not a public speaker. If anything at all, I'm a feeler and a dreamer and everything I say—that's what I feel." While visiting a former teacher, something she's been doing since she graduated, she was asked to stop by a class and talk to the students for a moment. She told them, "You should be really grateful and excited about what you have in this school, because a lot of people grow up to be thirty, forty years old and still don't know what they want to be when they grow up. Here you are in high school already making your choice. You've got this facility here and what it is saying is, 'Use me to be who you want to be.' So take advantage of that."

Questions and answers went back and forth. It's easy to get caught up in listening to Dawnn. Her thoughtful nature and warm personality draw you in. A few moments became a whole period. Another teacher asked her to come by one other class before she left. She smiles. "I spent the entire day in school, going from class to class."

"I would be sitting in these rooms, and people were so eager to hear what I had to say, I started crying in the middle of talking. I couldn't believe it. It meant so much to me that they were actually listening and they cared enough about themselves to ask a serious question. It was deep." On a later visit to her elementary school, Dawnn got the same response. Her mother, a nurse who works in several different schools, also asked if Dawnn would come to her schools and talk to the kids because they needed someone they could relate to. Many kids felt pressure to do things just to be part of the crowd. Something Dawnn understood very well.

"*I* was a 'good guy' when I was growing up. I wasn't a goody-goody, but I did well in school." (She graduated magna cum laude from the University of Miami.) "I liked school, but at the same time I was this kid who wanted to have fun. I wanted people to like me. I would do my homework and do well on exams. I prided myself on being able to pull A's all the time, but I couldn't tell my friends that." She laughs with a warm smile. "I got beaten up enough as it was!

"I was being two people at one time," Dawnn recalls. "I was this good student undercover, and a troublemaker on the other hand so I could hang out with everybody. It was hard."

It was obvious to her that the kids she was talking to needed an outlet and an empathetic ear. Dawnn created the Good Guys' Club in order to give kids the opportunity to talk about their problems, fears, and the pressures of growing up in a society that, at its best, is trying even for adults. The purpose of the Good Guys' Club is to give encouragement and support, "and to show kids the benefits, the power, and the strength in being the best person you can be."

At each school or community center she visits, Dawnn establishes the club so the positive effort can continue after she leaves. "I pull out some representatives from each class who are not necessarily the best students. I did well, but I wasn't the best student when I was in school, either. I was just somebody who was trying. I sit and I rap with them—besides having the big assembly where you sit and you talk to everybody."

Dawnn and her celebrity friends who sometimes join her in her travels (like Marsha Warfield and Michael Jordan) talk about everything from peer pressure and substance abuse to physical abuse at home. "Some of the people who are doing so well in school have family members who are drug addicts or alcoholics, who are in prison, who have been molested, or who *molest.*"

One issue that Dawnn deals with regularly is teen pregnancy. "I've gotten letters from some kids saying that they were thinking about having a baby because they were bored with school. Or they wanted to have a child because their boyfriend wanted to do it. But after talking it out with their boyfriend, they repeated something that I said to them. 'If your body parts work *now*, they will work when you're twenty or twenty-one and you have a choice.' Believe me—I know. *Mine* still work!" This approach might seem too direct or raw in some people's eyes, but Dawnn doesn't see it that way. "I'm talking to kids in junior high school. There's no reason to sugarcoat. There's no reason to paint juvenile pictures, because they know very well what we're talking about. They know *all too well* what's happening."

Dawnn's efforts are funded mostly out of her pocket, although occasionally she will receive an honorarium to offset her expenses. However, most of the groups she speaks to cannot afford even that. Her talks have been publicized through word of mouth. Each time she speaks to one group, someone there knows of a place that could use her inspirational spirit. Yet she tries to avoid publicity and doesn't generally sign autographs on these trips. "I'm not real big on the autograph thing because we need to *talk* to kids, and not give them souvenirs. The souvenirs should be what's left in their heads and their hearts after you're gone."

Her audiences are diverse; her speaking engagements take her from day-care centers to universities. For the last few years, Dawnn has been asked to be the keynote speaker at the National 4-H Conference meeting in Chicago. Operation PUSH has asked her to speak at the University of Chicago and Illinois State University, and the United Negro College Fund requested her presence at an alumni homecoming in Alabama. The Good Guys' Club travels to community centers and Boys' and Girls' Clubs, as well as schools. The communities represent all income levels because all kids face life challenges. In the project's first year, Dawnn visited over thirty institutions. "I'm hop, skippin', and jumpin' all across the country," she says laughingly, with a false Southern accent. All this traveling, speaking, and following up somehow fits around taping a weekly television show and writing and recording her own music. Then, of course, there are all the little side ventures, one of them being a series of public-service commercials she wrote and had produced through OSAP (the Office of Substance Abuse Prevention). The effort ("Stay Smart—Don't Start!") included posters that Dawnn personally signed and sent out to schools, clubs, and community groups.

Among her other honors, Dawnn has been recognized more than once by the National Black Social Workers Association for her work with kids and her community service encouraging family unity. It's Dawnn's firm belief that to reach the world's youth, you must educate their guardians. "Adults have spent so much time fighting for and protecting what we have, that we often forget to educate and encourage those coming up behind us. We just expect them to know. Everybody tries hard, but we all feel inferior to *somebody at some time*. That can keep you from trying, from wanting to shine, because you feel, 'I'm never going to be the one everybody thinks is the best. I'm just going to be satisfied surviving.'

"I grew up in Bed-Stuy, Brooklyn, and went to school with all kinds of people. That's how I was raised. I try to spread around a little hope, a little positivity."

One of Dawnn's goals is to create a school in New York for creative and cultural development. This facility would accommodate people from varied economic and ethnic backgrounds, including physically and mentally challenged students. Mandatory classes would include sign language for the hearing and Braille for the sighted. "So we can all communicate with one another."

Coretta Cosby and Shannon Greeley

Coretta Cosby looks at me for a second as she thinks about her answer to my question—and it *is* only a second. "That wall out there really motivates me," she says as she gestures with her hand to just outside the double doors of the cafeteria. Shannon Greeley, who sits across the table, smiles knowingly and nods almost imperceptibly. "That wall has pictures of all the graduating classes," she continues. "This veterinary school's been open since 1944, but they've graduated only three people of African descent, and that pisses me off." Shannon Greeley and her friend Coretta Cosby are students at the veterinary medical school at the University of Illinois in Champaign-Urbana.

The wall Coretta speaks of is lined with framed photographs of the graduating classes of U of I veterinary school going back to 1944. The faces are mostly white. In fact, a visitor would have difficulty finding much ethnic diversity of any kind in that wall of photos. The few

Black faces are almost consumed by the faces of the other students. Shannon and Coretta are two of a handful of Black students currently studying at the veterinary medical school.

"There's no way you can tell me there have been no African-Americans in this state interested in veterinary medicine except those three since 1944," Coretta adds. "One of whom was from *Nigeria* and went *back* to Nigeria as soon as he graduated. So he wasn't even African-*American*. I hate that wall. It bothers me a lot."

Shannon and Coretta are friends, both working toward degrees that will give them the qualifications to take their state exams and become veterinarians. The field of veterinary medicine is one that both agree few people of color consider as a viable career choice. For Shannon, it seemed an excellent choice. "I didn't want to go into any sort of traditional field. I sat down and tried to assess what I wanted to do with my life. I thought about working for people but decided it wasn't something I'd want to do forever, especially not a desk job. I thought, that's not for me, so veterinary medicine stood out as something I could do for a long time *and* enjoy. 'The wall' motivates me as well, because the numbers are appalling. Appalling."

Shannon has known since she was about ten that she wanted to work with animals. "We always had a lot of pets in the house," she says. "But I think the factor that influenced me most to become a vet was probably when my cat had feline leukemia. I had such a sense of being powerless. There was nothing I could do to save my cat. I thought, maybe if I was a vet I could have done something.

"In sixth grade, when I was eleven or twelve, I'd go and hang out at my local vet's, just to see what it was like. At that point I found it to be . . ." she pauses, looking for the right word, ". . . it was neat. Really neat. It was going to be a long road, but I stayed with it all through high school."

Living in a city like Chicago, Coretta didn't have quite the access to animals that Shannon had growing up in the more suburban Decatur, Illinois. But, she was able to spend most summers on a farm her dad's family owns in his native Alabama. "Every summer from the time I was six months until I was sixteen I went down there. When they had to go do something to the pigs, I went and watched them. When they had to go feed the rabbits, I went. I always liked animals.

"From the first time I can ever remember saying what I wanted to be, it's always been a veterinarian. I liked science in school, so I did fairly well with it. I liked animals, too, so I figured I should be an animal doctor," Coretta says matter-of-factly. "My parents have always been like, 'Don't do that. Be a *medical* doctor. You can make so much more money.' Up until the summer before I started here, my grandfather was telling me, 'If you go to medical school, I'll pay for *everything.*'

"When I was in eighth grade, I was calling around trying to get veterinarians in town to let me come in and watch. In Chicago they probably thought I was crazy," Coretta says, and laughs, "or they were worried about malpractice, but I never got that opportunity. It wasn't until I was fifteen when I went to the Society for the Prevention of Cruelty to Animals after school that I had the opportunity to work with animals. I was just looking at the puppies when I noticed they had a volunteer program. I filled out the application even though it said you had to be at least eighteen to work as a volunteer. When they interviewed me they said, 'Well, you seem like you're very interested and you're really motivated, so we're going to let you work, even though you're not old enough.' I worked there until I was eighteen, and then I came to the university.

"I was really fortunate because if I hadn't done that, I would never have had that sort of vital experience until I came down here. Once I got here I sought it out, because a lot of the students in vet school are kids coming from farms who've had hands-on animal experience. Whereas me coming from the city, I had to seek it out, because I felt I'd be starting with a deficit if I didn't. I did work-study all through undergrad; they were always animal-related jobs. It was basically changing cages, but I got to hold the animals. At least I'm not afraid of rabbits and mice and things."

The studies at the school are extensive. There is a pre-vet curriculum, which Shannon says offers the basic requirements for entering the vet school. It gives you some of the basic concepts you will need to use in your training, like science and biology. The first two years of veterinary medical school concentrate on learning and understanding the bodies of the various creatures you will be caring for as a veterinarian. These studies include anatomy, biology, and pathology, which is the study of diseases and how they affect the anatomy. There is a great deal of lab work, which involves dissecting animals, much the way medical doctors have to dissect human cadavers. But unlike a *human* doctor, the veterinarian has to learn and understand the bodies of many different types of animal—dogs, horses, birds, cats, and reptiles, to name only a few. Each has its own special problems and differences. Starting in your third year, you get more hands-on experience; you begin treating animals as patients.

The vet school is a teaching health facility, offering people in the community who have animals veterinary care. Those outside the school have come to trust the students with their animals, knowing that both sides will benefit from the experience. On a walking tour of the stables, a once-beautiful horse is seen in a large open pen. Most of his body is covered with sores. Some skin has come off in large uneven patches, and it is obvious he is in some discomfort. But pained as he looks, he is anxious to come over to see what Coretta and Shannon are up to. He is just one of many of the students' patients.

After completing her four years of veterinary school and passing her state boards, Shannon plans to go into private practice. Coretta is interested in medical research, an area she knows is cause for much dissension. "In laboratory-animal medical research, they develop animal models to study human diseases, or animal models to study animal diseases. I'm more interested in human diseases, particularly those which affect African-Americans.

"I get a lot of grief from people because of my interest in animal research. One of my classmates is in PETA [People for the Ethical Treatment of Animals]. I hear from her all the time. A lot of stuff goes on in animal research that is less than desirable. But I think the only way you can effect change in anything is by getting involved with it. So if it bothers me that animals are being used senselessly, then what better way to *stop* it than to be involved in that area."

The conversation comes back to getting more people of color involved in the field of veterinary medicine and other so-called nontraditional careers.

"You read the paper and they want nurses and all kinds of health professionals, and I wonder, why can't somebody train our people and explain to them that these things aren't as difficult as our teachers have lead us to believe? That we *can* do this. These are gaps that we can fill," Coretta asserts. "It really disturbs me that we have this great pool of people who don't see the many different types of things they can do because people tell them, 'Oh, man, that's hard. Science is hard.' *Everything is hard!* But that's life! I want that wall to have my picture on it, and I want it to have a whole bunch of Black people after me, because it shouldn't be the way it is now."

Coretta and Shannon are both involved in a student-run Multi-Cultural Student Association, which features an outreach program. "We go into the community and say to these kids, look at where we are, at what we've achieved. This is something that *you* can do, too. Just study and you can be here. Other vet schools have their minority students doing the same thing, and that's one way we can effect change," says Coretta. "I think that whatever field you go into, you have to be involved with the community. When I was in high school I joined the NAACP, and that's always a place where you can get involved and do things. I'm in a sorority and I can always do things with them, and I'm involved with my church at home. I think it's very important that we give back to our communities."

Coretta continues: "People always say, 'Well, I made it on my own.' You gotta go back and talk to people and let them know that there are things they can do, not only driving a bus or working at the post office. Not that we don't need those people, but I think we've been doing that for too long.

"There is one thing I would like to emphasize to high school students, having *been* a high school student myself and knowing what peer pressure is like," says Coretta. "You don't have to be an A student. Just do the best you can. I wasn't an A student in high school, and I went through college and I graduated. I wasn't an A student in college, either. I'm in vet school and I'm not an A student *here*. But I'm going to be a doctor!"

"Exactly," says Shannon. "Don't give up. Sometimes it may not feel like it's going to get any better; in fact it often feels that way, but it *will* get better."

Tim Francis

When you think about it, it might seem that Timothy Francis doesn't know what he wants to be when he grows up. I don't want to confuse you. Tim *is* grown up. It's just that he's done so many things, and *keeps* doing so many different things, that it seems as if he's trying them all out. Like he's thinking, "What's the best job in the world to have?"

Tim lives in Los Angeles, California, and works as an art publisher. This sounds very interesting, but what exactly does an art publisher do?

There are two answers to that question, he says. "One is what an art publisher does, and the other is what *I* do as an art publisher."

Most art publishers find an artist whose work they would like to reproduce as high-quality prints. They arrange to print the work and put up the money to pay for the printing. Then the publishers help sell the work to galleries or to individual buyers. For these services, they work out an arrangement with the artist; the artist will pay them part of the prints' selling price.

"In my instance," Tim explains, "I'm much more of an independent publisher. I give the artist the flexibility of working with the printmaker of their choice, or if they have printmaking capabilities, working within their own studios to create multiples of whatever they're doing. I will negotiate a deal with the artist, whether they're working with their own printmaker or whether I'm getting an independent master printmaker to work with the artist.

"In the typical situation, I'm working with an artist who does not have their own printmaking capabilities. I will work out an arrangement so the artist and the printmaker work together throughout the printmaking process. Once that is done, I market the prints to dealers and galleries, who then take the end product to the general public."

The other part of the business for Tim is helping the artist and printmaker figure out how to create the art at a reasonable price.

"One of the advantages of working with me as opposed to any other person or publisher," says Tim, "is the fact that I'm also an artist. I don't want to overglamorize what I do, but it's not simple. When you get an image where there are brush strokes, in each brush stroke there may be three or four colors. You really need to have a sense of identifying colors, because it's a *combination* of colors that will give you *another* color.

"You need to be able to say, 'There may be sixty colors, but there are a combination of ways we can do it. We can print sixty separate colors or we can do a sixty-color original image in thirty colors by combining, which is cheaper.' So that's an important ingredient in doing this whole thing. It's not only understanding how the printmaking process works."

Tim is the first to admit that he was very fortunate to be exposed to many things when he was growing up. "I had a very unique childhood, because I grew up on a college campus. My father, Norman Francis, is president of Xavier University in New Orleans and has been president since 1968. Prior to that he was executive vice-president, so from the time I was born I was on campus.

"My experience growing up was sort of hip because I was exposed to people from a variety of walks of life. The student makeup of the university was predominantly Black, but professors and folks involved in the university were white, Hispanic, whatever. At any moment at home there could be a dozen different people sitting at my mother's kitchen table while she's cooking red beans and rice with my five brothers and sisters sitting around."

Growing up on a college campus gave Tim a chance to check out a lot of things he might not have been exposed to otherwise. "I spent a great deal of time hanging out in the art department. In fact, one of my first jobs was polishing and grinding bronze and steel for an artist. I was making a dollar fifty an hour in ninety-degree weather and a hundred percent humidity. I was maybe ten." He laughs.

With an uncle who was a Catholic bishop, Tim came from a very religious family. Instead of public school, Tim went to a high school seminary, which was for boys who were interested in becoming priests. The thought of him being a priest makes him chuckle when he talks about it.

There were so many other things competing for Tim's attention that the idea of being a priest was forgotten. "A great portion of my time was spent at the gymnasium playing basketball. Part of my childhood was being a jock. I played baseball and football. Actually, I was sort of a decent baseball player in high school; I made all-state. I was most valuable player of the state AA baseball. I pitched.

"I was scouted and the whole bit, but my senior year I pitched almost every day. My arm almost fell off. That was the end of my career. I knew that ultimately, given my small size, I could not be a professional baseball player. But I think once you have that competitive spirit, you never let go. At least, *I* couldn't afford to let go."

He saw that the work his father did as a lawyer was stimulating, but art still held a certain fascination. The artist that Tim worked for was also a professor at Xavier. "He used to always tell me that despite those two jobs, he just didn't seem to earn enough to survive. So always in the back of my head was the need to develop another career to be able to pursue the art thing. Not that my parents said, 'You have to be a lawyer.' They were like, 'Do whatever you want to do; just be serious about whatever you're going to pursue and then we're happy.'"

"After college I got a job offer to work with Moon Landrieu, the former mayor of

New Orleans and then the secretary of Housing and Urban Development under President Jimmy Carter. At that point, how much information did *I* have? It was more of a learning experience." When the Reagan administration took over, all the political appointees were asked to resign. "At that point I went to law school."

Tim studied law at Tulane University School of Law and earned his doctorate. He took a job working in a large law firm as an associate, which means he was doing the grunt work. "You would get assigned to research projects, looking up case law. Real narrow mundane issues of law that would gag anybody. These were the things that had to be done to get a case going. To get a paycheck."

The money was good, so although he wasn't excited by the job, he stayed on. While working at the law firm, Tim learned there was a position available working for John Breaux, who had just been elected a Louisiana senator. Tim left the law firm and worked as an advisor to the senator on issues like labor, civil rights, health, aging, banking, and the judiciary. This even included advising on Supreme Court nominations. "It gave me an opportunity to continue to use my legal research and writing skills.

"More than just wanting the job, it was a great chance to really make a difference. And I think I did, in terms of giving the senator a fair and accurate sense of where people stood on these issues. Ultimately, he's answerable to the people who elected him. It's important to be able to take a step back, be objective about the whole thing—lay it all out—and then have an opinion. Which," Tim says, laughing, "I *always* have!"

After about two and a half years with Senator Breaux, the phone rang in Tim's apartment at 6:30 one morning. It was Stevie Wonder calling from China. While working in Washington, Tim had met Stevie through a mutual friend and they kept in touch over the years. Because of Stevie's interest in issues of the world, the two had plenty in common to talk about.

Tim remembers the phone call that morning. "He said, 'Hey man, I've been thinking, I want you to come work for me.' Who could turn Stevie Wonder down? I said to myself, 'Well, he's in China. He must be serious.' From the Hill to Hollywood—who am I to say no?"

Within a very short time Tim resigned from his post in Washington and was in Los Angeles. His new position was chief operating officer, running Steveland Morris Entertainment. "My principal role was to provide a check and balance of all that was going on. To make sure things were being done properly." Tim handled everything from music publishing to Stevie's tours and a film division.

One of Tim's last duties before leaving Stevie Wonder's company was to put together a charitable foundation. The Wonder Foundation, Tim declares, "hopefully will realize some dreams that Stevie has about funding projects and helping people around the world."

Now Tim Francis's time is spent concentrating on his art publishing business, his personal artwork, and developing movie script ideas with a friend. It would be pretty easy for Tim to feel very self-important, but that's not the case. After all his experiences working for powerful, rich, and famous people, there is a lesson Tim has learned. "If you think that working for someone like Michael Jackson, Stevie Wonder, or someone else who has achieved success will bring you happiness, you're wrong.

"No matter if you're working at a law firm or working at McDonald's, the bottom line is that happiness has to come from within. And I don't mean that to the exclusion of acknowledging there is a God and that God ought to exist within you. You need to explore your spiritual existence as it relates to God. I think that's all a part of finding the star within you and being very happy about your life.

"I don't think success ought to necessarily be measured in terms of monetary gains. Success should be measured in terms of how you touch somebody else's heart and nourish them as a human being and make them feel better. When that happens, this world is a better place for everyone. If you've done things right, legitimately and forthrightly, you should never have to look over your shoulder, and things will come together for you no matter what you do.

"I think if you're pursuing a dream and you're creative, the sky's the limit. Your dreams may bring forth things that you've never considered."

Latoya Hunter

"It is hard to believe that this is the day I have anticipated and looked forward to for such a long time. The sun still rose in the East and set again in the West, the crisis in Iraq is still going strong, and Oprah Winfrey still preached at 4:00 about other people's business. This may sound funny, but somewhere in the back of my mind I thought the world would stop for my first day of JH."

So begins the first published work of author Latoya Hunter, a diary of her freshman year in junior high school. Latoya did not wait until she was old and gray with a handful of children close by calling her "gra'ma," to write about her life. At twelve years old she was given a five-thousand-dollar advance by a publisher to chronicle her experiences as a young Black girl growing up in the Bronx, New York, and attending Junior High School 80.

While she is shy and soft-spoken, Latoya is a thoughtful and opinion-

ated young woman who, while excited at the prospect of writing a book, was wondering just who would buy it. "When I was first asked to do the book I was thinking, how could my life be interesting to other people? But I found out that my opinions and all young people's opinions count, and that people really want to listen."

Latoya has long had a love of writing. A native of St. Ann, Jamaica, she came to America with her family when she was in the third grade, and as she began writing, her teachers noticed her skill. "They used to tell me I had talent, and that's what made me feel like I could do it," says Latoya. "That's when I thought of being a writer."

Latoya had been writing outstanding essays in school for some time when a reporter from the *New York Times* was completing a series of articles about life at Public School 94. "She spent a lot of time in our class. My sixth-grade teacher, Mr. Pelka, told her about my compositions, and I read some to her. I won an award for best writer at graduation, so she wrote all about that in the article.

"A publisher saw the article in the *Times* and called my teacher and asked if I'd be interested in writing a book. Mr. Pelka called me on the phone because it was during summer vacation. He said, 'There's a publisher interested in doing a book with you!' He was really excited. I couldn't believe it, but by the way my teacher sounded, I knew it was really happening."

So this average twelve-year-old girl headed off with her parents to a meeting with Crown Publishers editor Richard Marek. Marek was very enthusiastic about the possibility of working with Latoya, and they discussed the project, a diary of her experiences entering junior high. "When I met with them," explains Latoya in a soft and friendly voice, "they said they would have to see two weeks of the diary first, to see if they would like it. When I wrote it, they loved it," she says with a shy but large smile.

Her first diary entries were wonderful. For anyone who has ever gone to junior high school, they should bring back vivid memories of those first years of feeling grown-up. For those still on their way, it's a primer. "I was starting junior high school, so I just wrote how it felt to be in a new school, with new people. There was a day called Freshman Day when the seniors would beat up on the freshmen and I was going through that during those first two weeks."

"I actually made it!" she wrote. "Something must have snapped in the minds of the older kids. Maybe they remembered when they were freshmen themselves because there were only a few fights today. . . . They didn't really bother the girls. I think that was decent of them. I'm really relieved as you may guess."

But what is most impressive about Latoya's book is her insight into the situations around her and her attempts to define herself as an individual. Her editor asked her to be as straightforward and honest as possible, and it is likely that may not have happened if things had continued as they started. "It was really hard during the first two weeks, because my mother would read what I wrote afterward. Richard noticed that I was holding back in some ways, so he talked to me about it. I told him that I didn't feel comfortable with my mother reading the diary. He said maybe she should hold off on reading it until it actually came out so I could be more comfortable.

"When she stopped reading it, I was able to say everything." And that she did, often giving her audience a look at a young person's perceptions of their parents' actions. The good, the bad, and the annoying.

"I thought they would be upset," Latoya says of some of the entries published from her diary. "But they weren't. My mother, maybe she felt bad when she read some parts of the book, but she didn't really discuss it with me because I guess she didn't want me to feel like I should regret writing it. I do think she learned how to understand me better, how the things she does affects me, and how I think."

Latoya has also gained something from the experience, she says. "I learned that my mother could be supportive. And I was impressed with how she dealt with the book." Latoya's friends, on the other hand, were not always as gracious. "A friend who I had written wasn't nice to me, told me she was angry for a month after she read the book. For a whole *month* she was holding a grudge!" Latoya says in dismay. "She finally called me and said she didn't want to be angry any longer. We talked about why I wrote what I did, and why she did the things that I wrote about. She didn't even realize she was behaving that way when it happened."

Some of Latoya's classmates were jealous and envious, she says, but most of her friends couldn't be more proud of her. Latoya kept the whole thing very hush-hush, not letting on that anything unusual was happening in her life until she told one of her high school teachers she would be late for class one day. She had to make a publicity appearance on NBC's "Today" show. "I had no idea I would even be going on *one* show or doing any interviews," she says. I just thought I would write the book and that would be it, because I never saw authors doing things like that. I was really surprised.

"When I did the 'Today' show, it was *live* and I was really scared. But then I saw that I was able to deal with it because the host made me feel comfortable. After that—national TV and live at that—I knew I could do everything else." She smiles.

Latoya did most of her writing in the evenings when things were quiet and she had time to herself, making her entries almost every day. Much of her writings deal with her interest in boys and the arguments she would have with her mother, who runs a strict home and has little tolerance for Latoya's attraction to the opposite sex. We witness the addition of Devoy, Latoya's first nephew, to the family. There were some days when she had nothing to say, and others that were boring. But Latoya thought it was important to point out to "Janice," as she called her diary, that life wasn't that exciting for a twelve-year-old. One day, however, she shared a tragedy that too often befalls people living in the inner cities.

"Today gunshots echo in my head. They are the same gunshots that killed an innocent human being right across from my house last night. . . . It turned out I knew the person who got shot. He worked at the store on the corner. He was always so nice to me, he was always smiling. He didn't know much English, but we still managed a friendship. . . . Things like this happen every day in N.Y., but not in my neighborhood, not to people I know."

Latoya has since skipped a grade and is now in high school. She plans to write another book or two, but right now she wants to concentrate on school. And although she has had an auspicious start to her writing career, having sold the paperback rights to her book for a substantial sum, at the moment it isn't something she sees herself pursuing full-time. "As a career I think I want to be a psychologist because I really like to see why people think the way they do. I would also want to write because I think that writing will always be a part of my life. I'm interested in doing fiction about 'real' people and their problems. But I don't want to make it a career, because I think if you have too much of something, you can lose the special kind of love you have for it."

Christopher Ewing

In our society, it is rare to find a Black youth pursuing a career with horses, particularly in Detroit, Michigan. "Somewhere around my twelfth birthday I got this big fascination with horses," says Christopher Ewing, who always seems to be in a good mood. "I think it started when I went to a camp for the summer and they had horseback riding. I just had fun hanging out on the horses, running the horses around. So I came home with this thing, 'Man, I want to ride a horse!'"

Chris admits, "A kid who grows up in a single-parent home, living in the city of Detroit, it was like, 'Boy, sit down! You're not gonna have a horse. Get out of my face and go read that book! Quit dreamin'.' But it was one of those dreams that wouldn't die."

Even without *owning* a horse, he knew he was going to need some lessons, and that was going to cost big bucks. So Chris became an entrepreneur. "At the time, I was selling newspapers—the *Detroit Free Press*

and the *Detroit News*. They were competing newspapers at the time. I sold them in the morning before school and at night after school, and made the money that way to pay for the lessons."

The more lessons Chris had, the more involved he wanted to get. He knew he had to have a horse of his own. This was no easy feat. Even if he could somehow raise the money to *buy* a horse, the upkeep—stable fees, food, and veterinary expenses—would make owning the horse next to impossible to manage. Instead he kept selling papers and made enough money so that he could lease a horse from the stable where he took his lessons.

At age fourteen, though he still didn't have much money, he was able to buy a horse that he liked. "Saving money and showing my mother, 'Look, I've got seventy-five cents of the dollar,' she would chip in," Chris says, explaining his good fortune. "And her seeing, 'Well, he does like it, and it's keeping him off of the streets.' I also got a lot of credit from the people that were involved with the horse, like the trainers or the people that owned the barn. Sometimes they'd let a lesson or two go by till I had the dough. Sometimes the boarding fees would add up so I would work it off or pay it off slowly. I used to ride horses for the guy that owned the place, and he would credit me.

"It cost me a couple of thousand dollars to buy the horse, which by horse means is not much at all. Not anything of any caliber. Looking back now," says Chris, "I'm surprised I got away with what I did."

Chris started taking his horse around to the various shows where they would compete in events like jumping and basic skills events. His horse, named Ta Cin Ca Fawn (Chris didn't name the horse) was an Appaloosa. Appaloosas have large dark spots on their white coats and are the third or fourth most common breed of horse in the world. Chris had been showing quite well with Ta Cin Ca Fawn and had been getting noticed.

"I came home from the barn one evening, and when I walked in the door my mother said some lady had called up and she was crying. She said she used to own my horse, and to call her as soon as possible. As it turns out, the horse's name was still registered to her, and she had received this invitation to compete at the World Championship Appaloosa Horse Show, which they hold every year in Oklahoma City. They just sent it to her address.

"She was crying and saying, 'You must have been doing great things with this horse. I'm so proud of you.' I had never met this lady, but she was so proud that a horse that she once owned had gone on to do some of these things. It seems that she couldn't control the horse. She was advised to get rid of it and get something that was more to her level."

If Christopher and his horse were going to go to the championships, he was going to have to sell a mess of newspapers. Somehow, between his efforts and his mother's, they scraped enough money together to make the trip. "It took two days to get there. We drove," he says of the trip he made with his mother and grandmother. "We found somebody who would take the horse to Oklahoma for next to nothing—we managed to get it on with some other horses, which made the trip cheaper.

"It was incredible," Chris recalls. "The coliseum was much like Madison Square Garden—huge! We were there for a week, and just to see these horses from all over the world was deep. To have gone from point A to point B was really something!

"I competed in the open jumper division, which is where the jumps are very high. Sometimes four and five feet high, by four or five feet wide. There were forty-some-odd people in the division. I found the crowd favorites of the competition were myself and this man who was seventy-something years old and had just got into jumping.

"And out of all these horses and all these people," Christopher says, still sounding amazed so many years later, "I placed sixth in the world. I went there with no trainer because he had to stay back in Michigan and teach, so it was just me, my mom, my grandmother, and my little white horse."

Chris continued to show his horse back at home in Michigan. He got better with each entry, and after four years of riding he entered the Appaloosa National Championships, which is a competition you can just enter without an invitation. Ta Cin Ca Fawn and Chris entered in the youth division because Chris was still under eighteen. He ended up as the number three junior rider in the nation, and in the open division, where kids can compete against adults, he ranked second in the nation. "I beat all the adults except for one and tied with another adult.

"I had only really been riding for a year when I went to the World Championships," he says as he thinks of his achievements. "Now, as I go out and train horses for people like Stephanie Powers, and I see how long and laborious some of these things can be—I was a *fluke*. I was not supposed to be anywhere within three years of learning how to ride. Certainly not at the caliber that I was. I've taught some people for years that still can't jump a jump. They just don't have it."

Either being Black in a sport where few Black people are found can make you a better rider or the pressure of proving you are as good as your predominantly white counterparts can send you running from the stables. For Christopher, it has only boosted his skills. "I've never thought about it until now. I don't know that that was what made me 'good' when I first started, but I know it's what has made me become even better as I've gotten older," Chris tells me. "Because I've noticed that people oftentimes will judge the book by the cover. I've gone to horse shows to compete against the best of 'em, and people will think I'm the groom. They'll come up to me and say, 'Excuse me,' some even say, '*Boy*, is the boss around here?' And I say, 'Yeah, he is. And he's looking right in your face!'

"I don't think it's been anything that's consciously forced on my part, but certainly, subliminally, I've found that I have exerted myself because of my race. Because I've wanted to prove that I *can* do this. And I've recognized in my mind that if I wasn't good, then they were going to

say, 'See! I knew that brother couldn't do it. They can't ride. They belong out in the fields.' So I think because of all that, it's kept me on my toes. What has made me get better in my riding is what people have said, be it negative or positive.

"I've heard all kinds of stuff. And 99.9 percent of it was false. But just the fact that it was said was enough to make me try harder. Now as I've gotten older, I sit back and think, 'Wow, those people didn't say all those bad things about me because they were *true*. They said those things because they *weren't* true.' They said those things because I am good at what I do, I've done very well with my horses, and they were *jealous*." For the most part, Chris says his experiences have been good ones. He has been treated with extreme kindness and generosity far more often than not.

Chris has made a point of not dwelling on any negative experiences he's had. They become little lessons and are filed away for future reference. They inspire and strengthen him. You might chalk it up to the fact that he's a spiritual person, or you can attribute it to his positive outlook on life. Positivity always seems to win out. And why shouldn't it?

Christopher Ewing has achieved goals that many people twice his age and experience wouldn't dream of attaining. He has become a sought-after and respected horse trainer who works with everyone from famous celebrities to young kids.

When he is not working toward opening his own training facility—a long-held dream—he is usually furthering his acting and music career. Something of which he is

justifiably proud. "I've probably done eighty TV and radio commercials, plus a number of industrial films," Chris offers. "I've worked on three soap operas: 'All My Children,' 'One Life to Live,' and 'Search for Tomorrow.' I've worked on a sitcom, 'Kate and Allie,' and as I have done those things, I have had the opportunity to meet a lot of young people."

Encouraging young people is one of Chris's favorite projects. He has written a song entitled "Hang on to the Dream," which he recorded with the pop group Peace. His song, about not giving up on things you aspire to, reflects directly back on his life.

"I tell kids I didn't have thousands of dollars to go out and ride against those people. They don't need it. Don't let that stop you. There's ways around everything. To the brother or sister that can paint, get out there. Let people see that stuff, even if you don't have thirty dollars for a portfolio case. Go somewhere and let somebody see that stuff. Things happen. If you work on cars, if you do anything, get out there and do as much as you possibly can. Make as much noise as you can. That squeaky wheel will get some oil just to stop it squeakin' if nothing else.

"Living in a single-parent home did not equip me to go out and start buying and selling horses and become a big rider, but the desire and the 'I'm gonna show you' got me into that and over those hurdles.

"To me," Chris says, "money isn't everything—the money can be spent. How I feel about what I'm doing is the biggest thing."

Paul Brunson

At fourteen Paul Brunson had just about every reason to let his life go into the toilet, and if he had, there wouldn't have been many people who would have been surprised. Almost everyone in his family had experienced some kind of run-in with the law. They had seen jail, drugs, and worse. In 1991 Paul's mother, who was fighting her own battle with crack addiction, was murdered in a drug-related incident.

In spite of all this insanity, something clicked in Paul's mind and made him decide which way his life would go. He was going to do whatever was necessary to make sure he was going to turn his life around.

The day I met Paul, he was wearing his Golden State Warriors cap, and he and his best buddy, Johnny Cochrane, and a couple of his uncles were getting ready to go fishing. This was a far cry from hustling "rock" right around the corner from his own house barely a year before.

"When my mom died, I could have went either way. You know, there's that little psycho stage where you just go crazy. I came that close to doin' that. But then I sat and thought about it, how life goes on. These things happen. You may not like it, but they do. You just have to go strong with your life. Go strong, finish strong, you'll get anything you want."

Paul's a little guy, lots of his friends call him "Shorty," but he has a certain maturity that comes with having to be a grown-up before you get to realize you're a kid. "He had a hard life," says his uncle Quinn. "He had to raise his little sister by himself, but still, he's a strong young individual."

"My background's been pretty hard, but if you let these things get to you, it just destroys you and then you just turn into a *nobody*. So you just gotta have common sense," Paul says, adjusting his cap. "Don't fall back into that little trap, 'cause you won't make it in life."

His uncle played a big part of keeping Paul straight. Having been released after doing a quarter of his sentence on a drug conviction, he refused to let his nephew make the same mistakes he had. "When I was young I was hard, I was robbing, doin' this and that. All of a sudden those folks said, '*Whaamm!!* Mr. Brunson—twenty years.' I spent five years of my life in a penitentiary," says Quinn, now thirty-two. "Paul looks at that. He's not gonna go through all that. He's gonna help people like me lead a better life. He's gonna help the younger generation and school 'em. He's what I should have been. Hey! Paul is *my* role model." Even so, things didn't

always look as positive as they do now.

On one of Quinn's weekend prison furloughs, Paul bought his uncle a fishing rod. Quinn thanked him, happy to receive the gift, but in the back of his mind he wondered where Paul got the money to afford it. "Paul asked me if I wanted money to go out. He'd give me fifty dollars and I'd go out and have a good time. He'd have a big ol' bankroll, and I'd ask, 'Whose money is that?' He'd say, 'That's John's money. I'm holding it for him.' It didn't smell right.

"The next couple of weekends, we're watching the NBA," Quinn continues. "Paul's ordering pizzas and buying beer for my friends and me. I asked, 'Where is this money comin' from?' He'd say, 'It's not mine.' Now, I know if you're holding money for somebody, you aren't gonna be spending it! I just said to him straight out, 'Man, you're selling crack.'"

I ask Paul what was his response to that? "I just said, 'Don't tell grandma!'"

Quinn couldn't believe what was happening. He knew he hadn't set the best example for Paul, but after all the little speeches he had made, and being sentenced to twenty years in jail, he had hoped it would have made some sort of a dent. "I had tears in my eyes when I talked to him. I grabbed him with both hands on his neck and I started crying. I almost choked him to death. I got so emotional, I didn't realize what I was doing. I said, '*Hey man!* You ain't selling no dope. You got everything you want! Get into those books!' He hurt me and he knows better."

Seeing his uncle so torn up seemed to

get the wheels turning in Paul's head, but he will tell you, only he could make the final choice. "I was hanging with gang members and making money and everything. I wasn't ripping anybody off, I was just selling dope. Everybody knew me, all the smokers knew me. I would make like a thousand a day. I started dealing in the beginning of the seventh grade. I was about thirteen. I stopped in the beginning of the eighth grade. That's when I started getting my good grades.

"I figured I could do what I *wanted* to do. If I wanted to get good grades I could have good grades. To be something, you've got to go up to that level. I wanted to do that, and that's what mom wanted me to do. My grandmother, she wants me to do it. She knows I'm going to make it because I'm doing these things that her kids should have done."

Paul made the decision that he was going to be somebody, and he knew he had to make a few simple changes in his life. "*Study*. Read books. Do what I was supposed to do mainly," he says. "Know what my teachers expect, and just do it. It's not hard. If you put your mind to it, you could do anything you want to do! It's as simple as that," he says confidently.

Those changes in his habits and a positive attitude worked well for him. "I never could get on the honor role for some reason. All my report cards I was getting D's—sixth grade, seventh grade.

"In eighth grade I really started thinking, 'Man, I'm gonna have to do something, I'm gonna have to get good grades.' It's just self-discipline. Then I got a 3.5, then I graduated with a 3.8. Now in high school, first quarter I got a 3.5; second quarter a 3.6; third quarter, 3.8. For fourth quarter I'm striving for a 4.0." An A average.

Paul already has his plans for the future locked in his mind, because at this point, there is little he feels will hold him back. "Master's degree!" he says enthusiastically. "In business or communications. I could be a counselor, talking with kids. I could help them a lot," he says. But Paul also has an interest in real estate. "I want that master's. I want to build and make them bucks!" he says, rubbing his hands together and smiling.

"John and I, we study together, we just try to get everything down pat. When we get older we're going to be tight. We're gonna have our cars. We're gonna have good jobs, our own businesses, and nobody's going to be able to touch us!"

John and Paul, like most best friends, spend a lot of time together, and in the end it certainly helps them both do the right thing. "We have fun all the time," Paul says with a big smile. John's smile back is equally large. "We always go fishing. Come home, clean 'em, cook 'em. Every weekend is like this—fish, fish, fish. That's the only way to stay out of trouble. If you sit at home, you're going to run into problems.

"If you just do positive things, you can't get into no kind of trouble. We play tennis, football, basketball, and chess. The only hard obstacle is school. That's the hardest thing for us right now. After school we might play Genesis or Nintento, or we might play tennis."

"We don't worry what other people say if

we do tennis," adds John. "A lot of people give us a hard time because they think tennis is a 'white' sport." He laughs.

"We just prove 'em wrong!" says Paul. "We got some of our friends to start playing. Now they can't *wait* to play! They see us and it's like, 'Dag! John, Paul! Let me see your tennis racket! Let me hit it a few times!' Then when they get their hands on the racket, they don't want to give it back, they want to keep playing. Then they go buy a racket and we *all* have fun. Now we

teach *everybody*, and they love it."

Paul has made a significant change in his life, and he appreciates the value of the way he's chosen to go. "We have a lot of friends. Some going this way, some going that way, good, bad . . . If you're bad, sell dope, and make all this money, all these things sound good now, but in the future— if you have one—you're not going to have any Social Security or nothin'. Then"— Paul starts to laugh—"all those people are going to wanna come live off me!"

139

Mustapha Khan

Several years ago, Mustapha Khan was making follow-up calls after sending out some résumés at a friend's suggestion. He was dressed in a suit and holding onto a briefcase as he made the calls from a pay phone. Although he looked sharp, if you had turned all of his pockets inside out, all you would have found at the bottom was lint. He was broke. He wasn't even sure how he was going to eat that night.

Mustapha was making a big change in his life. Fresh from earning a combined degree in comparative religion, psychology, and anthropology, he was planning to become a filmmaker. He had deferred his entrance into Columbia University's graduate program for a year so that he could check out film school at an intensive eleven-week course at New York University. He was presently looking into making documentaries but needed a grant to fund them.

"It was depressing," Mustapha says, smiling and shaking his head.

Vincent Walter, Photographer
828 Main St.
Lafayette, IN. 47901

"First, you need to be a not-for-profit organization to get the grants. Otherwise you could borrow the not-for-profit status of some larger organization, meaning you'd have to join, which is gonna cost a couple thousand dollars." He shakes his head again. "The funding organizations were only giving individual grants to people who'd already made films, or people who were finishing their films by doing editing and other post-production work. Everyone said, 'Good luck. If you go at it full force, but with no work to show them, you'll maybe get five thousand dollars three or four years from now.'"

Mustapha couldn't wait; he needed to eat. A friend had mentioned a job that would pay him cash and get his feet wet. "My friend said, 'I'm working at this company for fifty bucks a day as a production assistant. I heard they need some help. You should take a résumé around and drop it off to a few places.' Fifty bucks sounded like a lot of money to me then," Mustapha says as he remembers the conversation.

"So I dropped off my résumé to the places he suggested, as well as some places I looked up in a book. A couple of them didn't even exist anymore; I just slipped it under a door anyway. At the time I didn't even know what a production company *did*. Just that they did it in film."

So there he stood at this phone booth, in a suit, calling each of those production companies until he finally got through to someone. "They asked me, 'What are you doing right now? Can you work today? Right now?' I said sure. I was flat broke. They said to just come to the office.

"The woman on the other end said,

'What's your rate?' I didn't know what she meant by 'What's your rate.' I asked her. She said, 'How much do you want to get paid today?'

"I said, 'Fifty bucks would be great.' There's a silence on the phone. She comes back on the line and says, 'Okay, we'll pay you seventy-five.'

"So I walk into this office in a suit and tie. Everybody just stared at me." Working as a production assistant is not a suit-and-tie kind of job. Being a PA is grunt work. You could be doing anything from getting doughnuts for the crew to loading trucks with film equipment to mopping floors.

"She told me to go to the bank, pick up this, drop off that. I went out to the bank, walked up to the teller, and gave her the note and a check, and the teller handed me back three thousand dollars in cash.

"I said, 'Damn!'

"Instead of going to Rio, I went back with the three thousand dollars. They said, 'Great. Thanks a lot for today. Can you come back tomorrow?' I said yeah. The woman said, 'We're probably going to need you all week, but do me a favor—jeans and a T-shirt tomorrow, forget the briefcase.'"

After working with the production company for three or four weeks, Mustapha started to understand what they did and the relationship between the production company and the client. The production company, he learned, is responsible for physically making the film shoot happen. They provide the services of a director, art department, film crew, the equipment, editing facilities, and whatever else is necessary to take a

client's idea and put it on film or video.

Even with this break, Mustapha still needed to find other work. "I'd done some research and consulting for *Essence* magazine, because a lot of my focus in college was looking at the situation of young Black men in the inner city and their patterns of self-destruction. While I was in the *Essence* offices one day, director Spike Lee walked into the office. His film *She's Gotta Have It* had just come out. Susan Taylor, *Essence's* managing editor, introduced us. I said I was interested in film, could I give him a call? He said, 'Sure.'"

A letter from Mustapha went unanswered for some time, and then, after talking with contacts who'd worked with Spike, Mustapha received a call from Lee's office. He was hired as a production assistant on the film *School Daze*.

"Working on *School Daze* is where I got a lot of good practical experience, because it was a low-budget film, so everyone did everything. They became very dependent on me after a while because I knew the camera, so if they needed a second assistant camera person, I knew how to do those things. If the sound man went away for a day, I'd handle the boom mike. I also worked as an assistant editor because I knew how to splice things together from that film class." All the while, Mustapha was making contacts. Every time he'd help somebody out, he'd get to know them and they'd exchange phone numbers. It was always, "Anytime you need help, man . . ."

"I made thirty dollars a day for two and a half months. I couldn't afford to stay in Atlanta for the shoot because they were paying me peanuts, so I came back to New York. Now I know the film industry, and now I know for a fact I'm on the bottom rung of the ladder."

"I waited tables for a little bit," Mustapha continues, "then things started flowing. I started working as a production assistant on commercials and even on some music videos. I was trying to figure, how do *I* start making films? How do I get somebody to give *me* two hundred thousand dollars to make something I want to make? While working on documentaries, I could see it's all about juice, about power."

Mustapha began to see all the money being poured into commercials. He had a vision of a style of commercials that he thought would be novel and interesting, one clients would be anxious to use. But Mustapha couldn't afford the three-year film program at NYU to sharpen his skills and create a reel with sample work. "I figured if I become known as a commercial director, then people might say what do *you* want to do? Maybe then I'll be in a position to push through the documentaries I really want to make. It's the reverse of the way a lot of people do it."

He borrowed money from old college friends and his father, ending up with about eight thousand dollars to make speculative, or "spec," spots. These were commercials written by Mustapha and done as if they were shot for a real client. One was for Big Brothers of America, and the other was a fashiony perfume spot.

"I shot those over a weekend. People who I worked with in the industry when I was a PA, I got to work with me as crew members because they wanted to move up the ladder. The assistant cameraman on a shoot wants to move up and become a director of photography. Maybe if he works for me free as a DP, that helps him. Production assistants get to be producers or coordinators, and so on down the line."

Everyone got something out of the trade, and everyone had something for their reel. And Mustapha finally had his. "It was really through the kindness of a lot of people whom I barely knew," he says. "I'd work for a week as a PA and then at night do a film-to-tape transfer-and-edit session and blow all the money I made that week in an hour. It was like four hundred dollars an hour to rent the edit room. It took me five months to complete the spots.

"As soon as I got them done, I took them around to people I'd met while working as a PA: producers, heads of production companies, and people I'd driven to the airport or something. The response from it was great! People would say, 'Let me show this to the head of the company.' Within a week I had all these offers to be signed as a director with the same companies that I was working for as a PA.

"Within a couple of weeks I had a signed contract and a guaranteed retainer with a major company to shoot commercials for them. Then people saw that my work was musically oriented and began to ask me about shooting music videos."

The head of the company Mustapha worked for did a lot of documentary work for Public Broadcasting Service. He asked Mustapha what it was he really wanted to do, and Mustapha told him. There was a project his boss was working on for PBS. He said, "If you want to do something about inner-city Black youth or whatever, I'm doing a show and there could be a film in that show. If you want to make a film that would reflect that experience, it's already slotted and arranged. Let's do it."

They did, and Mustapha's short film about the coming-of-age of a sixteen-year-old boy in the South Bronx was featured on "American Playhouse."

Aside from the work he has done for clients like McDonald's and Coca-Cola, shooting a commercial that featured actor/comedian Bill Cosby and jazz singer Betty Carter, most of Mustapha's work is centered around children. He writes and directs many of the short film pieces featured on "Sesame Street," often composing the music that accompanies them himself.

"What I'm working on now is a feature-length documentary on children throughout America, and this is being sponsored by the Children's Defense Fund, the children's advocacy group. CDF tells people, our kids are not taken care of. We neglect them, they're ill-educated, they have no rights, they're abused all the time, and we let this happen. A third of the children in this country live in poverty.

"With the artistry of a filmmaker and the research of a social scientist, I try to bring it all together in a piece that will work on an emotional level. Hopefully it will open people's eyes to certain things. Tell people how wonderful these children are. Charm them and say, this is a precious natural resource. Then show them how endangered that resource is at the same time."

143

Victoria Johnson

During most of her life, food was Victoria Johnson's enemy, and her battle with it almost killed her.

"I hope you're not gonna be standing around like that for long," Victoria says with a laugh into her wireless microphone as she strides across the front of a room filled with people in exercise gear. She is wearing black nylon bicycle shorts and a multicolored top that exposes her taut stomach.

She starts a steady, rhythmic side-to-side movement, with a little knee bend on each side to the beat. The class follows her warm-up eagerly. *"COME OONNNN!!"* she bellows into the mike as the beat pumps through huge speakers in the mirror-walled exercise studio. As they continue the warm-up, the custom-mixed tape picks up the tempo and Victoria starts throwing in some hand and arm moves to make it harder. "All right!! Squeeze those buns!!"

Just watching this can get your blood pumping. The music. The movement. The energy. *BAMMM!* The music changes and Victoria has everyone in the room doing what amounts to a funky dance move. *"Ho!"* she yells as the combinations get more complex. "How are we doing back there?" she shouts to the sea of bodies moving in unison behind her. "Okay," a few say between breaths.

"Not enough of you are answering." Her five-foot-three-inch frame moves toward the tape deck with determination, keeping the beat all the while. "I'm gonna have to 'pitch' it," she says, turning a knob on the deck that increases the speed of the tape. A collective groan erupts from the group at the River Place Athletic Club in Portland, Oregon. "Let's go!!" she urges her class, smiling while she barely breaks a sweat.

This goes on for another fifty minutes: moving, bending, lunging, laughing, and flexing with weights. When it's over, her class leaves sweaty and panting but energized. Victoria Johnson towels off, pops a different tape into the deck, greets another class, and does it all over again.

"I don't teach class to get thin; I teach class for emotional strength. Because when you're walking and there's oxygen and you feel good and there's energy inside you, all of a sudden you can knock down walls. But when you're depressed, your shoulders are slumped, your oxygen is cut off from your diaphragm, your head is low—you have nothing. You have no emotional hope, you have no physical hope. That's what I'm trying to bring to the surface of people. The emotional and physical, as well as the increased energy strength that comes from movement."

Only after years of fighting bulimia and anorexia, two eating disorders that affect vastly more young women than young men, has Victoria come to this realization. Bulimics will eat huge quantities of food and then force themselves to throw up to avoid the weight gain and to make room for more food, but most importantly to relieve themselves of the guilt of overeating. This is known as bingeing and purging. Anorexics avoid eating altogether, partly because they see themselves as too heavy. Even as they become unbelievably thin they will continue to refuse to eat, often to the point of starving themselves to death. Typically, one eating disorder leads to another. There are many psychological factors involved as well. Anorexia and bulimia are complex illnesses that doctors don't completely understand. The one thing they *are* certain of is that, untreated, these illnesses will almost always lead to death.

Searching for more work for their migrant farm family and better educational opportunities for the eleven children, the Johnsons moved from Louisiana to the Yakima Valley area of Washington State when Victoria was eight. She and her parents and ten sisters and brothers crammed into a one-bedroom house. Abruptly, she found herself in a new world. She didn't realize that the odd looks she was getting in class were because she was the only Black kid in an all-white school. It was because she was overweight. Wasn't it?

"I walked into a classroom, and the first thing I saw were all these skinny white legs. I didn't even see skinny *white* legs, I just saw *skinny legs!* 'How come *I* don't look like that?' I almost killed myself trying to look like those bodies."

Growing up in a community of Blacks, Victoria was used to seeing a particular body type: round, with full hips. Just as her new white classmates had nose and lip shapes that were different from hers, many of them had body shapes that were different because of their ethnic backgrounds. Hoping to lose weight, she went on an all-lettuce diet at the suggestion of a friend whose mom ate it all the time.

Still, other things in her life made her unhappy and food became a way to feel better. "I always felt inferior because of my financial situation, not because I was Black. I felt I didn't have the same advantages, and that was psychologically devastating.

"We all had set chores. If we didn't get them done we didn't do extracurricular activities. Along with going to school I had to get up at four o'clock to do extra chores so I could stay after school for dance class." Often Victoria would be packing boxes of freshly picked produce at nine o'clock at night in the rain to earn money for dance shoes. Getting the secondhand shoes that someone else's daughter grew out of hurt her. "That pain was what I was always trying to cover up with food. Food was my comfort. I could snuggle up at night with food and feel better. Of course I gained weight, so somebody taught me how to throw up. Get rid of it."

When Victoria's high school track coach became pregnant, she asked Victoria to fill in for her and teach the phys ed class. Victoria brought music to the workouts, combining her dance skills with exercise. "I got addicted. Helping other people—they would laugh, they would smile. To help someone else not have the pain that I had—my pain was gone.

"I lived in migrant camps where there was violence, killings, death, rape, and incest. Such a painful childhood. I would do anything to erase that pain. Music was one way, movement was another. And being in a crowd of people. Every time I stood in front of a crowd I was devastated, but I didn't have the pain. I had *fear!* Well, I would rather have fear than pain, so it was a trade-off for me. It was a really incredible time for me during those periods."

Even so, Victoria still didn't feel very good about herself. Being in the spotlight of a fitness class only made her more aware of her physical appearance—a negative image that her mind wildly exaggerated. She constantly went on "surefire" diets, even avoiding body lotion for fear that oil would get into her system. "If I didn't try it, it hadn't been invented," she says, laughing. "I even got one of those suits," she says, almost laughing herself breathless. "You hook it up to your vacuum cleaner to suck the fat off you!" She tried a spinach and egg diet. She tried cow placenta injections.

Victoria went from bingeing and purging to simply refusing to eat, and it was really taking a toll on her body. Her mother would call Victoria her "little sickling." She

was always in bed, weak from fasting or too light-headed and dizzy from throwing up to do anything. "Through the anorexia period I ended up losing bone. I was going to have to have jaw surgery. I had knee injuries because my ligaments were wearing down from of lack of nutrients. My body was a wreck."

People with eating disorders are very sneaky. They hide what they are doing because they know it's wrong. When Victoria was growing up, anorexia and bulimia were just being discovered. With only a free clinic available and not having much money for better medical attention, it was hard to get an accurate diagnosis.

Victoria's triumph over her problems allows her to laugh at how crazy she was. She remembers being thrilled she had lost so much weight during her hospital stay. "It was the greatest diet I ever went on—this is how *sick* I was!" Her dark eyes squint with the laughter. "My pants were baggy. *Yesss!*" Victoria pumps her fist with mock approval. "I absolutely loved it."

She ate an entire batch of cookies a girl-friend brought her in the hospital. "I'm talking like, forty, fifty cookies. I *crawled* out of the bed because I had stitches and bandages, and I went over to the sink and I threw up. *In the hospital.*" All this just so no one would ever know.

"When I was in college I started to go to the clinic again and actually talked to a counselor about my problem. I don't feel I got qualified help. 'Do you need birth control?' '*No!* I need *food* control! You're not listening,'" she says, chuckling at the absurdity. All the while she was teaching

others aerobics but was unable to get a handle on her own needs. She got sicker and sicker.

"I couldn't teach my classes and I couldn't make money. I went to a new doctor that a friend referred me to, and he's the one that said, 'Listen, I've looked at your teeth. You throw up.'" After so many years of forcing herself to vomit, the acid coming up from her stomach and the lack of nutrients going into her body were making her teeth rot. Victoria denied it.

"He put his hand on my shoulder and said, 'Victoria, you're lying.' No one had once said to my face, 'You're not telling the truth.' I was sinking and it's almost like I wanted him to find out.

"That day, going home, I drove a completely different route." When she got home, "I started writing, writing it all out and crying. And that was the healing.

"I have taken every positive motivation course in America—how to do this, how to do that. I had all the tools. I wasn't ready. But this guy scared me so bad; when I listened to my own heart, it went '*da-da-da-da-da—da-da-da-da-da,*'" she says, imitating her fast and very irregular heartbeat. "I was ready to admit myself into a ward. The night before I had called the suicide hot line."

With Victoria's new attitude and rebirth in the church, she knew she could beat her problems. She set goals for herself, and among them was to create fitness videos and get into competitive bodybuilding. "Going onstage in a little swimsuit, you couldn't hide anything. I'd done the mind change. That was body change."

Victoria hired a trainer for a year, even

though she didn't have the money to pay him. "I just taught extra classes, did whatever I could to get enough money." She knew she needed the discipline if she was going to change her life. If she was going to live. "This guy was with me six days a week. That was part of my counseling right there."

Her trainer, Davis McGinty, a former Mr. Oregon, also taught her how to eat properly. Eating small amounts of healthful foods all day long, every two hours, leaves Victoria satisfied and properly nourished. "So far today I've had a muffin, an orange, a nectarine, three egg whites for protein, and cereal. Later I'll have some chicken and rice, a salad, and later a bagel," she says as she sips on some fruit juice. "He taught me not to be afraid to eat.

"You know what else he taught me? Dieting is positive because it makes you feel good and it gives you control over your physical body. I could eat all the time, I had energy all the time, and I was losing weight by doing it. *His* method of dieting *gave* me power versus *lack* of power."

Besides the butt-kicking aerobics classes she teaches, Victoria Johnson delivers a message promoting exercise and healthy eating—particularly to the Black community, whose cultural traditions don't lean that way. "I'm teaching this class, there's all these little heavy Black women working out, and they're like, 'Oooh, girlfriend! I gotta stop. I'm startin' to sweat.' *You're supposed to sweat!!* What do you mean you have to stop?

"Look at our food," she adds. "High fat, high starch, white flour, no fiber. No nutrition. My mother fried everything. I swear, she fried Kool-Aid. 'Get some gravy on that!' That's why I ended up so huge. I wasn't eating for survival.

"Let's not change the culture, but maybe let's change what we're eating and what we're *putting in* what we're eating. How do we take recipes and change them? Well, instead of adding whole milk, which is four tablespoons of butter in every cup, what about using skim milk? McDonald's has chicken sandwiches now, and salads. You can get a hamburger without the cheese. They have fat-free frozen yogurt instead of ice cream. It's there for you, it's the choices. Now it's creating enough self-esteem to want to make the choices to feel better."

Victoria is working to get more Black aerobics teachers into the community. Meanwhile, she has created a line of videos with a funky twist that fit the budget of the average American. *The Jane Fonda Workout* looks weak next to Victoria's *TechniFunk 2000* video. "You'll go put on the new Hammer record and dance to that. Why can't you do it for thirty minutes and make it an exercise? Organized exercise was never a part of our culture. We've come from slavery to being overworked on the job."

These things will change. With Victoria's books, fitness videos, her traveling across the country to teach people to "squeeze those buns!" and being a consultant and featured spokesperson for L.A. Gear sportswear, her message of health, fitness, and self-esteem will motivate anyone who gets caught in her wake.

John Lyght

It's safe to assume that a visitor would think nothing much goes on in the small, picturesque community of Grand Marais, Minnesota, just a stone's throw from Ontario, Canada. But Cook County Sheriff John Lyght does see some action, although not with the frequency of places like Detroit or New York. Well, that's just fine for Sheriff Lyght. The wall behind his desk is covered with awards, plaques, and commendations for his service, much of it for aiding the DEA (Drug Enforcement Agency) and the FBI.

John, an African-American, is the sheriff of a predominantly white community. More accurately, he is the *only* Black resident of Grand Marais. And while he is quite comfortable living that way, it doesn't mean he has forgotten or tries to deny his ethnic heritage.

"My dad was born in Alabama, but he didn't like the way the people treated you, didn't like the life-style of Alabama. So, he went to

Pennsylvania, worked there in the coal mines for a while until he saw he wasn't gonna make any progress working in the coal mines, either. See, working in the coal mines back in those days was just like you giving your money back to the company store. You work for a certain amount, and then everything had to go back to them because you got your groceries, your clothing—everything—right there from the mining company.

"Then he had read in different papers about the Homestead Act, so he thought he'd venture out and try it." The Homestead Act would give 160 acres of unoccupied public land to each homesteader, for which they would have to pay a small fee after five years of residence. John's dad headed for the homesteads in Minnesota and traveled to the north shore area just south of the Canadian border. When he arrived in Lutsen in 1913, there were no other Black people in the area.

"The first winter he just took care of the family and got things lined up, cleared land, and got us settled in. He started working on the road gang, working and building the roads," John recalls. The main artery, Highway 61, was nonexistent back then, "nothing but a deer trail on the side of the lake. When he come up from Duluth to Lutsen, he came up on the old *America* boat—that was the only transportation they had back then."

John grew up in Lutsen. He was the fourteenth of fifteen kids—ten boys and five girls. With so many brothers and sisters, there were plenty of people to watch your back if you got into a hassle. And there were

a few instances where they had a hard time because they were the only Black family in town. "You know it's a funny thing," he says, "kids will fight each other, and they'll call each other names and all that kind of stuff, but after they get poked in the nose once in a while, and they get to 'wrassling' and tussling with each other, kids will mingle good. That's one thing I can always say about kids—kids will eventually get along. It's the parents that sometimes give you the problems. Most of the parents started to get along after their kids got to be friends. But let me tell you, though, it wasn't easy the first go-round."

By the time John was born in 1927, the Great Depression was on its way. His dad was running his own private summer resort, and John eventually worked there, helping with the logging, clearing off the land. There weren't a lot of jobs around; some of John's brothers got into Work Projects jobs that the government set up. Most of those jobs were building roads and clearing land.

When he was about twenty-three, John was working in one of the various ski resorts in the area as the main gatekeeper. He would collect fees from the tourists and handle some security duties. At the end of the day he would turn in the large sums of money taken in at the gate. Weekends meant work as a bouncer at the resort dances. "I guess the owners of the ski resort thought that I should be deputized, because there was a lot of liability involved in the job," John says with a laugh. "So they talked to the sheriff and had me deputized for bouncing at the dances."

Dan Ross, a local conservation officer,

started talking to John about the tourist boom in the community. With the newfound popularity of the area, more and more of the local youth were getting involved with vandalism, alcohol, and other things that meant a need for more law enforcement. Dan suggested that John, and another young man who was also a part-time deputy, be fully deputized so they would work for the Cook County Sheriff's Department. It seemed like an interesting idea to John, so Dan spoke to the county board and the deal was done. The board outfitted their cars with some basic police gear: lights, sirens, and radios. John and his partner worked the night shifts.

"I worked as a part-time deputy until 1972. When the old sheriff retired," John says, getting comfortable in his chair, "then lots of people decided that I should put my hat in the ring and run for sheriff. So that's what I did." Five people put in their applications to fill the spot left by the sheriff, who resigned before the end of his elected term. It was up to the county board to choose a temporary successor until the next election. Three of the competitors were locals, while the other two were from outside areas. They all had impressive credentials. John lets a smile slip. "I was the lucky winner.

"In 1974 I had to go up for election and I won with ninety-five percent of the votes. I had three people running against me at that time. And every four years after that I've always won by a high margin." John has never had less than 75 percent of the vote.

"One of the things that helped me in that election and in being appointed was that I was always a go-getter and a good worker, and I always got along with people." One thing that gave him a big advantage was trust. John was driving the school bus in his late twenties. He got to know the kids and their parents and was recognized by his neighbors as someone they could trust with their children's lives. They knew that when their kids got on the bus with John, he would see them safely back home that night. "And—not to be bragging or anything else—but I always did a real good job of taking care of the kids. You give respect, you get respect.

"I've always been an early riser, so I get to work 'bout quarter after seven or seven-thirty in the mornings and I stay to five, six o'clock sometimes. When I took this job I said that I would do my best, and that I was on call at any time. So I get bugged at home, I get bugged away from home. I'm constantly working twenty-four hours. I'd go out and be out on the road all day long. But in the last ten years it's changed." The people job has become a paper job.

"Paperwork is killing all these police departments nowadays," he says with a sigh. "One of the reasons I liked this job was because I could be out on the street meeting people. But with the paperwork, you don't get a chance to get out as much. If I get called out, that's about the only chance to go out. Otherwise I'm just processing papers and running back and forth to the courthouse all the time."

The Cook County Law Enforcement building is pretty small. From the outside it resembles a storefront. On the inside is a small waiting area with bulletin boards thumbtacked with notices and items from various police and law-enforcement agencies. There is an alarming number of photos of missing children. On the other side of the glass is the main command center. Two officers handle the phones and radio calls. If you think being in a small town means nothing is going on, you would be surprised by the activity in the communications area.

When Sheriff Lyght is out on the street, everyone is anxious to greet him. As he drives by in his patrol car, people wave from their bicycles, trucks, or front lawns. Pulling up to an overlook, he spots a bunch of local residents enjoying the view. When the half-dozen or so senior citizens see the cruiser, they throw up their hands. A few "assume the position" on the hood of their car. "We didn't do it, John!" they say, trying not to laugh. John, with his own laugh, waves them off, somewhat embarrassed but obviously enjoying the attention.

With six officers working under him, John and his men and women cover 1,364 square miles and protect a population of about 3,820. It's 85 miles from one end of the county to the other. Grand Marais has only one traffic light, and it's right in the middle of town. Most of Grand Marais consists of small roads and trails leading to homes tucked away in the wooded areas.

A great deal of John's and his officers' police work involves intercepting drug traffic coming across the Canadian border into the States. Smugglers assume it will be easy to slip into the country through such a small community. The numerous commendations on John's office wall would tell them otherwise.

Burglaries, sexual assaults, speeding cars, and domestic disturbances are the most common crimes in Grand Marais. There has been an increase in suicide and alcohol-related problems, which troubles the sheriff. "We're on the international highway, and we have a lot of drug and alcohol problems. They are also due, in part, to the fact that this is an old pioneer county. Many residents, they work hard and they play hard. The parents, grandparents, great-grandparents, they all drink heavily." He says very seriously, "Alcohol is a dominant thing here in this county."

Grand Marais is a beautiful place, situated on the shore of Lake Superior. The views are spectacular and the air is clean. Many people head to its wooded and peaceful shores to change their environment. "I notice the people coming here trying to get away from the life-style in the cities. They have got a problem of their own which they're trying to outrun. I tell 'em all, don't think that you can come here and a change of scenery can change your problems. No, you gotta get your act together, get your problem solved *before* you come up here."

This is John's last term as sheriff. "I've been in the public's eye ever since I was about ten or twelve years old; that's enough. My dad ran that resort for years, so I've seen enough of the public." It's easy to forget this tall rugged man with the warm smile is in his sixties. "It's been fun and it's been interesting. Like I tell people, I wouldn't take a million for the experience I've had, but I wouldn't give a dime to go back to do it over again, either!" he says with a laugh. "It's been really nice."

Jimmy Jam and Terry Lewis

There is absolutely no reason for James Harris III (best known as Jimmy Jam) and his partner, Terry Lewis, to move from their hometown of Minneapolis, Minnesota. People who try to tell them they should be in New York or Los Angeles simply don't know what they are talking about. Having been honored with a star on Hollywood's Walk of Fame in March of 1993, they regard that as the most permanent presence they care to have in Los Angeles.

Terry and Jimmy grew up in this midwestern community, and that's where their families and many of their most important friends are—friends they grew up with and work with today.

You could easily drive by the offices and studios of Flyte Tyme Productions—which are located in a small, nondescript one-story building in Edina, Minnesota—and never know you had passed the creative home of one of the music world's most respected and

talented writing and production teams.

There is something very special about the environment at Flyte Tyme, the home of Jimmy and Terry's own record label, Perspective Records. Most people think of the entertainment industry as glamorous and pretentious—populated by people with lots of money and attitudes to match. When visitors walk into Flyte Tyme, they are warmly greeted. The building is cozy. It features winding, carpeted walkways lined with artwork and photos. And TVs. There are lots of TVs. Jimmy admits he's hooked, and being a big sports fan, he's got to be able to catch the important games. The actual recording studios and control rooms are unusually large and comfortable. Intimate sitting areas dot the facility—places to take a break during typically long recording sessions.

"We try to keep it very comfortable because we have to spend a lot of time here," explains the affable Jam. "Comfortable, but there's not a bed here, because we never want to get to the point where we're actually spending the night here. We want to keep home and business separate. There's no studio in our houses. And there's no bed at the studio."

Artists working in studios run by other musicians or producers usually just get the facility—a nice place to work, and maybe people to do it with. Flyte Tyme runs on the Motown concept. You come to Flyte Tyme for the whole package: writing, production, musicians, whatever you need to create the recording you want. The Flyte Tyme crew can supply everything but the artists' God-given abilities.

Although he's easy to talk to in a casual setting, Terry isn't much for interviews. Those duties are usually left to the gregarious Jimmy, though you can tell *both* have a sort of shy streak in them. Maybe that is part of the reason for the trademark dark sunglasses that accompany their forties-style hats.

The two met in a high school Upward Bound peer-teaching program. The school cafeteria, closed during the summer program, was always dark, but it didn't prevent Jimmy from finding the piano. "I never knew where the light switch was, but I knew where the *piano* was," Jimmy says with a smile. "And I would feel my way in the dark, and I'd go in and play. People would hear me play and say, 'Wow,' but I never felt I could play well. I just enjoyed the piano."

Jimmy figures his talent came from his dad, a jazz and blues musician and keyboarder. At the time Jimmy really thought of himself as a drummer. "When I was really young I used to hit on things around the house. I think when I was like four or five I got a little drum set. I grew up around pianos and organs and stuff because my dad played, so I would always mess around with them."

Jimmy sat in with his dad's group on a regular basis from the time he was thirteen. Terry was putting a band together when he met Jimmy. Terry tried to recruit a reluctant Jimmy to join his band and play keyboards. Jimmy insisted he was not good enough.

Eventually Terry talked Jam into borrowing his dad's keyboard and doing a year-end party for the Upward Bound group. Jimmy remembers, "We had about two days of practice. We didn't have a singer, but we played all the songs instrumentally. It was cool, it was a lot of fun.

"And that's what really got me into playing keyboard," he continues. "But the band wasn't making any money, and my dad was making the steady money, so I said, 'I'm going to keep gigging with my dad.'" But Jimmy and Terry kept in touch.

Two years later, at sixteen, Jimmy joined another band as the keyboarder. A school counselor, Michael Dixon, happened to have a piano in his office, a former music room in the school. Jimmy experimented with songwriting for the first time, as he and Michael, who sang, wrote songs together for the group. Their style was heavily influenced by their idols, Gamble and Huff, Thom Bell, and the Stylistics, all famous for the "Philadelphia sound."

"When I was eighteen, nineteen years old, I got fed up with the band," Jimmy tells me. "I was the youngest cat, and I was writing all the songs. There was a little friction and resentment from the other guys. They weren't serious about the band, and I was. I was like, "Hey, I want to do this for a career.'"

Jimmy left the group and worked as a DJ at skating rinks and different clubs around town. Terry's band, Flyte Tyme, was playing downstairs at one of those clubs while Jimmy happened to be spinning records upstairs. "One time Terry came upstairs and he said, 'Man, we got this new keyboard player, you've got to check him out. He's bad!'"

Jimmy liked the sound. Terry told him it would sound even better with Jam on a second keyboard. "Terry was always poking at me. 'Come on, Jam, join the group, you're not a DJ.'" When Jimmy broke up with a girlfriend soon after that, he was devastated. "I was walking home from her house and I walked by where Terry and the band were practicing. Terry was on me: 'You gotta join the group. Join the group.' And I said, 'Okay, but I can't right now. My head is really messed up from the break up.' And Terry said, 'Well, this will be really good for you.'

"About every two days Terry would call me and say, 'You've got to join the group,'" recalls Jimmy. For every excuse Jimmy had for not joining the band, Terry had an equally good answer. "I would say, 'Look, Terry, I sold all my keyboards 'cause I'm not doing the music thing.' Terry would tell me, 'That's cool, man. We'll buy you the keyboards. Whatever you need.'

"I took the girl that I broke up with to a concert that Flyte Tyme opened. So we're sitting in the audience watching them, and I'm going, 'Damn! These brothers are bad! They really cook.'

"So, it was like fate. I took her to the concert and she broke up with me. The next concert they did, Flyte Tyme opened for Cameo. By that time I had joined the group, and Terry had bought me the keyboard." That's when Morris Day from a rival crosstown band got together with them, and they formed The Time.

The Time did well with their first album and had been working with Prince, who was a strong influence on Terry and Jimmy. Terry was getting restless. Although he was very happy working with the band, he wanted to go to Los Angeles to push his songwriting, and asked the band to join

him. The only person crazy enough to go with Terry, who had no place to stay and no idea how to get demos to people, was Jimmy. They had tried writing songs together before, but their musical styles clashed. Jimmy was more the smooth style, while Terry had a heavy P-Funk, George Clinton, Bootsy Collins edge. They couldn't be sure they could make it work this time, but Jimmy trusted Terry's vision.

A guardian angel followed them to L.A. They hooked up with some friends of Terry's living in Los Angeles and shared a tiny spare bedroom in the friends' house. "Terry sold his car or something, for like seven hundred bucks," recalls Jimmy. "We bought a four-track recording system out of the classified ads. We had a little Casio keyboard, about one hundred bucks, that I had bought, and Terry had his bass. We had a microphone, which we hooked up in the bathroom so we could get some echo. And we recorded our demos—we had about four or five tapes."

The team eventually met the right people and several of the songs on the demo were recorded by different artists. Most of them were "flops," in Jimmy's words, but two songs, "When You're Far Away," recorded by Gladys Knight and the Pips, and "High Hopes," by The SOS Band, caught some ears.

Clarence Avant, president of Tabu Records, The SOS Band's label, called Jimmy and Terry into his office and asked them what they would have done differently if they had produced the SOS song. "We played him a demo of the song, which was a lot looser than what actually ended

up on the record. He said, 'I like that. I want you to do two songs on the next SOS record.' We did 'Just Be Good to Me,' and 'Tell Me If You Still Care,'" Jam recalls.

"Meanwhile, we were getting a lot of criticism back in Minneapolis, because it was time to start rehearsing for the next Time record. We would rehearse and do the tour and then fly back out to L.A. on our own money to do the productions.

"It wasn't about a money thing, it was about a creative thing. We were in a group where the creative force was Prince and Morris, which was fine, because that's a great creative force. But if you're a creative person, you're still going to create and you need an outlet.

"We were losing money because we were taking our own money and flying back and forth, and we were getting fined for leaving on top of it. They would call a rehearsal while we were gone and they would say, 'Well, you weren't here, so you're fined.'

"During the middle of the second tour," Jimmy remembers, "was the famous snowstorm in Atlanta. We had gone down to Atlanta to record The SOS Band, got snowed in, and missed the gig, and subsequently got fired. The night we were fired from The Time we mixed 'Just Be Good to Me' and it took off. And we were into our production careers full-time."

Clarence Avant became a friend and mentor to Jam and Lewis and is still important to them today. When they met Clarence, someone was trying to work out the deal for them, and Jimmy remembers what happened: "Clarence calls us up and says, 'Come to the office; don't bring your manager.' We go to the office and Clarence says, 'I got a problem with your manager.' And I say, 'What's that?' He says, 'The amount of money she wants.' I'm thinking, Oh, she asked for too much money! And he says, 'She didn't ask for enough money. You guys are worth more than what she's asking, so that's a problem. Here's what I think you're worth, and here's what I'm going to pay you.' We walked out of there going, 'WOW!'"

Whenever Terry and Jimmy asked Clarence if he wanted to hear something they were in the process of writing, unlike other record execs they had dealt with, he told them he didn't want to hear it until they were finished. It's a philosophy they have stuck to today. Terry explains, "Because we think what we do is a form of art. You know, it's like seeing a painting in the works. An artist wants to show you when it's all done. And that's the way we feel. That's one of the advantages of being up here in Minnesota as opposed to being in L.A. Nobody can just drop by the studio and say, 'Hey, how you doing?' and be in our business. We keep everybody in the dark, but they all trust us now."

They have been quick to share their knowledge and good fortune with others who have asked. When producers L.A. and Babyface asked to be introduced to Clarence, Terry and Jimmy obliged. Terry says, "The thing Clarence said to us was that Black people have this thing where they want to see everybody else fail. They want to be successful but don't want anybody else to do good. And that shouldn't happen. That thought always stuck with us. So when L.A. and Face asked us about Clarence, people had already started say-ing, 'Well, they're going to be the next Jam and Lewis, and they're going to be your competition.' I never thought of it like that. I always thought, here's another cre-ative Black entity and we don't want to see them fail.

"There's that syndrome where, and I don't mean to generalize, Blacks are very quick to criticize and very slow to praise. So if something goes wrong or somebody is not doing well, people are quick to jump on them. I don't like that. And if some-body's doing good, we don't want to give them their propers.

"That's wrong and, unfortunately, I have to say that I sometimes find myself doing it. So I think it's something that just became a part of our people, and I don't know why. But the whole key to anything like that is to recognize that it is a problem and try to do something to correct it. I think Terry is aware of it, and we try to keep it out of our formula for success."

Jimmy and Terry began their own record label, Perspective Records, in 1991. This was another step, in part, to change an inequity they see in our society. Jam continues, "Up until our label deal, the record company would give advances, but they wouldn't really go into business with you. Then you wouldn't really own anything at the end of the deal. That's the crux of the problem. Black ownership. We really don't own any-thing, so we really don't have anything to sell. We're selling records, but we're making money for Sony or whoever it may be."

The arrangement Jam and Lewis have with A&M Records to work in partnership has set a precedent for other producers to do the same thing. For the first time in the history of the music business, Black writer/producers are becoming owners of the material they create. Jimmy and Terry, for example, have been the force behind such artists as Karyn White, Johnny Gill, Janet Jackson, Herb Alpert, The Human League, and Sounds of Blackness.

Many producers "inflict" their style on the artists they work with. Terry and Jimmy have gained the respect of other producers because they don't work that way. "I like to think that our process is like a tailor who makes a suit from scratch," says Jimmy. *You pick the material that you like, you measure and get the size, and you actually make the suit.* That suit is made especially for that per-son. The fit, the color, the texture—the whole thing. We have a way that we play as musicians, but when an artist comes in, we don't have a style for them. We try to create a style from scratch that the artist is a part of.

"I remember when we were working on Janet Jackson's 'Control' album, and John Mclain, who developed the R and B depart-ment at A&M Records, asked me, 'What do you want to be doing in five years?' I said, 'I want your job.' He asked, 'What do you mean?' I told him, 'I want to be sitting behind a desk listening to demo tapes or whatever, not full-time, but that's what I want to do.' Well now, five years later, that's exactly what I'm doing. I'm listening to demo tapes, sign-ing groups, signing writers and producers. We're turning the reins over to other people to give them some creativity. We're giving them the freedom to do what they want to do and telling them, like Clarence told us, 'I don't want to hear it till it's done.'"

As an art dealer, Alitash Kebede has kept her focus on the creations of
African-American artists. She laughs a bit at this because she herself is African. "You'd think I would be featuring the work of other Africans," she says in her lilting Ethiopian accent.

The gallery, which displays the work of the artists she represents, doubles as her home. It is tucked away from the busy streets of Los Angeles; the entrance is shaded by leaves set in perpetual motion by the cooling breeze.

Alitash came to the United States when she was sixteen years old. Her father had told her of his travels abroad when he was sixteen—that the experience had made him responsible. She thought traveling would be a good idea for her as well. When her father died, she found it difficult to live with his absence, so she contacted a boarding school listed in an American magazine and was accepted.

Her American experience gave her access to many of the things she

had only read about or had a slight taste of in Ethiopia. One of the things she had liked even back at home was art. "The first art exhibition I went to was when I was twelve years old. I went to an opening at a gallery which was part of the Haile Selassie University. I was staying with my cousin and her husband at the time. My cousin and another Ethiopian artist, Skünder Boghossian, had an exhibition at this gallery. I don't know if she really wanted to take me to this exhibition, or had to because I happened to be at the house and there was no one to leave me with. Either way, it was lucky for me" she says, and smiles. "I remember walking into the gallery and saying, 'Wow . . . this is wonderful!' For me it was a turning point in my life and has shaped who I am today.

"I couldn't believe the artwork. Talk about tapping into your own heritage. This guy, Skünder, he had taken a regular Ethiopian chair and made *art* out of it. He was a European-trained artist, but he was still true to his roots, because everything that he did, you could tell *who* this guy was—you know what I mean?

"And not only was I admiring what was on the wall," she adds, "but the people that were there were equally fascinating because Addis Ababa is a truly international city. They have the United Nations Organization, the ECA (Economic Commission for Africa), and there is the Organization of African Unity. People from all over the world live there. There were many international organizations, so there were people from the embassies. There were people from all walks of life in that place. And

between the artwork and the people, I was saying, 'Wow! This is what I'd like to be doing!' But at that age I didn't know that such a thing as an art dealer existed, but I wanted at least to be like one of the people in the crowd. Because whatever they were doing, they looked like they were doing fine to me!" Alitash laughs.

When asked, Alitash told her uncle she wanted to study photography. Her uncle thought it was crazy, telling her there was no such thing as a photography major. Even though he was incorrect, he convinced Alitash to find another major, and although she wanted to major in art, she ended up taking only a few courses as a minor. Her major was history, "Twentieth Century China, of all things," she says.

"My doctor, knowing that I was interested in art, used to always say to me, 'I have to introduce you to Mitzie Landau.' He used to be one of her clients. She and her husband started a gallery, like, in the early sixties or late fifties. They were one of the first galleries on LaCienega Boulevard—that's where *all* of the galleries were in Los Angeles. They represented some of the best artists in the country. Every time she had an opening or something, there was always some reason I couldn't make it. Then one day I had something important to do, but I said, 'No! I'm gonna go meet this Mitzie Landau.' So I went to her opening.

"Whenever I would go to galleries, they used to snub me because they knew I wasn't going to buy anything." She laughs as she almost shyly brushes her skirt. "They just knew by looking at me. When I went to meet Mitzie, I remember she was talking to

the actor Jack Lemmon. But when my doctor says, 'Mitzie, this is Alitash, I've been wanting to—,' she stops her conversation and says, 'Excuse me one second,' to Jack Lemmon. I said, 'Oh God! I'm not going to buy anything! She can just go ahead and talk to him!'

"She said, 'Oh, it's so wonderful to meet you!' And I said to myself, 'Wow, art dealers can be like this, too? Well this is the kind of art dealer *I* want to be.'

"She was a role model for me, because most of Mitzie's clients were Jewish people. And I remember standing at her gallery, and usually I'm the only Black person there. And I thought, wouldn't it be wonderful if I had a gallery and my gallery was filled like this with Black people!

"It was just a dream!" says Alitash, becoming very animated. "Everything starts with a dream! No one can stop you from dreaming anyway. You're better off dreaming something good because it might happen! But dream *realistic* dreams."

There is one thing in particular to which Alitash credits her success: the artists. "I got words of encouragement from the artists; I got belief from the artists. You have to have that. You have to have the artists believe in you.

"I identified the artists that I admired, and contacted them. One of them was Vincent Smith, so I talked to him. You know what," she says with surprise, as if this just happened yesterday. "He sent me some work— that I didn't even pay a *dime* for. He believed in me and set me up. He's one of the people that sent me work to start my business. Then I called a dealer in Detroit named David Zellman. He publishes artist Romare

Bearden's prints. I told him I was interested in becoming a dealer and I wanted to sell some of the things that he published. He sent them to me. This man never met me; we just spoke on the phone and he trusted me." Alitash's eyes become moist as she tells this story. "And I lived up to what they expected of me," she finishes. "You have to be honest in this business—in any business. That's what's going to carry you on, because this business is built on reputation."

Her passion for art, and for bringing it to other people, was what kept Alitash going. There is no way, she says, that she could have kept up her enthusiasm if her interest in becoming an art dealer had been based only on making money. "I remember many times I said to myself, 'Well, you know what? This is just not going to work!' Selling art—come on! It's not a necessity, you know what I mean?

"But I remember being in here when I was starting and people would come, and I would tell them about this art, and tell them about that, and tell them about *another* piece, and they would walk out without buying anything." Alitash looks around her gallery, which at the moment contains several paintings and a few small pieces of sculpture by new artists. "But you know what," she says with a look of satisfaction, "I have not had a single person come in here and walk out not appreciating what they saw. Usually the reason why they don't buy is because they can't afford to, but the fact that people appreciated the art kept me going. I felt that was worth it, because I knew one day somebody would come who could appreciate it and also be able to buy it." After surviving the first year,

she decided to try a second, then she tried a third and a fourth .

"Artists are commentators about the world that we live in. How would we know about anything from the past, whether it's about the Egyptians or the Aztecs? It's all through art, yet art is less important to today's society than ever before. It wasn't always like that. Artists had much more importance in past times than they do now. In the past they were the documenters of history. Today we have television, which doesn't really serve us well.

"When I'm in New York I visit lots of galleries. I want to see what other galleries are doing, who they are showing, who are the new artists."

There isn't a day Alitash doesn't go to a museum, a gallery, or visit an artist's studio. "It is very rewarding for anyone to be in this business, if they know what they're doing, and if they look at it for the art and the artists. You cannot go into this business thinking about making money and how glamorous it is. I really want to emphasize that to young people. I would say eighty percent of the time it's a lot of fun, but there's a lot of work involved," she says, unconsciously pushing back her sleeves. "Most of it has nothing to do with meeting fancy people. Sometimes, when I pick up paintings by myself, and I mean *big* paintings, I go to the storage room, and I'm putting this stuff in the car, and I say to myself, 'Oh, for all those people who say to me what a glamorous job I have, I wish they could see me now with my sweats on!' It's tough!"

Alitash volunteers a lot of her time to museums to arrange lectures on multicultural

art issues, and has even curated a few shows. She tries to enlighten the public about not thinking of the artists as Black artists. If you were to look at their work, you would never know what their ethnicity was. "They're just *artists,* and I hope by the time the kids my eight-year-old nephew Zelek's age grow up, we can be able to show artists without saying this is this, this is that, and this is the other."

In her gallery on this particular day is the work of Emilio Cruz and Nanette Carter, one of Zelek's favorite artists. "People don't know that for a lousy five hundred dollars you can buy a piece of art by an artist who's going places! *And* you can pay for it in installments. This is what I want to communicate to people," Alitash says, with her hands now doing much of the talking. "Art is not just for people with money. It's for people who are *interested.*"

For the ten years she has been in the business, Alitash Kebede has satisfied something inside of her that she doesn't think she would have been able to satisfy working at another job. "I love when people come here with their kids. Kids have a lot of sense. Adults are sometimes intimidated by art because they feel, 'Oh, what is it? I don't understand, I mean, I like this, but . . .' You're not *supposed* to understand everything. Kids are free with their feelings, and they see all kinds of things. Their comments are comments that I would love the adults to make. Sometimes you don't know why you like something, you just do.

"I feel like I'm contributing something to society. I really do. I have kids coming in here and . . . I feel *great!*"

Dudley Edmondson

"_Freeze!_" yelled a voice from within the woods. Dudley and I instantly and instinctively ducked down and froze in our tracks. This we did for different reasons. Dudley Edmondson knew the shout meant an incoming bird was about to be trapped by the team at the banding station just out of our view. If it saw us, it might fly away.

I thought we were going to be shot.

The same voice yelled again. "Clear!" I followed Dudley's lead and stood up. As we walked through the brush, we came to a small clearing. There stood a shack not much bigger or any more attractive than an outhouse. Four or five young men were crammed into the dark space looking out through two six-inch-high, two-foot-wide openings in the wall.

In front of the shed was what looked like a volleyball court cut into the woods. Several poles rimmed the perimeter and supported fine black netting. Sitting in the midst of all this were a starling and a pigeon

attached to a specially designed line. They were the bait. Just behind the tiny shack were noisy cages filled with other starlings and pigeons, as well as sparrows, "waiting their turn," as Dudley says.

From August 15 to November 15, the Hawk Ridge banding station is manned twenty-four hours a day. The job of the crew is to trap birds of prey—falcons, hawks, and owls, among others—and examine them. They are then checked for size, weight, approximate age, and health. The information is recorded in a log that includes the date and time the bird was captured. Finally, a small numbered metal band is attached to its leg. If the bird is found again, dead or alive, the U.S. Fish and Wildlife Service is notified, and the information is compared to the notes made when the bird was first banded.

Dudley Edmondson moved from his home in Columbus, Ohio, to Duluth, Minnesota, so he could be a little closer to the things he loves—the outdoors and birds of prey.

"My art teacher back in high school got me into birding. He was a bird-watcher—absolutely crazy about birds. He formed an Audubon Club in high school." His teacher decided to take the club to Texas, an excellent place to watch migrating birds during certain times of the year. By holding a fund-raiser they were able to finance the Texas trip and observe dozens of different bird species. It was a special experience for Dudley: "That was pretty much the beginning of my bird-watching days." Columbus, Ohio, is not jam-packed with wilderness, so Dudley knew he would have to move to a different location if he was going to be able to *really* check out the types of birds he was interested in.

"I had a pretty good job—a pretty good *paying* job, as a matter of fact—with Ohio State University Hospital. I worked in the pharmacy. But I was bored. I'd go bird-watching and nature looking, but it wasn't fulfilling, so I started traveling, seeing other cities around the country." Visiting first the East Coast of the United States, then up to Canada, Dudley eventually came to Duluth. "I had read about Duluth for hawk migration and decided it was a pretty nice place. There's a lot of wilderness around here, and the people are pretty decent.

"I had read about Hawk Ridge in a book about hawk migratory spots around the country, so I came here in 1987 and talked to the bird counter at that time, who told me more about their operation. We became friends. The next year I came back and visited with him." The third year Dudley visited Duluth, he decided to move there.

Shortly after Dudley arrived in Duluth, he heard the banding station needed some help, so he signed on. "I knew this wasn't the job that was going to keep me in Minnesota, particularly in Duluth, because it only paid six hundred dollars for two months of work." Dudley eventually got work as a pharmacist in town to cover his living expenses.

In the meantime, Dudley was gaining experience and earning the trust of the folks running the Ridge. Dudley quickly became involved with the whole operation and eventually became a member of the Hawk Ridge Preserve board of directors. The board develops a budget and plans the year's events, such as talks at schools and weekend events for the people who visit the Ridge in droves every weekend. They also oversee trail maintenance.

Dudley's talent as an artist has been an added bonus to the Hawk Ridge Preserve. He has designed dramatic T-shirts and other souvenir items, the sale of which helps to raise money for the upkeep of the Ridge.

"My father had the artistic talent; that's where I got it from. I used to draw everything—people, dinosaurs, superheroes, and animals. Then I specialized in birds of prey and that's primarily all I draw now."

Another creative avenue that Dudley has explored is photography, which for him goes hand in hand with his other interests. Aside from capturing exciting views of his favorite subject, the photographs are the perfect reference material for his drawings. "If you're going to get a good photograph, you need to work at either a nest, a place of heavy concentration of food, or a migratory spot through which birds have to pass because they have no choice. Those are the three places that I usually work." The combination of these art disciplines has evolved into a venture Dudley calls Raptor Works. He offers for sale art and writings based on his love of birds of prey.

While we were waiting in the shed, another bird was spotted high in the sky. Everyone knew it was large because it was high up but it still looked to be a good size. It cut back over the clearing a couple of times before it began to make its dive. It had seen the bait. The question was, what was it?

One of Dudley's colleagues began working the lines attached to the pigeon. The pigeon had been fitted with a vest that is attached to several control lines but allows its wings to be free. By pulling on the lines, the team in the shed can control where the pigeon flies, enticing birds of prey toward the target. Pulled on certain lines, the pigeon is brought closer to the net, just where they want the incoming bird to land.

Everyone in the shed is trying to figure out what kind of bird it is, which is impossible to tell because the dive-bombing bird is coming in head-on. All they can see is the top of its head and its wingspan—an incredible wingspan. The only thing that is certain is that birds this size often destroy the nets and escape in the process. Once the incoming bird flies into the net, it panics and forgets about the meal. It wants only to get out. A bird this size is usually trapped in a bow net, a circle of strong mesh folded in half and triggered by garage-door springs. The nets they are using today are for smaller specimens.

The wings dip as the bird banks into a final high-speed approach. All at once it looks beautiful and graceful, calculating and deadly. It does not make a sound. Suddenly the team shouts in unison, "It's a goshawk!"

A prize to be sure, the goshawk is the bird bird-watchers drool over. In this instance, however, it means trouble. If any bird can do damage to the nets and still get away on top of it, this is the one. With a body approximately twenty-one inches long from head to tail, it has a wingspan nearly four feet across.

"Get ready to run for the door!" yells biologist Dave Evans, who runs the sta-tion. Someone must get to the hawk as soon as possible to keep it from destroying the nets and escaping.

One final last-second tug on the pigeon and . . . *WHAMMM!!* The hawk is in the net.

One of his partners beats Dudley to the door. *"Go! Go! Go!"* yells Dudley as his friend scrambles for the net.

In a panic the hawk has already gone through the bottom of one net and has become tangled in a second. The captor uses one hand to distract the hawk as he tries to maneuver closer to the bird. He must not let it "foot" him with its talons; they are needle sharp, the hawk's best and most dangerous weapon.

While the bird is momentarily confused by the hand hovering over its head, the captor quickly slips his other hand in to grab the legs. Using both hands to control the bird's wings and feet, Dudley's coworker subdues the hawk, which is then gingerly removed from the netting and brought back into the shed.

The hawk is surprisingly quiet as it watches every move made by the group. The head turns, looking at each of us with disdain. "Good going," someone says to the hawk's captor. He smiles proudly as the bird is slipped headfirst into a tube made of two coffee cans that have been secured together with duct tape, with air holes punched into the bottom end. Once in the cans, the bird is easy to control. Dave can now examine its tail feathers and talons. It is then removed from the can and other measurements and information can be recorded. Finally, the small identifying band is attached to its leg, and Dave care-fully hands the hawk to Dudley.

After taking the bird to a favorite lookout spot, Dudley Edmondson releases it back into the wild. "He's going to sit in a tree and count his feathers," Dudley jokes. "I have a feeling he won't do anymore hunting today."

For Dudley, being in the wilderness offers more than just a chance to see animals. He wishes other people of color could see what he sees every day. "Black people I know tend to spend a lot of time in the city. When they do venture much outside of the city, they tend to go to other large metropolitan areas to visit friends and relatives. It's a shame that I see so few people of color in the woods looking at animals, studying birds, whatever.

"Camping for weeks on end by myself in the wilderness gave me a lot of self-confidence, a feeling that I could do virtually anything I wanted to do because, hell, I survived in the woods! I don't think young people in the city have the self-confidence they need to succeed. A wilderness experience could build up a lot of their self-confidence. I'd like to help others go through that same experience to build up their self-confidence so they can begin to take on some of the challenges of life.

"You could take anything in nature, whether it is a bird, a plant, a reptile or whatever, and you could study it for the rest of your life and still never learn everything about it. To me, that's what's so interesting about nature. Go out and enjoy the outdoors and the wilderness and feel comfortable out there, because it belongs to you as much as it does anyone else in this country."

Gordon Henderson walks into the vast loft space that is his showroom on West Thirty-ninth Street in Manhattan. A firm handshake greets me. "It's nice to meet you," he says with a questioning glance. I'm almost certain that he doesn't really remember the reason for our appointment. This is a busy man. Just a few moments before, a rather boisterous creative meeting—it could be heard throughout the showroom—was going on in his office.

As we enter his office, three or four casually dressed people turn from what they're doing and smile at us. "Hi!" they say in unison.

"Okay, kids. It's time to go," he tells them.

"Awwww . . . ," they moan in mock despair as they leave. "We were just starting to have fun," someone says.

The office is big and comfortable. One wall is covered with Polaroids, magazine covers, clippings, drawings, and photographs—faces of women

wearing clothes designed by Gordon. Against the adjacent wall leans a huge mirror, almost the length of the wall itself and about six feet high. A dress form is modeling in front of the mirror, waiting for clothes. Opposite the mirror is a wall of windows and a large oval desk made of slate with wrought-iron legs.

It's a pretty nice office for someone who's been in business for such a short time. It's rare to find someone this successful, this young, and this *nice*. Where's the attitude? It's there but it is very good. Gordon likes what he does and he likes the people he works with. Most importantly, he doesn't think being a successful fashion designer means getting a fat head. "It's better to keep yourself down here," he says. "It's just better to try to keep yourself focused on what you're doing and where *you're* going."

Gordon's parents divorced when he was three years old. He and his mom lived in Northern California in a small town called Winton. His dad lived in Berkeley, California, so Gordon spent a lot of time traveling back and forth to visit him. His parents' separation made him mature faster because of the added responsibilities of being the "man of the house."

"After I got out of high school I went to Davis University. I was studying zoology with intentions of going to medical school, which I quickly realized was something I was not going to be happy doing.

"Everyone was so *detached* from the world, just studying, which I thought was a poor way to educate someone who was going to be taking care of the welfare and health of the world. It just wasn't interesting to me. I was very good at it; it was easy for me, but I wasn't dedicated."

He decided to take a year off and think about what he wanted to do. He had some ideas, but he didn't know how to go about pursuing them. He left for San Francisco and lived there for a year.

While Gordon was in school he made many of his own clothes, mainly because "I was pretty small then, just starting to grow, actually, in high school and college." It was the only way to get clothing both in his size and in styles he liked. This exposed him to a large fashion community, which taught him what went on in the industry. "I became very interested in it and found myself becoming more and more involved with doing clothes, the idea of clothes. I started to realize that it was not just a hobby, that it could be a career.

"I had my mother start investigating schools; where should I go if I really want to get involved in this? She found out about Parsons School of Design in New York City. While I was in San Francisco, I applied to Parsons and did the portfolio that you had to put together for them." This included sketches of clothing designs and ideas for fabrics that Gordon might use to create a garment.

"It was hard. I couldn't draw," he says, laughing as he thinks about the old pictures he still keeps. "There really aren't many successful designers who can't draw. Drawing is getting your idea down on a piece of paper so that you and other people know what it is. But somehow I got accepted, and it's still baffling to me. I guess it was just good enough, and they saw something they felt was worth cultivating." Gordon headed to the East Coast with a chance to pursue his dream.

"'New York! Just like I pictured it,'" as Stevie Wonder's song says. . . . Well, not exactly. "To my dismay I was not happy with what I found. I thought, this place stinks! These people are not at all nice, it's dirty, and everyone's so intensely *motivated*, there's no way I'm ever going to penetrate the system here. That's how I felt initially.

"So I locked myself into school. For the three years I was at Parsons, I basically just studied. I really didn't go out very much. I didn't go out to clubs. I missed that whole scene in the seventies, or the end of it. I was really a timid, quiet, reserved kid."

After graduating from Parsons, Gordon received an offer to create a small line of sportswear. Unfortunately, it wasn't very long before the two company partners started arguing with each other and the business fell apart. But his misfortune there led to a job as a designer for Calvin Klein.

"Somehow, the job before I went to Calvin was a blessing in disguise, because it gave me a taste of doing my own thing. Although my experiences at Calvin's were really good ones, that little yearning, that twisting desire was still there. Calvin offered me a lot of opportunities, but none of those chances to do my own thing were happening. We discussed it. I said, 'I'm not really excited by what I'm doing now, versus what you offered me in the beginning.' He said, 'You're going to do this for three years or forget it.'

"I said, 'Fine.' To me, what I felt was I

could go out and free-lance and be an assistant to a designer at any point, but what I really wanted to do was be involved in the creative process, design in a company or try something on my own.

"Previously I had met a woman named Sabina Allison. She had a sample room, and we became very fond of one another and always talked. I started doing samples on my own, putting a line together with her using her sample room. Soon I was doing a million dollars' worth of business—who knows how! It just happened that way."

Gordon was selling his clothing to major stores like Saks Fifth Avenue, Bloomingdale's, Macy's, and The Limited. Again the company he worked under folded, but he still had lots of contacts. He got magazine editors and people who buy goods for department stores to come and see his work.

"Selling the clothes, making them—it was all me doing that stuff. Which proved to be a very good education for me to run my business. I have a very good handle on it, because I had to do all those things."

One thing Gordon Henderson has learned is that if you want to stay in business, you have to give the people not only what they want, but also what they can afford. His clothing is not only stylish, it is not terribly expensive. The garments are comfortable enough for work and hip enough for a night out.

"I started in the designing business doing clothes that were affordable, not outrageously expensive. With the condition our economy is in now, it's really a blessing in disguise that I took my intuition and followed it." Gordon thinks comfort and practicality should be your guides to dressing well. "I *have* expensive clothes, but I wear T-shirts and jeans. I am a person who feels like someone really looks good if they have a good watch on, or a good pair of shoes. The rest of it can be whatever you want.

"In the designer market, if you're going to buy a pair of pants, skirt, jacket, dress, a couple of blouses, you're at four grand easily. It's unreasonable, and there are too many people out there that want to look good and dress well, and I'm going to give that product to them."

A line of less expensive but greatlooking clothing is available from Gordon Henderson. The line is called But Gordon and came about because people kept telling him, "But Gordon, you can't sell a low-priced line of clothing." These people thought it would ruin the sales of the more expensive collection. It didn't. "The look of But Gordon is not as expensive, but the attention to detail is very much the same.

"We're hard-working people," he says, looking at the bustling crowd outside his office window. "We have to walk, get on the subway, do all this kind of stuff to get where we want to get. And there's that many people," he says, making a tiny space between his thumb and forefinger, "who have Lear jets, Rolls-Royces, and chauffeurs who drive them back and forth to work, or have very high-paying jobs and do whatever they want to do. I'm not really trying to cater to those people." Gordon starts to laugh. "Most of them have the worst taste in the world!"

Gordon is a good businessman, and he prides himself on that more than on his fashion achievements. Although he gets awards and is regularly praised in fashion magazines, that's not what makes him happy.

"I'm much prouder of articles in *Newsweek*, *Time*, even the *Wall Street Journal*. Those things are much more important to me than *Vogue* or *Mademoiselle*. My father doesn't read *Vogue*. Some financial person doesn't read *Vogue*. They don't even know what's *in Vogue*.

"It's a very difficult business. It's very cliquish. You have to be willing to go in and do all that cliquish stuff," he says, referring to the parties and hanging out with the "right" people. "Or you have to have confidence enough in yourself to live your life as you want. That's what I chose to do.

"I like it that way. My whole life is not going to be based around the fashion industry, Seventh Avenue. My picture is a much broader one." Gordon wants to create entire looks for singers and films. "I think it would be very nice to win an Academy Award for outstanding costume design," he says with a winning smile.

Angela and Ronald Trigg

There is something very cool about trains. I don't know what it is, they are just cool. Think about it! Whatever train you have the chance to ride on, whether it's the Chicago "el" or an Amtrak going across the country, it seems as if everyone wants to sit or stand up front. *All the way up front.* You want to see what's in front of you, where you are going. You want to see those tracks rushing underneath your feet.

Even better, you want to drive the train. Angela Trigg wanted to do that when she was a little girl. Her dad, Ronald Trigg (everyone just calls him "Trigg"), has been a conductor on the Long Island Railroad for over twenty-one years. The LIRR is the only commuter and freight rail system of its kind in the United States. The railroad carries more passengers each day, runs more trains per hour, and has more track per square mile than any other railroad in the country.

"She used to come to work with me when she was ten," Trigg recalls. "How come you're not driving the train?" Angela would ask her dad. "Because I'm the conductor. The conductor don't drive the train! The engineer drives it."

"I want to drive it!" said Angela.

Trigg continues: "I said, 'One of these days, baby, you might get to drive it.' I was saying this, but I never thought it would really happen because there were no women even doing what I was doing. The only women they were hiring were for clerical jobs. Oddly enough, Angela was getting pretty tired of clerical work.

"It seemed like a good job," she says. "*He* worked there. I put in a résumé and they called, and I applied as an assistant conductor." Angela had a month of classroom training and tests before she could work on the train. Assistant conductors can qualify for conductor in three to five years; instead, Angela opted to interview for engineer.

"That led to fifteen more months of training," recalls Angela. "Memorizing the tracks, the book of rules verbatim. All kinds of interesting things. Learning how to operate the trains. After the training was the qualification. And now I've been operating for two years."

Lots of aspects of training to work on the railroad are tough, but Ronald and Angela agree that one of the most difficult is memorizing the miles and miles of track. "I couldn't believe that you had to know every mile of track," says Ronald, sitting in the employees' cafeteria with his daughter. "I didn't think it was possible until I did it.

"I had it on a wall in my bedroom. I'd be doin' it in my sleep. And I'd wake up, turn on my light, and see something, then turn it back off. And that's how I remembered it. All around the wall in my room. The whole railroad."

"And I did the same thing," adds Angela. "It's funny how you get into it. I had my posters up and my blackboard. You go out for the holidays and you're writing on napkins," she says with a chuckle.

The LIRR is a unique train system, Trigg explains. "You have to always know where you are. It's not like working for Amtrak or Conrail, where they go state to state—that's easy. This one is all bunched up together. Compact. Branching off this way and that way, it's like an octopus. That was kind of hard, to cram all that in your head."

Knowing the tracks isn't just something they make you learn for the heck of it. Heavy fog is a regular occurrence in the far reaches of Long Island, and "sometimes," Angela explains, "you just can't see. You just go by, I remember that tree, that telephone pole."

There is a kind of friendly rivalry between the first father-daughter conductor-engineer pair on the Long Island Railroad, and possibly any rail line in America. Although the engineer is like the pilot of the train, it is the conductor who is really in charge.

"The conductor makes sure his equipment is clean and safe and all the cars are connected properly," says Ronald. "You make sure that all your equipment is in proper working order—air-conditioning, lights. And make sure your help shows up. . . ." Trigg looks at his daughter with a teasing smile as she sits across the table. Angela just laughs at him and lets loose a big smile. ". . . your engineer, brakeman, all the other people," he continues. "The conductor is sort of like the captain of a ship."

"It shouldn't be, but it is," Angela says, teasing her dad.

"*Somebody's* got to be responsible," says Trigg. "Pretty soon it's gonna be nobody on the train but the engineer. Then they'll be in charge." Angela laughs. "They're going to eliminate us," Trigg continues. "They'll make the engineer the conductor; they'll take the train out and everything else will be automatic. That's what they're working on."

Both Ronald and Angela were among the first on the LIRR to do what they do. Angela is among the first female engineers, and Trigg was one of the first Black conductors. However, they are not firsts in their clan. Their family has an amazing tradition of working on railroads. Trigg's dad worked twenty-nine years on the railroad as a brakeman, *his* father worked another fifty years, and Trigg's mother's father worked forty-seven years. All of them for the Norfolk and Western Railroad in Virginia.

"My grandfather used to work on trains, repairing them. Oiling the wheels, making sure that the trains were kept running. He invented something on one of the trains but he never got credit for it. The railroad had a locomotive and they couldn't make it run. So they gave him a scale model. He took it home, brought it back, told them what he did. He got a bonus. That was it."

Angela said she had thought of quitting when the training seemed too tough, but "my grandmother said, 'Oh, no, you don't quit! You keep goin'. It's in your bones. There's no way you won't pass.'"

Ronald Trigg looks proudly at his soft-spoken daughter. "Your grandpa would have been tickled to death to know that you and I both work for the railroad," he says to her. He passed away even before Trigg had started working on the railroad.

Even with all this family railroad history, Ronald Trigg wasn't really planning on a railroad career. He had put in a couple of applications to the Long Island Railroad, but they weren't hiring. He found other jobs with the telephone company, United Parcel Service, and as a cab driver. He figured if he really wanted a railroad job he would have to go back to Virginia, which he didn't want to do. "If you've got a railroad history it's good on any railroad, which at the time I wasn't aware of." Working for railroads is like working for family. Once you work for one, it gets you in the door at just about any other rail line.

When Trigg was hired, there were not a lot of Black conductors on the LIRR. For Angela, she had to deal with pigheaded men who didn't want women driving trains. "I didn't know prejudice till I came here. That was odd. While I was qualifying to be an engineer, certain guys wouldn't let me operate because they thought I should be barefoot and pregnant and their son should be sitting next to them.

"It was tough because one guy makes

you sit on a crate, another guy doesn't want to have anything to do with you; he wants you to disappear. 'Go study before I'm going to let you operate.' And on the other hand, some people are very cool, but they talk too much; they want to share everything with you. It was real odd dealing with all the different personalities."

Every now and then something will happen to remind Angela it was all worth it. "A little old man gets on and he says, 'You're operating this train?' I said, 'Yeah.' He said, 'I'm not getting on it!' Then he gets on another car. At the end he walks up front and

says it was a nice ride." She chuckles a bit.

Angela already has a motorcycle license, a tractor-trailer license, and a bus license. "The only thing I can't operate is that heavy equipment for construction. I'll get to it one day. I want to be a pilot. I'm going to take the one-hour lesson to see what it's like."

Ronald and Angela Trigg have become one of the most unique father-daughter matchups around, and that has a lot to do with their shared philosophy. "Follow your intuition," says Angela. "Do what you know is right. Have patience, persistence, and peace from the inside."

MAD DADS

John Foster was tired. He had just returned home to Omaha, Nebraska —a long drive back from Winston-Salem, North Carolina—and all he wanted to do was rest. As his body finally began to wind down, there was a knock at his bedroom door. When he open it, his twenty-year-old son stood before him, beaten and bloodied. John flipped out.

John's rage built as his son told him about the gang that had wanted to take his Suzuki Samurai from him while he gassed up at a service station in North Omaha. Five or six guys had decided they wanted his jeep. He resisted, and they beat him severely. John's son was fortunate to get away not only with his life, but with his jeep as well.

"I became livid, out of control. I wanted to retaliate," John says, only now able to tell the story calmly. "My son told me what he remembered and described some vehicles and people, because I planned to take the law into my own hands, which was stupid on my part. I loaded up my

licensed .44 Magnum and a .357 Magnum and laid them on the front seat of my car. I then took to the streets of Omaha."

John cruised all the areas where these guys were likely to hang out: housing projects, fast-food restaurants, parking lots, and even back alleys. He questioned people on the street. "Did you see these guys in a brown 1978 Monte Carlo?"

It was very late when John stopped at the corner of Patrick Avenue and Twenty-ninth Street. He was frustrated and angry, and he began to realize that he was also completely out of control. "If I had seen anybody who resembled these individuals," he says, remembering his emotions that night, "I'd probably be in jail or dead. I would have shot 'em. There's no doubt in my mind. I would have shot them."

He sat in his car thinking for a long time. "I got to talking to myself out loud," he says, and chuckles. "'We have got to do something about this. We've got to organize the strong men in this community.'

"The following day I sat down at home and wrote up a flyer. A local television station, KMTV, was having a rally against drugs at North High School, so I headed there and handed out about five hundred flyers about a meeting at my house. Nothing materialized; only one person showed up."

Because this was so important to John, he contacted some people he knew from his job as the vice-president of the civilian employees union of the city of Omaha. One of them was Eddie Staton, the human relations director on the mayor's cabinet. "When John called me and told me the story of what was going on and said we were going to meet," remembers Eddie, "that was right up my alley! And what we found was there were a lot of good men that felt the same way, but nobody had ever tried to pull them all together."

John strongly agrees: "For too long the Black father figure has been absent. It has been the strong Black woman who has had to be everything to her family. There have been some good fathers like myself, Eddie, and all the men in our group, but we were diffuse. We weren't organized enough to speak out against what was happening in our community. And in many cases against what was happening to our families. But what happened to me started a fire in all of us, and after we got organized, it just took off.

"We are not an organization, so to speak; we are a movement. And this didn't start with me," John says, laughing again. "God brought us all together. In August 1989 we officially kicked it off." They became M.A.D. D.A.D.S.—Men Against Destruction Defending Against Drugs and Social Disorder.

At their first meeting the group talked with the North Omaha Ministerial Alliance, which is an organization of local clergy, and told them what they wanted to do. "They were apprehensive at first," John says with a laugh. "They thought we were going to be vigilantes. When we assured them that wasn't the case, they gave us their blessings. We then met at Eddie's house and stayed long into the night, trying to put together a workable, reasonable solution. And we did.

"We came up with the four committees that made up MAD DADS—administration, mobilization, communications, and security. People from all over the city of Omaha and neighboring communities are involved in MAD DADS. The only thing we require of new members," says John, "is that they *please* check their egos at the door. We don't care if they are Black or white, rich or poor, young or old. The only qualifications are that they be a loving and caring parent and, of course, that they be drug free, because we want to set an example. We want to be good role models."

From the start, the idea of MAD DADS was to bring together the *Black* men of the community to deal with the problems facing its youth, Eddie says. "We quickly realized that we had omitted very important parts of our community from MAD DADS, and we've since taken the phrase *Black fathers* out of our literature. Now we simply say *fathers*, because we've come to realize the problems facing the Black community are not unique to Black folks. The lack of positive role models and positive stimuli for *our* youth was also apparent in the Hispanic community, among Native Americans, and in white America. *All* fathers felt the same way. We needed to come together to ensure the perpetuation of each of our races through social defense of our youths."

MAD DADS's objective is to identify the problems facing the young people in the community and to create solutions, or at least give the kids alternatives. MAD DADS has persuaded the city to bring a movie theater into the North Omaha area, because there was not a single theater there. One sure way to curb the crime born out of boredom is to give young people recreation within their own community. It's easy for people to say, "Hey, they can go into the next town to catch a movie," but when you live in an urban area with little to do and no means of getting around, it's not that easy. And why should they have to travel to the next town when there is enough money to support businesses that choose to be located in North Omaha? Many times their only alternative has been to make their own fun—often at someone else's expense.

MAD DADS provides outreach—someone to talk to if you have a problem you can't seem solve on your own or through school counselors. MAD DADS is also a place to get information and educational assistance. They are not a social-service program, but simply parents doing whatever they can to help where they are needed, while trying to help educate other parents along the way.

"When we first started out, we painted over gang graffiti," explains Eddie, MAD DADS's president. "This sent a strong message to the gangs: 'We don't like this and we want it stopped. We refuse to buy into the Bloods', Crips', and the Vice Lords' propaganda. These are *our* young men, and we want them back.'

"Our goal is to let 'em know that if you're doing something illegal, we're gonna drop a dime. We *will* testify against you. We want you in jail. But we will do *everything* we can to help you if you want to come out of that situation. As fathers, that's what we're here for; we're here to help."

"Being out here for almost three years," John adds, "we've seen a lot of our kids who used to play sports and go to school together grow up and turn into cold-blooded killers. We still can't figure how it happens. What has disrupted their reasoning process so much that they can shoot somebody down in cold blood, go home, eat, go to sleep, and show no remorse? It's those kids we're trying to reform or redeem, going into correction centers and talking to the ones who have been incarcerated and saying, 'Now you have a support group out there that really cares about you. When you get out, you will have someplace to come home to.'"

Block parties are a good way of getting the word out that there is help. MAD DADS sponsored the premiere of the film *Boyz 'N the Hood*. After the screening, they held a meeting with the audience to discuss the messages in the movie. They created a game called Money for Your Knowledge, since cash prizes can be a real incentive to attain knowledge. "We have a stack of cards with different questions and"—John laughs—"a stack of money. The age group determines the type of question that's asked. We might ask an eight-year-old, 'Who's the mayor of the city of Omaha?' If they win, they'll get, say, two dollars.

"We constantly try to come up with new ideas. We're tired of basketballs, baseballs, and all the other trinkets people pass out with which we are expected to solve the problems of our community. It's much deeper than that. Gangs and drugs are the symptoms of problems that are much more firmly rooted. We've got to get to the root of the problems."

One of their successful methods of cleaning up the streets is the Hot Spot Sheet, a five-by-seven-inch form that asks citizens to report information about illicit activity in their neighborhood. It asks for dates, times, locations, and especially the name of the person or persons involved. The Hot Spot Sheet can be turned in anonymously, and it helps MAD DADS to try to take action to rectify the situation, but MAD DADS always encourages people to call the police in an emergency. Getting the community to cooperate with the police will foster better understanding on both sides. The only weapons MAD DADS carry are their portable phones and radios, their anger, and a desire to keep their kids alive.

They have been criticized by social-service groups, who thought they would take funding away from them, and by local residents, who don't do anything in the community besides complain about how important MAD DADS thinks it is. One of the keys to MAD DADS is that they don't close at five or six o'clock in the evening like regular social programs. "One of our biggest advantages," John tells me, "has been *how* we attack this problem. We are dealing with the night culture that no one else wants to deal with. A lot of these kids are out on the streets when the adults are in their beds asleep. So we start going out at nontraditional times, getting up at one o'clock in the morning and going out in the street and staying out there until three, four o'clock in the morning—whatever it takes to deal with the situation.

"They saw we were consistent in doing this, and that we weren't going to go away. We were becoming a problem for them. They couldn't figure out what we were. And when we started messing with their livelihood, that's when they started trying to say we were narcs, a rival gang, or any other nonsense. All we were, and still are, are fathers concerned about their children."

Mothers also get involved in MAD DADS. Another very successful effort was the Mothers' Midnight March. "At midnight," says Eddie, "we marched right through town, past this car wash where the gangs were hanging out. Those mothers were going in there, talking to those young men. They were pulling them and saying, 'You come out of there and march with me, son!' It made an impact."

MAD DADS also highlights the achievements of those youth who choose to excel, a pat on the back that Eddie says happens too infrequently. He has even put together a security service that makes constructive use of the talents of the young people who have turned their lives around.

Reverend Robert Tyler, known to all as Bob, is the group's vice-president and treasurer. He has his own all-too-familiar story to bring to the table at MAD DADS. "I have experienced the downward spiral of a young person's life because of crack; my sons were addicted to it. I've had to go through the pain other families are facing when they deal with a loved one's addiction. It's a pain most people are not voicing, because they don't want others looking down on them or their family members. The addicts and families of addicts alike are forced to mindlessly follow the dictates of that drug. What we have discovered is most of the treatment programs around here are thirty-day treatments. That's the tip of the iceberg in terms of treating crack addiction. Most crack addiction has to be dealt with on a long-term basis. We also know that most insurance companies will pay that five-thousand-dollar-a-month inpatient fee for the first month, and after that you're on your own.

"We're telling local administrations," says the reverend, "'You've got to spend some money on care—especially those federal dollars coming in here.' We try to be the thorn in the administration's side in terms of economic development.

"We have gotten a few commitments out of the city administration to build some much-needed things in this community. One of them is a recreation center for young people—designed with *them* in mind—which will also employ community people. It's not the whole answer, but it's a step in the right direction."

MAD DADS has opened chapters in Denver, Colorado; in Houston, Texas; in several cities in Florida, and in New York City. They also expect to have others in Maryland and Mississippi soon. Their goal is to have a chapter in every city and state.

Bob designed the logo for MAD DADS: a fist against an open hand. It is a very important message to the young people, says John. "We let 'em know we're out there like the hand of reason to help turn them around, but there's also that fist of determination."

John B. Williams

Friday night is Cuban food night. The musician known as Nancy Wilson's favorite bass player, John B. Williams, walks into his favorite Cuban restaurant in Los Angeles after waiting on line for nearly twenty minutes with the rest of the crowd. Others with the status of John B. would have made their presence known and expected to be escorted to "their" table.

John B., a regular, smiles a big, warm toothy smile at the pretty woman who seats the customers. Inside, the din of Cuban music, hungry people chattering, and the bustle of waiters greeting and serving their guests make for a comfortable atmosphere. His distinctive features—bald head, Fu Manchu mustache, and tall frame—attract glances of recognition from the other patrons.

Food is ordered and soon arrives. He swallows a taste of his favorite chicken dish and looks up at the guests he's invited to join him. "Oh

man!" he says, putting his fork down. He speaks just like you think a jazz musician should. Very cool, very smooth. His voice is rich and lilting. After a week of working on "The Arsenio Hall Show" as The Posse's bass man and resident poet, this is a welcome treat.

This is a good town for John B. "Right now there's a lot of music happening here. New York used to be the place. So many of the guys from New York have come to L.A.; most of the music business is here these days."

L.A. has given John the chance to explore the new musical ideas he's developed from his years playing with many of the greatest musicians and vocalists in the world: Louis Armstrong, Count Basie, Billy Cobham, Jon Hendricks and Company, Dizzy Gillespie, Freddie Hubbard, Nancy Wilson, Gloria Gaynor, Roy Ayers, Benny Carter, and Louis Bellson, to name a few.

When John was growing up on Harlem's Sugar Hill, his family lived in the same building as saxophone legend Sonny Rollins. There was always a jam session in the backyard to check out. His four older sisters were musicians. One already played bass, so John took up the drums. It wasn't until his early twenties while he was in the Marine Corps that the bass became his instrument of choice.

As a kid "the gangs were always trying to recruit you. They would tell you if you didn't join they would hurt your family." He shakes his head. "It was rough." Somehow he kept away from all that, forming a group with some guys he grew up with. They played at the Apollo Theater with John B. drumming before the toughest audience in the world. "We won the amateur night two weeks in a row. We were all so young, in junior high school, and playing jazz. We caught their hearts," he says, beaming proudly.

John gently attracts the attention of a waiter. "Can we get some sangria for our table?" he asks. Sorry, no sangria, he's told. "Okay, just bring us a nice red wine." The waiter nods and is gone. "Is everybody cool?" he asks in that jazz voice. Heads with full mouths and busy jaws bob up and down in unison. "Cool!"

Latin food goes with John's passion for Latin culture and music. Growing up in Harlem exposed him to sounds and feelings that he loved. He often played at Puerto Rican dances and West Indian parties. "I love salsa! There is a rhythm and a spirit that lifts you and moves you." While traveling in the Middle East, John was influenced by the sounds and instruments of that region, like the sitar, and incorporated them into his compositions and style. "It's a pure sound."

John is always trying something different. Much of what he likes to do breaks from the mold that he is expected to fit into, considering the people with whom he's played. "People," he pauses, then clarifies, "record executives—are always asking for something 'complex.' 'You should do classical jazz. That's what you're known for.' It's easy to be complicated," he says, a little annoyed. "It's very hard to be simple. To keep things simple and offer something new and exciting—that's a challenge."

After six years as the bass player for the "Tonight" show, he left to work on other studio projects and formed the group Expectations, featuring the vocals of his wife, Jessica Williams. Far from conventional, they combined various jazz styles with rap and electronic sounds.

When he decided to try his hand at acting, he landed a role playing himself on six episodes of the television series "The Days and Nights of Molly Dodd." "They wanted jazz musicians to play these parts, for the main actors to feed off expressions that we use, the way we talk, and how we are.

"I got a great knowledge of acting. I got great lessons from Blair Brown [the star of the show]. She's incredible." John continues to audition for roles and takes acting lessons in spite of his hectic schedule.

When Arsenio Hall was offered the chance to host a syndicated talk show, he asked keyboarder Michael Wolff to put together a band for it. Wolff told Arsenio that he didn't want to audition bass players. He wanted John Bernard Williams. "Arsenio said, 'Well, that's fine,'" says Wolff. "He knew John B. from his Nancy Wilson days." In the late 1970s and early 1980s, Arsenio Hall was the opening act for Wilson. His first break.

In addition to John's bass for the show's Posse, "The John B. Williams Poetry Moment" has become a regular and well-received feature on "The Arsenio Hall Show." A straight-faced John reads outlandish and sometimes overly sentimental poems written by the show's writers, pausing occasionally to flash a glaring look at the snickering audience. The audience laughs harder at the out-of-character mock demand for respect. However, John will have you know that he writes real poetry on his own. "I get the muse from time to time," he concludes.

With a schedule that includes five nights a week on a talk show, various gigs around town, and his solo work, John tries to find time to help others who need some guidance and someone to look up to. In the past he has gotten together with other musicians and visited prisons.

"Me and some of the fellas do concerts in the penitentiaries. We spend some time talking to these guys. Some of them are kids. You hope they're going to get a second chance when they get out." His face is serious and thoughtful as he speaks. "We want to keep them from going back. It's no kind of life for a young soul, and many of these kids have good hearts.

"There are too many young people getting caught in a really bad game and listening to the wrong people. They have got to believe in *themselves*. When they see us come in and talk to them, and play music for them, they can't believe that somebody cares like that."

John and company reassemble after dinner at the Williams's cozy apartment on the outskirts of Hollywood. As the group settles, John pops a tape into the deck. A wicked combination of classic jazz and fusion pumps out of the speakers in his living room. "This is the new album we're shopping around," he informs his guests. Everyone is staring at the speakers, expecting the performers to materialize before them. It feels live.

The room is full of smiling faces and bobbing heads as everyone starts to hum the underlying melody. We are surprised when a familiar, liquid velvet voice starts to sing a love song. *"John!"* exclaims a female on one side of the room, "is that you?" A smile lights up his face. "Yeah," he says proudly.

He sings, too!

Kwame Tyrrell

As you enter the house with the strange green door, it's hard to know where to step. The floors and furniture are covered with amazing artifacts. Fifteen-year-old Kwame Tyrrell and his mother Gloria inhabit what can only be described as a live-in museum. Between the two of them they have collected virtually every form of African-American and Native-American memorabilia imaginable, from golliwogs, which are grotesque dolls mocking Black people, to actual slave shackles.

It's rare to find someone as young as Kwame with such an incredible collection of Americana. At four years old, Kwame would be safely tucked into the shopping cart seat while his mother pushed him along the grocery store aisles. When they got to the cereal section, Kwame immediately motioned to his mother that he wanted a box with a Black face on it. "He would say, 'That one. Gimme *that* one,'" recalls Gloria Tyrrell. "I would wonder, 'Is he that conscious so early?' He

always wanted somebody brown."

Ms. Tyrrell may have been slightly surprised, but she knew that it wasn't too unusual; she had been collecting memorabilia for years. Some of that interest and pride was bound to rub off.

Kwame has a very impressive collection of packages that feature dark-skinned people; his passion, however, is cereal boxes. He has everything from Walter Payton and Michael Jordan on Wheaties boxes to a rather unflattering minstrel face on Darkie toothpaste, which is sold in Europe and India. There are giant cutout Black Campbell's soup kids, Mr. T Cereal, and a Kellogg's Corn Flakes box with Vanessa Williams on the front, sporting her Miss America crown and an armful of roses. The collection is not only limited to big stars: There is a box of Cheerios with a tiny picture on the back of a Black boy who raised money for his homeless family by taking pictures. In the beverage department, there is Famous Amos's chocolate soda and a can of Cherokee Red featuring the face of a Native American in full headdress.

But these are not the only things that young Mr. Tyrrell loves. "I collect first day covers of important Black Americans like Martin Luther King, Harriet Tubman, and Frederick Douglass." First day covers are commemorative stamps on distinctive envelopes specially postmarked on the day

they are issued by the post office. He smiles broadly, showing his braces, then exclaims, "Oh yeah! I collect posters and buttons." Far from being ordinary posters or buttons, these political memorials chronicle much of the contemporary Black American experience. Kwame has buttons from rallies where the keynote speaker was Malcolm X, as well as Jessie Jackson presidential-campaign buttons.

"I think it's important to know about the people who fought for our rights. A lot of the kids in school don't understand. They just think it's stuff I collect." Kwame's face is serious for the first time. "I try to explain to them who these people are. Not everyone thinks it's important."

Many older items Kwame finds while traveling to different cities with his mother, who performs dramatic interpretations of famous Black Americans. "I've been to the Carolinas, Washington State, Florida, Pennsylvania—all over," he says. Besides being fascinated with memorabilia, Kwame designs much of the clothing he wears. Choosing from traditional and contemporary African patterns, he picks the styles and fabrics, then a friend of the family puts the clothing together. "Mom always says"—he affects a falsetto—"'That fabric is ugly, why don't you use the same one *I* used.' Later she comes back and says, 'Oh, Kwame! That's so beautiful. I

wish *I* had used that fabric.'" Kwame smiles.

Despite all his energy and enthusiasm, Kwame has to deal with the everyday challenge of sickle-cell anemia, a disease that is often as painful as it is debilitating. Kwame frequently finds himself missing school, which makes it tough to be just another kid growing up. "I have to be careful what I eat. Some foods are not good for you when you have sickle-cell. Most of that is stuff my mother doesn't want me to eat anyway," he says through a giggle.

Kwame follows a regimen that includes taking vitamins, minerals, and antibiotics, along with Tylenol, to help his body deal with the illness that has slowed his growth. Because it's a blood disease, many people—particularly kids—don't understand Kwame's illness. "They think I've got AIDS," says Kwame. "A lot of kids won't play with me because they think they can catch it. You can't catch sickle-cell!"

Despite all this, Kwame has a spirit that motivates others around him. Like any other fifteen-year-old, he's out playing, causing trouble, and collecting Teenage Mutant Ninja Turtle paraphernalia. But his true passions are his buttons, stamps, and Black memorabilia—his memorials to the Black American experience.

"It's about where I come from. It's about my family. It's about who I am."

Ladysmith Black Mambazo

As Joseph Shabalala and the other nine members of Ladysmith Black Mambazo traveled through New York on their first trip to the United States, they expected at any moment to be asked for their identification papers. "It was something new to me. Always at home we had to carry something like a passport," says Joseph in a soft melodic voice. Home is South Africa. "But it is not a passport; it's called dompass [pronounced *DOME-pass*]. It's a pass. Yes, you must always carry that thing. When you walk around, the police would always come and ask if you have the pass with you. You must show them that."

"And what if you don't have your pass?" I asked Joseph.

"Oh, then if you don't have it they take you into jail," he responds very calmly and nonchalantly. The white citizens of South Africa did not carry the pass, only the Blacks. "Ya, ya, that's all, that was very bad. But nowadays it's coming good. There are many things that are changing."

The end of the dompass is one of them.

It is hard to believe this gentle man, the members of his singing group and all the Black citizens of South Africa have been subjected to regular and incessant disrespect, violence, and abuse at the hands of a minority-run government, police force, and military. So much so that tribes turn on other tribes, and Black people begin fighting among themselves to establish what little superiority they have left in their world. The land Joseph and the other members of Ladysmith Black Mambazo love so dearly seems, to most outsiders, a place to flee and never return. But for the members of Black Mambazo, it is their inspiration, their reason to spread the joyous message they have to share with the world. It is their home.

"Our mission," Joseph explains, "is to spread our culture and its tradition. Also to encourage musicians and composers to let their music and their composition remain as close as possible to their African roots. We want to spread the gospel of love, peace, and harmony, and to identify our Lord as the answer to most questions. Because it's most difficult to answer all the questions," he says with a chuckle. "Yes."

Joseph speaks in a quiet, peaceful, but strong voice. His eyes dance with ideas and emotions as he talks. Even though his words come deliberately and carefully, they still roll off his tongue. Although some of the group's recordings have included musicians, the songs of Ladysmith Black Mambazo are mostly a cappella, performed without instruments. The percussion, bass lines, and melodic overtones are all provided by the voices, hands, bodies, and feet of the members of the group.

"This type of music, its origin is from Zulu dances and songs. It has evolved from its ancient form to its current style. The music I sing originated where I was born, in Ladysmith. Other people from other places, they began to know this type of music when they came together to work in the mines." Diamond mining is a huge industry in South Africa, and it is one of the main sources of income for the Black people, who are generally relegated to living in townships. Townships are not unlike the reservations Native Americans were forced to live on, separated from the rest of the country's population. To work in the mines, the men generally traveled far from their homes.

"The music was in Ladysmith for a long time," he continues. "We were singing together, boys, girls, old women, old grandfathers, and aunts. We used to sing together at home. But when we left our home and traveled to work in the mines, then we began to sing alone, only the men. The people who didn't know this type of music, they said, 'Oh! They just came together and composed songs in the mines.'"

Watching Ladysmith Black Mambazo perform is both hypnotic and exhilarating. There is no doubt that they are having a good time. They move their hands and feet in unison while looking at each other and laughing as they sing. Theirs are fluid motions: A leg kicks up powerfully and freezes, then comes down gently. The movement is based on the tradition of the music and came out of necessity. "When you did that at home—picked up your foot—the people are waiting for the sound of *stomping!*" explains the lead singer. "When we were stomping the floor while we were singing, neighbors complained. When we stomp the floor hard, the wooden floor breaks, even the cement floor cracks. Ya, and then neighbors would complain. We were avoiding those people's complaints." Joseph laughs mischievously. "Because of the action, people said, 'What are they doing? They are singing like us, but the action. They walk lightly on toes!'" The performers were given the name *Cothoza Mfana*, which means, "tiptoe guys."

As he speaks, it is hard not to feel as if Joseph Shabalala is actually singing. His voice is soothing and warm. "There was something moving in my mind—that I must compose songs and sing for the people and tell them what I want and encourage them, bring them their dignity. Because they lost the confidence—they lost the respecting, respecting each other, because of trouble. And I discovered the only way to conquer the world is to respect each other. Just bring the dignity. That's why I used to tell them about their kings, their warriors, and ask them to forgive each other and work together. And encourage them. Yes."

While they were very popular in their own country, the rest of the world had little knowledge of the group's existence. Then in 1985, American singer/songwriter Paul Simon traveled to South Africa looking for musical inspiration and artists to work with. Being a fan of Ladysmith Black Mambazo, he sought them out and asked Joseph if they would record with him. Joseph was amazed that a famous American singer would know who Black Mambazo was. He was delighted to accept the offer.

Simon wrote and recorded songs with Black Mambazo and released them on his "Graceland" album. It would have been very easy for him to go back to the United States and reap the benefits of this collaboration, leaving the South African musicians where he found them. On their own, it would have been virtually impossible for them to leave the country. Simon knew this might be the only opportunity for them to travel to the United States. He arranged to bring Black Mambazo to the States to tour with him. For that, the group is eternally grateful.

"I used to say Paul Simon was sent by God. I gave him the name *Vulindella* [pronounced *Voo-LIN-day-la*], which means 'he who opened the gate.' Because this is the only way to talk to the world and tell the people what's going on, what happened, what God gave us to share, our ideas, our music.

"Paul Simon came to South Africa and opened the gate for all musicians. And now we discover that we have many friends, lovely people who enjoy our music, who love our music very much. This is very nice!" Again comes the easy smile.

When they arrived in New York, Joseph, who is the spokesman for the group, had one big concern. "I was thinking about the language. That people would not understand what we were talking about!" He breaks into laughter. "I was not speaking English at home. I began to practice English in 1986. In 1987 there were many interviews. I understood what they say to me, but it was very difficult to answer them," he says, then lets out a long sigh. He pauses for a second and reflects.

"It was very difficult, very difficult."

Joseph now speaks excellent English, and the group has traveled to many countries all over the world—Australia, Japan, Switzerland, and Russia, to name a few. The singers of Black Mambazo enjoy these experiences. "Oh, we discover the people are very happy, and so far everything is going very well. I agree with those people who say music is universal. It's amazing. It knows no boundaries."

That lack of musical boundaries has caused many artists to seek out Ladysmith Black Mambazo, and the group has eagerly collaborated with all sorts of musicians, experimenting with sounds, styles, and textures. "Now, since we have many friends around the world, we like working together with other groups, like the Wynans, because I love very much the gospel music. Then the funk music man George Clinton; it was very nice working together with him. I like his music—funny things, wild rhythms carry on," he says, and starts to imitate the strange rhythmic sounds found on many George Clinton tracks. "These things sound like Ladysmith Black Mambazo! Because Black Mambazo, while they were singing, you could find a sound . . ." He makes more incredible sounds with his voice. "I like funny things, that's why I work together with George Clinton."

Joseph has an amazing ability to create sounds it seems no human could make. Part of it is simply because the words of his native language use sounds not heard in most languages familiar to our ears. But most of his ability is due to the fact that he is simply very talented.

Ladysmith Black Mambazo hope their work will inspire younger artists to develop their own styles. But, Joseph says, "lately I discover that they imitate Black Mambazo instead of learning and nurturing their own talent.

"That's why now we plan to build an indigenous-music academy in South Africa. In fact, I have been walking around South Africa, talking to the people, and they accept what I say." Joseph was given a large plot of land. "Now we are looking forward to planning how to build and to raise funds. Because now we want to plant our music and watch it grow in our country. Maybe the youth will come back to their roots, because they all ran away from it, from African music, and began to sing Western music. But now they are starting to come together and to make many groups, but they are imitating Black Mambazo. That's why we want to build the school and teach them how to produce their own music."

The group works well together, and much of that comes from their respect for Joseph, who instills in them a spiritual as well as an artistic commitment. Ladysmith Black Mambazo is made up of family and friends—three Shabalalas: Joseph, Ben, and Jockey (the fourth Shabalala, Headman, was killed in 1991); and two Mazibukos, who are cousins: Albert and Abednigo. And there are four friends: Geoffrey Mdletshe, Russel Mnthembu, Inos Phungula, and Jabulane Mwelase. They are all like brothers.

There is a saying in the Zulu language: *Umcolo uthokzisa abadabukileyo*—"Singing makes all the sad people happy because it is the voice of happiness."

Lisa Young

The sounds coming from the stone yard tucked behind the Cathedral are at once irritating and exhilarating. There is a constant din. Grinding, hammering, the sound of someone sanding a piece of stone by hand.

Every weekday morning, Lisa Young goes off to a job that most women would never think of doing. In fact, most men would not consider it either. Stonemasonry is an old and, until recently, dying art. The stonemasons of Cathedral Stoneworks are hoping to revive it and in the process are giving the European masters a run for their money.

One Hundred Tenth Street is known on the west side of Manhattan as Cathedral Parkway. At Cathedral Parkway and Amsterdam Avenue stands the one-hundred-year-old Cathedral of Saint John the Divine. A massive structure, it is still working its way toward completion, even though construction began December 27, 1892. If the Cathedral suddenly received one hundred million dollars, the remaining towers

could be completed in three to four years. Odds are it will take a lot longer than that.

"When I was little I wanted to be an astronaut. As kids we had these little one-piece pajamas, and they were our space suits. We used to go in our linen closet and pretend to be astronauts. It's hard to compare that to what I'm doing now."

As a stonemason, Lisa cuts and shapes the stone used to build columns, bases, and the areas of detailed stonework that will be added to the spires, doorways, and windows of the immense Cathedral. Her work keeps her covered in dust, but Lisa doesn't mind. "I like working with my hands. You can see what you're creating," she says.

In some ways this seems like the perfect job for Lisa Young. For the most part she is a quiet person who seems to be happiest when she is on her own. Behind the dusty goggles and smudged face mask protecting her from the stone dust, which finds its way into anything that isn't sealed, is the focused mind of this Harlem native. Lisa wasn't always focused, however, and she will tell you so.

"I dropped out of high school, I wasn't motivated," she explains with surprising honesty. "It was like, why go to school? If I'd known all the opportunities I could have had with an education, I would have stayed in school. But back then I just couldn't see it." Lisa spent a couple of years "hangin' out. Wasting years, wasting time. At that time, I preferred to stay home and watch 'The Munsters' or something like that," she says, laughing at herself.

When she finally decided to get her life going, she enrolled in a vocational school for electronics. The job it led to didn't work out for her; she was unhappy there. Lisa had been looking for an alternative when she caught a TV news story talking about the apprenticeship program at Cathedral Stoneworks. In 1979 New York businessman David Teitelbaum had put up some money not only to bring in skilled stonemasons to continue work on the Cathedral, which had stopped one week before Pearl Harbor was attacked in 1941, but to create a program to train local people to do stonemasonry.

Cathedrals have always been focal points of the communities they were built in. Teitelbaum wanted to bring that true sense of the Cathedral back to Saint John the Divine. He hired as apprentice stonemasons young people who lived, for the most part, in the local community, and watched as the building began to take on a new personality, both inside and outside. Earlier pieces featured faces of people who looked as if they were from Eastern Europe. That was because the artisans came from that part of the world. The new pieces look like people of African, Hispanic, and Asian descent. They are a reflection of people from the community and of the city. And as such, Lisa Young's work has become an important part of that transition.

"When people ask me what kind of work I do, I say I'm a stonecutter. It never fails to start a long conversation." Lisa says although her two older brothers are proud of her, "they wouldn't say so." And they like to tease her about her work. "'Oh, you're making tombstones,' they like to say."

The work at the stone yard is noisy and dirty. By the end of the day, Lisa's dark skin has become the color of the gray stone she has been shaping all day. "It's challenging. I like making things. I walk down the street and see buildings, and I notice they all have detail work on them that I can do or have done. These are things I would have walked past a few years ago and wouldn't have paid any mind. I see them now; it's like, 'Wow! That looks like the windowsill *I* did!'"

The tools Lisa uses range from simple hand tools like hammers, chisels, and sanding blocks to heavy power tools. To watch her work, you can see how easily this skill comes to her. She is completely engrossed in the piece she is working on—as though she is a part of it. "I was good at drawing and stuff like that, but never something as developed as this," she admits. "At first it was difficult; now it's easy. The more comfortable I was doing it, the better I got."

Lisa's first years of work at the stone yard were as an apprentice. After five years of work she is about to become a journeyman stonemason, but she isn't content to pat herself on the back and say, "I've made it." She plans to become an apprentice carver, which means she will be going back to being a trainee all over again, but this time in a different discipline of the art. Carving is a highly skilled aspect of detailed stonework. Having come this far, Lisa Young figures it is worth the extra time. She's almost certain she will want to be in this field for the rest of her life.

While most of her colleagues are men, there are several other women who now work at the stone yard. Several have come from other parts of the country as word of the stone yard project has made its way across the nation and abroad. All the stonemasons have different skills and specialties and are assigned jobs by the foreman accordingly. "I may be able to do the stone, but they may give it to a person that's been cutting a longer time than I have; it depends on the degree of difficulty."

The stone yard has increasingly become a source of quality stonework for clients across the nation and has begun competing against the established stonemasons in Europe for work overseas as well. One recent contract was to complete work on the Jewish Museum in New York City.

Lisa is using her earnings from her job at Cathedral Stoneworks to continue her education. She is a communications major at the College of New Rochelle. "I probably will stick with stonecutting, but this is just in case the stone market collapses," she says with a smile. "It's sort of like my insurance policy. If I plan to go to college ten years from now, lord knows how much the tuition is going to be. I figured that I wanted to get a college education, so I might as well get it now."

When I ask her what advice she would give to other young people, Lisa doesn't miss a beat. "Stay in school, try to go to college. The opportunities are there for you. If you can work wearing a suit—*do it!* If you could have a job in engineering, go for it. You can make more money doing less heavy work. I'm doing interesting work, dirty work, but interesting work. And what a way to make a buck," she says with a smile.

Ta-coumba Aiken

"It's a weakness of our country that's created this quick-fly-somewhere- else-and-leave-your-nest mentality. There's no nurturing of the community you come out of, and it's a big mistake. It's going to be costly to this country. The Italians try to hold on as much as they can. Different groups of Asians try to hold on. Clearly we're a melting pot, but you've gotta be able to respect each other's contribution. And if a group of kids don't respect where *they're* from, when they go someplace else, they're tearin' it up. And when they get to that other place, they might be adults with their fingers on the buttons to bombs. So it's a thing of getting them to have respect for themselves *now,* so later they can have respect for everybody.

"I guess I took that on as a responsibility of mine, coming out of Evanston, Illinois. I *ran* out of Evanston. It was like, 'Get me out of here as quick as possible.' But later on, I saw the benefits of being there with my parents.

"I do murals on grain elevators and walls showing the histories of towns and communities. I want to give those communities self-pride, for their kids to be able to come back and contribute something to a community that now they know has done something for them."

The soft-spoken Ta-coumba Aiken loved to draw as a child. "I got mats and little frames and stuff from an art store and gallery that was about ten or fifteen blocks away from my house. I drew on every piece of paper that we had; we didn't have a lot, but I drew on them anyway."

His first art exhibition came when he was six years old, an art show he hung in his basement. "Art wasn't my dad's favorite thing. He wanted me to be a lawyer." The owner of the neighborhood art store and gallery, where Ta-coumba would spend much of his free time, had encouraged him to keep up his interest in art and prove to his father how much he wanted to pursue it. Ta-coumba's father had made it very clear that art was to remain just a hobby.

To publicize his art show, Ta-coumba had his older brother help him make flyers, which he gave out to people, telling them to make some copies and give those to their friends. The day of the show, Ta-coumba noticed a line of people outside the kitchen window, wrapping around the side of the house, as he and his family ate dinner. "My dad looked out the window and said, 'Boy, you are in trouble now! What in the world did you tell these people? I ain't givin' away nothin'!'

"'I just sent them this flyer!' I had looked at it but I couldn't *read* it, so I was afraid to give it to him. I thought maybe my brother had played a trick on me. My brother looked at me like, 'I don't know.'

"My dad said, 'What are they here for?' And my mother said, 'Maybe to look at his artwork.' That was the *first* time she backed me up about my art. So my father told me, 'I'm not opening up my doors until we finish dinner.' So then it was like, chow down! I was downstairs with a stomachache."

A woman, whom Ta-coumba never saw again, had asked to go down to the show before they finished eating. She was a relative of a friend, and a well-known artist. She told Ta-coumba's dad she had a plane to catch but wanted to see the work by the artist she had heard so much about. She was allowed in. Unbeknownst to Ta-coumba, while she was alone in the basement, she changed all the prices on his artwork—adding zeros, and raising the prices from five cents to five dollars.

"At the end of the show there were pictures all over the place. I had hundreds of pictures, because all I ever did was draw. My dad said, 'I'm sorry you didn't sell anything.' I said, 'Dad, I *did* sell stuff.' I showed him the cigar box my brother was watching. He pulled the nail out of it. It popped open and there was all this money. I had made $657.36. The show was up for three days from six P.M. to eight P.M., so it was the equivalent of over one hundred dollars an hour.

Ta-coumba kept practicing and developing his skills, because the one thing he knew he needed to do was learn how to draw people's bodies. "I could draw a portrait of somebody and it would look like them. The line would be there—minimal lines, but it would be there. But when it came to doing the body, it turned into a stick figure automatically. I hadn't looked at anybody's body.

"I remember when I got some *Playboy* magazines from underneath my dad's car seat, and I'd take the centerfolds and a piece of oatmeal paper, and I'd tape it together and draw them in crayon. The human body was just *fascinating* to me because I didn't know *any* girls that were shaped like that. I would buy those bodybuilder magazines to draw from. Anything I could get my hands on. I used to keep my drawings under this couch–converted bed kind of thing in the basement, 'cause I always drew in the basement. One day I was pulling them out to draw, and I noticed they were gone.

"I didn't freak out because they were *gone*, I freaked out because they were *found*. And my mother, being this religious entity, I just knew *she* hadn't found them, because I would have heard about it. So I asked my dad, 'What did you do with my drawings?' He said, 'What do I want your drawings for?' I dropped the subject and went to my brother.

"When I told my brother what the drawings were he freaked. He couldn't believe I was drawing pictures of naked women, and he was certain I was going to be killed by our parents if they found out. Especially because I stole my father's *Playboys*.

"So it turned out my mother had found them and got rid of them. I was sitting at the kitchen table one day, and she simply said to me, 'You know, sometimes even when you're really, really good, once you know it, you don't need to do it anymore.'

"I said, 'Yes ma'am.' So I *knew* they were good!" Ta-coumba laughs at the thought.

The Twin Cities area eventually became home for Ta-coumba, as he found life less hectic in St. Paul than in many other metropolitan areas, while still maintaining access to the things that big cities have. Minnesota quickly came to greet his talents with open arms, as he collaborated with other artists and became a much sought-after art instructor and "inspirer" for young people.

The mural is Ta-coumba's passion. Big surfaces cause his mind to reach farther for ideas. And there was one idea that had been in his mind for a long time. "Anne Christensen, whom I had dealt with when I was an artist-in-residence in Olivia, Minnesota, teaching art to kids, contacted me because this arts council wanted to do a national competition to get a mural on a wall in Good Thunder, Minnesota. They wanted me to help them organize the contest. I told them, 'This is going to take a long time. When do you want to get this done?' And they said that fall, and here it was May or June. I told them it was going to be a little difficult.

"I explained that the easiest way to do it would be to get the designs from the entrants already scaled, and you then choose the winner from the designs. The first prize would be the mural. So Anne said, 'Okay, but how do you draw a grain elevator?' I said, 'A *what?*' She said, 'A grain elevator.'"

Grain elevators are used to load, unload, clean, mix, and store grain. Often the grain is unloaded from trucks and stored in huge bins.

"I said, 'I've been looking for a grain elevator to do a mural on for *thirteen years*. I want to do the history of America. The farm, people could see how farmers get "dogged" all the time, how nobody respects what they do. You could take a loaf of bread, and it would start with wheat, then you show how it becomes bread. You see all these faces of the people of the community. Amber waves of grain, you know, the whole deal.' I was talking so fast because it was my dream.

"She said, 'That's a great idea!' But I said, 'You can't use it!' Then I asked her, 'This competition I'm setting up for you, I'm setting up for somebody else to *win?*' Then I told her, 'Here are the names of five experts. They will lead you through this process. I'm getting out of it now so I can compete. And when I compete and win, I'll do the mural on your grain elevator.'

"She said, 'I don't understand how you're going to win . . .'

"'I'm going to compete and I'm going to *win*.' She called me back four or five weeks later and said, 'This is Anne Christensen.' I told her I didn't think we should be talking. She said, 'Ta-coumba, we're not going to do the competition.' My heart just fell as far as it could go. It was in the ground.

"'It was going to take too long, and it would cost too much money. Part of the Minnesota Pride thing is that it has to be done this year. We have another solution, though.'

"I told Anne, 'There is no other solution. It's a grain elevator, that's what you should be doing. It's the perfect representation of the farm community for a mural—' She interrupted me and said, 'We want *you* to do it.' And then I dropped the phone."

It seems as though everyone in Minnesota knows of Ta-coumba's grain elevator in Good Thunder. It is his interpretation of the history of a small community that typifies the growth of American towns. Each section of the structure features people who do different types of jobs and contribute to the town. The piece, which he began in the summer of 1987, took him seven weeks to complete. At its highest point, it features a portrait of Chief Good Thunder.

Several of the residents of the town of 650 helped Ta-coumba by filling in large areas of paint, supplying lunch, and offering moral support. In return he used many of their faces as models for his mural.

"I did a scale drawing based on the size of the panels that were already there when they built the grain elevator. The panels measured two feet across, two and a half feet high. Nobody knew what size the grain elevator was, so I counted the panels up and across and was able to formulate the area of the walls. I don't know how I did it. I had never done anything like that before in my life," he says of the approximately seven-story building.

"I knew I *had* to do it." There was only one thing that made his dream-come-true a test of his will, and even today it makes him laugh.

"I'm scared of heights."

Paul Adams

"First impressions are usually lasting impressions. I really think that the simplicity of what we do is overlooked."

The simplicity he's referring to is the essence of Paul Adams's philosophy of running Providence-St. Mel, a private school on the west side of Chicago. When he became principal of the high school, which was then run by the Catholic Archdiocese of Chicago, Providence-St. Mel was in trouble. To shore up financially strapped Providence High School, the archdiocese merged it in 1968 with St. Mel, run by the Christian Brothers. They tried to operate two schools in one building. Girls on the first and second floors, boys on the fourth and fifth. The third floor was a buffer zone.

"It was an unhappy marriage," Principal Adams reports. "Each group had a different door to come in and different administrations. It just didn't work, and it did more harm to the school than good."

Ten years later, the archdiocese decided to cut the school's subsidies. The neighborhood was changing. Crime in the area was high, the cost of running the school was high, and enrollment was getting lower. Most of the students were not graduating, and few of those who did went on to college. Without the financial help from the church, it was very likely the school would be finished. Paul Adams did the one thing he thought would work—he went to the press. When he explained to the public the dilemma the school faced, donors came forward to help save it.

"They want to do a thesis on it. They want ten consultants to sit down and write a report that nobody's going to read," says Paul incredulously. "The objective is to make sure these students go through an academic environment that is competitive, that will get them a job—and that's called survival. I mean, this is real simple and everybody wants to make it complicated!"

The key to change at Providence-St. Mel was discipline—discipline for the students, and the teachers as well. Instructors working with different rules cause confusion and chaos. "Basically, the rules are quite simple—you do as you're told, now, not later. If you can't conform to the rules, you leave. I think it ends up being a level playing field for all the students, because the rules are applicable to everyone in the school. We don't have any favorites, we don't allow any people to have clout.

"Each year the administration will go over the handbook of the rules and regulations to find out the ones that are not working and get rid of them," explains Paul. "If it's just not a good rule or if it's not enforceable, we take that out and then we review the rules with the students."

Often, the best way to deal with problems is in a way everybody can understand. "We're very strict about attendance, tardiness. For example, if youngsters are tardy five times, unexcused, there is a two-hour detention and a ten-dollar fine. You get five more, we double it to twenty dollars and a three-hour detention. You do it again, it costs you forty dollars and a four-hour detention. After that you need to see the principal or some administrator, because we're not trying to raise money through the tardy fines. If you really don't understand it by then, something's missing and you need to be somewhere else."

Although there are no uniforms worn by the students, there is a dress code: no earrings for boys, no short skirts for girls, no creative patterns cut into people's hair, no torn-up jeans. "We try everything to keep the focus on why we're here."

Despite the beautiful park right across the street from the school, Providence-St. Mel is not in a great neighborhood. In fact, if you walk down either side of the school, or a block north or south, you will find the familiar signs of a neighborhood gone sour. Vacant lots appear like bald spots, and abandoned buildings sit, drafty and forbidding, just steps away from this proud building.

The gang problem is something that has been handled well by Paul and his staff. "The students have to be in a safe environment. See, the philosophy of the gang is intimidation. So we intimidate them, we shine the light on 'em."

"We keep in good contact with the police department, keep in contact with political people—we try to be a role model in the community. And I think, even the so-called bad guy will respect us. If one of our kids is harmed or attacked by someone—and it's rare—we're gonna insist that a police report be made. I'm gonna insist that I be in court. I go to court when parents don't go. You know, it's unbelievable when I think about it. I have gone to court probably in ninety-five percent of the cases. And in ninety-five percent of those cases parents haven't shown up. But we were there. If I was not there, some representative of the school was there. Our presence says, 'You can delay this case as much as you want to, but somebody is gonna be here, so we might as well get it over with.'"

There is no way Paul Adams can be accused of lack of commitment. He moved into the school building (the site used to be a convent, with quarters for the nuns) when the security guard began seeming like just a way to throw money out the window. "We were losing thirty thousand dollars' worth of equipment. I said, 'This is crazy.' I was divorced at the time—still am—so I moved in the building." The equipment stopped vanishing.

"You know, we're not going out here to do anything stupid"—Paul laughs—"but we are standing up, and we're not letting people run over us. The youngsters feel safe in this building—this is our turf. We control it."

Providence-St. Mel has added classes down to grade five, growing from around 300 students to 540. Well over 90 percent of the graduates go to college. Paul would like to see classes from kindergarten to twelfth grade. "The kind of structure we have should be offered at an early age, because the most formative years are birth to five."

Providence-St. Mel costs money for the students to attend, but there are various ways those expenses are covered. The tuition for the high school is $2,800, and elementary school is $2,200, but it costs Providence-St. Mel $4,000 to keep each child in school for a year. And even though 35 percent of the students don't pay any tuition at all, the expenses manage to get paid. Most of the students are from low-income families. "We have about twenty to twenty-five students from these families that we pick up in the morning—they're fifth and sixth graders. We keep them in school, we tutor them till about five o'clock, and we take 'em home. The expenses not covered by tuition—we go out and raise money ourselves.

"Because of the reputation of the school," Principal Adams explains, "we could easily say, 'We are gonna raise the tuition to five thousand, six thousand bucks, and if you can't pay it, tough!' Then we become an elite Black school. I don't think we need that. Because if you're really gonna do something about poverty, you have to get those people who are living in it. See, the challenge is to take the ones that don't have, and give them the tools to have. And that has been the biggest challenge ever. You know, we have a girl who's from the Cabrini Green housing complex. Her family has very little money. She's on full scholarship at Phillips Academy in Andover, Massachusetts. We have kids from the west side who are now doctors, lawyers, teachers.

Give the opportunity to people who want the opportunity. See, this school is really not for the needy, it's for the greedy."

The school's summer program was started by one of Providence-St. Mel's patrons. At first, forty or fifty students spent time at prep schools and colleges outside of Chicago, from Harvard to Arizona State to Oxford University in England. Paul remembers that first year of the project. "I kind of waited until the end of the summer with my fingers crossed, and the reports came back and they were all good. So we wanted to do this again. We called it 'Soul.' And this past year, we had almost two hundred youngsters in programs all over the country."

This is a wild experience for kids who have never left Chicago. "We've got kids that fly into Heathrow or 'gay Pa-ree,' and this is their first time there." Kids go camping in places they only saw on TV. "At the end of the summer to see these kids come back . . . You walk down the hall and there's T-shirts and smiles, and their heads are a little higher, they're much more confident. I think every school in the country should do it."

The halls and grounds of Providence-St. Mel are immaculate. The grass is perfectly trimmed, and the halls are quiet during class and completely graffiti free. Like the school, Paul Adams would like to see the neighborhood clean and proud. He decided that the school should set the example, so it has been steadily buying up nearby property. A separate corporation set up for this purpose will oversee the development of about 250 new units of housing around a six-square-block area. "Now, I thought," says Paul, "who wants to move over here

because of new housing—nobody! Why would you move to hell because there's new housing? I needed to attract young couples to the neighborhood. If you attract young couples, where are they gonna send their kids to school? So I thought we'd better open up the best grammar school/kindergarten in the country. And if they moved for that purpose, then they would be investing in this community for the next sixteen to seventeen years.

"We need to change the economy of this neighborhood." Instead of knocking buildings down, Providence-St. Mel will rehab the ones they can save and rebuild when it's appropriate. Prices for the housing will be kept low so that those who want to rent can stay and those who want to buy may be able to afford to. "Now some people are going to be displaced," he adds with a matter-of-fact shrug. "I hope they *are*—they don't need to be here. But we are not trying to turn this into a white neighborhood. I hope that many of my graduates will move back."

Not everybody likes the way Paul Adams does things. They say he's too tough, he's a tyrant, and that fining children is out of line with what a school should do. The problem with that argument is, his approach seems to be working. Providence-St. Mel is one of the most respected schools in the country, even earning Principal Adams a phone call and personal visit from former-President Reagan. "When I get all that together, then I think my job has been done. We will have proved that you don't have to gentrify the neighborhood. Within the inner city, Black people and Black students can fortify their community."

Michael Williams

For millions of people watching courtroom dramas, or the events of actual court cases, there is a fascination with the courtroom reporter—the man or woman sitting quietly in the corner of the room tapping away on the weird little typewriter, most commonly known as a transcripter. The transcripter is rather square in shape, and fairly small; the keys look somewhat off when compared to a typewriter's keys, and the paper streams out the back into a tray like a calculator. The job of the courtroom reporter is to listen and to write down everything that is said during a hearing or trial. Michael Williams is one of those people sitting to the side of the room, quietly hammering away on his transcripter.

Michael started his own firm to provide the services of court reporters, not only because he saw a great deal of discrimination in the business, but also to gain business opportunities. Legal reporting was not his first career choice. Michael was planning on becoming a doctor.

"I'd always wanted to be a doctor," he explains in his cheerful manner. "When I went to college, I didn't feel I had the passion for medicine necessary to be successful as a medical student *or* a doctor. I came out after a year and a half and traveled for about seven months, staying with my buddies until I ran out of money. After I had been home for a while, my parents started saying, 'What are you going to do? You just can't hang around here and do *nothing.*'"

Michael was interested in acting, so he thought he would pursue that. But at about the same time, a court reporter he knew told him about reporting. He could learn reporting, and once he started working, he would have plenty of time to pursue his acting career because he could make his own hours. Michael took the test for reporting school and did very well. After taking classes, he found he enjoyed the challenge. It changed his career plans completely.

Michael became skilled in the various forms of reporting, and after his graduation, began working as a court reporter in his home state of New Jersey. "My mother always said, 'If you can make it in New York you can make it anywhere,' so I figured that would be the proving ground for me. New York is one of the toughest states for reporting. You may do well anyplace else, but once you can work in New York, you're a master, because in New York City you've got everything. People talk faster and you've got all sorts of accents to deal with." But those weren't the only things that made Michael see that being a successful court reporter in New York was going to be difficult.

"There are two types of reporters. There are the 'official' court reporters, who are hired by the state. That's the reporter you see in the courtroom. Then there are the free-lance reporters, who do what I do. We are the reporters who take discovery work, or work before a case gets to trial. So most of our work is in the depositional stage. We also cover arbitrations, stock meetings, town hall meetings, and even tape transcriptions.

"I wanted to work with this gentleman who was an official reporter and was starting a free-lance agency," Michael explains. "And he said to me, 'Mike, no one is going to hire a Black reporter.' Just like that. Well, that was the best thing he could have said to me, because I realized at that moment that this is a very racist field. That statement motivated me to think, *someone* is definitely going to hire me. I'm going to make sure that I am *so* good that even when they don't want to give me work, they'll have to because I'm going to do a damn good job! They'll have to cut off their nose to spite their face. And when it comes down to money, *most* businesses will even put aside their prejudices.

"I knew my background would make me more solid in this field. I had more education than some of these men who *owned* the businesses. But they would look at my face, and you could see the stereotypes running through their minds. 'Is he going to comprehend proper English? Is he going to understand polysyllabic words? Is he going to understand punctuation?' You could *see* it," Michael says with some residual animosity.

"When I got out of school I knew I was good. I understood that I was the new kid on the block, but I looked around and thought, 'Nobody ever gives you an unsolicited compliment around here!' They always wanted me to be at a higher level than I was, no matter how high I got. I looked around me and said to myself, 'Nobody seems to be working as hard as *I* am, but they're telling them *they're* great.' Meanwhile, I'm 'okay.'

"One day I got mad and I decided to stay late at the office. At my office then, the guys were twenty or twenty-two years old. So I'm looking at their transcripts and comparing them to mine. I must have read about ten or so. When I finish I'm saying, 'Hey! These aren't so great!' So I said to myself, no man's opinion of me will ever mean more than what I know about myself, as long as I'm truthful to myself.

"From that day on I made up my mind that I was going to have an agency of my own. One: because I wanted to give African-Americans in this field something they weren't getting, and as far as I was concerned that was an even shake. Two: because I wanted to be sure that the African-Americans who got into the field would be better prepared than any other court reporter in the business—especially if they were going to work for me."

Despite the racism that he saw in the field of court reporting, he found his skills were hard for the major employers in New York to pass up. He knows this firsthand because he's worked for many of them, primarily on a free-lance basis. Occasionally his encounters with these employers, while annoying, became quite humorous in their own ironic way.

"I worked for this one firm and the owner said to me, 'Michael, you can end up making a lot of money in this field.' So," says Michael with a charming smile, "I'm wondering what he thinks is a lot of money, because he doesn't know what *I* think is a lot of money. The guy added, 'You could end up making fifty thousand dollars a year.'

"What stood out in my mind were the words *end up*. Then he said, 'You can have your own apartment, a car, and nice clothes.' Now, he thought he was giving me a compliment. I took that as an insult, because first of all, to 'end up' making fifty thousand dollars a year says that is the figure African-American males should be content with, even pleased. *He's* making one hundred thousand a year. *End up* making fifty thousand—I want to *start out* making fifty thousand," Michael says as he starts to laugh.

"Of course I want a nice apartment—so I can have a place to take a woman to have sex, because as you know, *all* Black men live with their mamas. Maybe he didn't *say* all that, but that's what he was saying in *my* mind!" Michael cracks up at this, laughing harder than before. "Bring a woman home to your nice place, in your nice car, have sex with her, and tell her you make fifty grand a year, with a nice suit on! What else could you want?

"I said to myself, I can't work somewhere where they're going to put a cap on my salary, and they're going to cap my salary because of the color of my skin. I knew then that I'd rather work for myself.

"I had worked for a small agency owned by a woman who really handcrafted her people. I used my experience working for her as the model for my own business. She sat you down and told you, you had to correct your own work and you had to bind it when it was completed. When I tell people I'm a reporter—*I'm a reporter*. I can do everything. When kids come out of the schools now, they use the computer and they don't really do anything."

The next step was research. How do you start your own reporting business? Michael needed to know things like how to find clients and what kind of fees were being charged for various services. So he'd ask. He would go to the billing department and find out what a case he was working on cost a client. He asked what kind of package of services that came with. When they told him, he'd write it down. Then he would call other shops and, posing as a potential customer, find out what they would charge.

"I wrote everything down in a book until I felt I had enough information to set myself up. I then had to figure out how I was going to be able to put out my product. I wanted to be computerized, so I looked into that and leased a system. I figured out how much money I'd need to get my supplies and to pay my own bills. The best thing was, I figured I could do this from my home, especially since there was no way I could afford an office."

Working from his home, Michael was able to receive calls for the reporting jobs and then go to the locations where he would be recording the events. If he was not able to cover a job, Michael would farm the work out to other reporters he had met, or he would subcontract the jobs out to other reporting firms he felt good about doing business with. Though the reporters on his roster are primarily Black, he works with reporters of all ethnicities. He has certainly learned *his* lesson from his encounters on the way up.

Another type of transcribing service Michael provides is closed-captioning, also known as real-time reporting. The transcripter is hooked directly into a computer, maybe a laptop, so that a deaf litigant can *see* exactly what is being said on a screen at his or her table.

Michael Williams doesn't plan only to expand his company around the world, he wants to do something for his community with some of the fruits of his labor. "I want to create a place where young African-American males can come and grow as individuals," he says of his plans to build a retreat for inner-city kids.

Michael appreciates how his sense of self-respect allowed him to accomplish all he has, and he hopes by teaching young people to work with the land, in a new environment, they may gain something. "If young people develop a respect for the land, if they are proud of the work they *do* to maintain the land, I think it will help kids learn to respect themselves. Respecting myself was the only way *I* could have come so far.

"I want for my Black sisters and brothers the same thing I want for myself, and that's to be the best person they can possibly be."

Danny D. Wilson is preparing himself for greatness. He is doing his homework by learning all he can about television production. Part of doing that homework meant doing something difficult—leaving the familiar surroundings of his hometown, New Orleans, Louisiana.

There is a vision that is driving Danny, and in realizing it he wants to make a contribution to the Black community. "Documentaries," he says definitively. "I love history, and history is part of documentary. I mean, you don't have to be dead to have a documentary made about you, although most people say, 'Oh well, that person's dead. Let's make a documentary.' My thing is to educate."

Danny works in St. Paul, Minnesota, as a free-lance news producer. His job is to get the facts of the story and put them together with pictures and words for the viewing audience. Dan didn't start off with TV. As a kid he always had an interest in being a disc jockey.

"I got a taste of the business when I got into the tenth grade and a buddy of mine was doing part-time work at a radio station. He used to sneak me in at night 'cause he worked the late-night shift. He showed me how to run the controls. I did that for a while and one day he said to me, 'You oughta come in for an audition.'

"I went for the audition and it didn't work out, so I left it alone for a while. About four years later I went back again. My friend was gone by that time, so it was up to me to say, 'Hey, this is what I wanna do.'"

When he was in college he decided to apply for a job at the local R and B radio station. The day before he went in, he called and got the name of the program director, Jay Stevens. Upon arriving he asked to see Stevens, but without an appointment he was told to fill out an application and leave it with the receptionist. While he waited, someone else, "who must have had an appointment," Danny says, asked to see Mr. Stevens. The receptionist asked him to wait and said Mr. Stevens would be right out.

"By that time, I had finished my application, so I had to make a choice. Either I was gonna turn in my application and leave, or corner this guy when he came out. That was the only thing I had to do.

"I let him meet his guest, and before he went back to his office I said, 'Excuse me, Mr. Stevens, my name is Danny Wilson. I'm interested in an internship here—I will do anything. I want to learn the business, can you help me?'

"And he said, 'Yeah, I like that.' He was impressed with my directness. He told me, 'I need you to get a letter or note from one of your professors at school saying that you will receive credit for doing it. And as soon as you do that, we'll start.' At that time the station didn't have internships there, because the internship program had just started in my school. But I was able to get the note. I started the next week in production."

Danny bounced back and forth between two rival radio stations. As program directors changed, staffs got fired and new ones were hired. With each new job, he was getting another experience in a different position. Though it took him a while, he finally became on-air talent instead of a studio engineer.

His interest in radio was beginning to wane when Danny received a notice from the National Black Media Coalition of Louisiana telling him of a position at a public television station, WYES. "I figured I'd try it out. But before all that happened, I got selected by producer/director Warrington Huddlin, of the Huddlin brothers, to work on my first film as a intern in Dayton, Ohio."

When he returned to New Orleans, he found there was a cameraman trainee position at WYES. "There weren't any qualifications for the job; it was basically, 'Hard-working person wanted. Will train you.' That November I had the job. I beat out one hundred and four people."

Danny had the advantage of working in a city where unions didn't restrict what he could do. Although he was a cameraman, he got his hands into a bit of everything. This gave him great knowledge to apply to his current aspirations. "Not only was I a cameraman, I was a set designer and I had to paint. I had to work lights, I had to work audio. We went on different shoots because this particular station had one of the best mobile trucks in the state.

"My first big shoot was working with MTV during Mardi Gras, and I met Keenen Ivory Wayans when his first movie, *I'm Gonna Git You Sucka*, came out. I've even got a picture at home taken with him. That was cool."

Chances to work with the cable sports network ESPN came along; a shoot with Hammer for BET. All these things from one job. "So as the apprenticeship went on, my opportunites got better and my skills improved in the production end of it. But I never wanted to be a cameraman, because their jobs are vanishing now except for the field-camera operators. Television stations are getting into this robotics thing now, where they can control studio cameras from the control room."

Danny knew to survive in the quickly changing world of television he would have to find something else he wanted to do. A former coworker, David Jones, had moved on to an independent station to produce a magazine show like "20/20." Dan knew he had nothing to lose by asking David if he could produce a piece for his show. "He said, 'Yeah, sure Danny, sure, what do you wanna do it on?' I told him I wanted to do a story on those guys that have those giant car stereo systems that they spend thousands and thousands of dollars on to make the systems go louder and louder. So he said, 'Yeah! That'd be good. Go ahead, do it.'

"It just so happened one of the stations that I used to work for was holding this 'boom box' car contest called Crank It Up. Guys from all over the country brought their cars to the community of New Orleans East."

It was perfect timing. David got Danny a camera, and Dan was off to put his story together. It was basically putting sound bites and scenes together. Sound bites are short, interesting quotes from the people Danny was interviewing. "I didn't have to do any scriptwriting or anything like that. It aired and I got a good response from it.

"I was the commentator; it was like the Spike Lee kinda thing. I had my little Brooklyn hat on and my Lakers shirt on. I stuck my head in their face onscreen. It was well organized, and it ran for about three minutes."

The apprenticeship was over, and without a guarantee of a job, Danny approached Peggy Scott-LaBorde, a producer at WYES, about doing some more work. She offered him a chance to produce a piece about a sculptor at Xavier University. *Bor*-ring! he thought. Dan told her he had already produced a piece, and she said to him, "No you didn't. That wasn't a produced piece. All you did was put sound bites together. Danny, its more intense than that. You've gotta do research, you gotta write a script, you gotta edit it. You gotta do all that."

To his surprise, sculptor John Scott was not boring. Danny came back with four tapes full of stuff from his interview. Now, he had to transcribe them—write down everything interesting that was said, so he would have a record of what was talked about and when it was said. This would help him pick out information on the videotape and assemble it for the final story. As much as he hated the tedious process, it was another learning experience for Danny. Soon he developed computer skills and was able to write his transcriptions in a more professional manner with the word processor. With each story he produced, Peggy helped him a little less.

His move to Minnesota has given him a chance to work in a larger market with better facilities. His skills are becoming sharper and his goal is now clear to him. "Everybody says, 'Well, I guess you wanna be another filmmaker.' My medium will be television films. That's my market.

"As the films go to theaters," Danny says, "the prices are going up. People are waiting for them to come to video now. Studios are turning them into videos two months or three months after they're released.

"I'm not saying that I couldn't compete in that market," he adds. "There's a lot of room, but I don't see many Black filmmakers trying to get to people through TV. Our community, the Black community, watches more television than anybody. And if my stories are going to be seen by anyone, I think the television-watching people oughta see them.

"I want to take the novels that Black writers are writing and turn them into films, because unfortunately, everybody doesn't read. It's a chance to bring some good literature and strong culture *by* our own, *to* our own. Just like *Roots* was a novel before it became a movie. It captured a huge audience. I think my idea will work." It can't hurt to try. There are certainly enough *trashy* miniseries on television as it is.

Minnesota may seem like an odd place for a young Black man from the South to move to. Of the 6 percent nonwhite population in Minneapolis, only 2 percent are Blacks. Dan decided he would challenge himself as aggressively as possible. Living in a community that is very different from the one he grew up in, and a huge physical distance away from it, makes it that much harder to give up and head back home.

Confidence is the thing that Danny exhibits to any person he meets. He understands his own ability and has a desire to succeed. "For you to survive in this world, you gotta have a confidence level; you gotta have confidence that you can go out there and take on a challenge. You know, I got this gig in Minneapolis, even though its not *the* gig I would like, but I felt that I could send my résumé almost two thousand miles away from home and they would dig it. I don't have a problem going to people like Jimmy Jam or Terry Lewis and saying, 'Hey man, you all need to hire me.'

"You just gotta believe in yourself. And I believe in myself. It's not that I'm cocky or anything. People talk negatively about Bryant Gumbel—and I *love* Bryant Gumbel—and it's not that he's cocky. It's that the man has *confidence*, and there's a big difference between confidence and cockiness."

The exuberant Danny Wilson removes the familiar Brooklyn Dodgers cap from his head and wipes his brow. "I've been blessed to make a way out of no way. And if the folks in New Orleans don't want to give me a shot, then maybe I'll get a shot up here, and if it doesn't work out, that doesn't mean I'm gonna go home. I'll just have to wait it out and see what happens, you know, and just deal with it. Like the slogan says, 'Just do it.'"

Barbara Brandon

In her typical style there's just a head. A young dreadlocked Black woman is adjusting her headphones. She is listening to a speech by Martin Luther King, Jr., and she has a very peaceful look on her face. "Finally," she says, "the man who helped raise the consciousness of a nation gets a day in his honor.

"Yet on Friday," she says as she removes her headphones, "my boss announced, 'The office will be *open* on Martin Luther King Junior Day.'

"Then he added, 'If any Blacks want to take off, you may—after all, it's *your* holiday.'"

The young woman looks stupefied and says to us, "Now am I wrong, or is he missing the point?"

Barbara Brandon's "Where I'm Coming From" is a slice of life from the Black woman's point of view. The topics she tackles range from

dating to respect for women in the workplace to Martin Luther King, Jr.'s birthday.

For Barbara, her dad's cartoon strip, "Luther," was an inspiration and a source of allowance money. After her father, Brumsic Brandon, would ink in the outlines of his characters, Barbara would put in the shading and add other finishing touches. But for her, getting a strip rolling was not that easy, and there were plenty of distractions. While she is the eighth Black cartoonist ever syndicated in the mainstream press, she is the first Black *woman* to have her cartoon syndicated in the mainstream press. Her style is definitely influenced by her father's and that of cartoonist Jules Feiffer. Feiffer also used the technique of having his characters talk directly to the audience, something that Barbara's characters do on a regular basis.

After studying at Syracuse University she eventually decided to show her cartoon ideas to various publications. One of those publications was a magazine called *Elan*. They loved her work. Unfortunately, their love for her work did not keep the magazine afloat, and they folded before ever publishing a single piece.

A year later, in 1983, Barbara sent her work to *Essence* magazine. "They were like, 'This is great! It's an interesting style and a great point a view. How would you like to be our fashion and beauty writer?'" Barbara laughs an infectious kind of laugh that seems to come easy to her. Although it was not what she wanted to do, money was tight and the idea of a regular paycheck was very inviting. So she took the job, and put her cartoon ladies on hold.

"I was into it! I got to travel all over the place. A week or two in the Caribbean to be on a photo shoot. There were lots of perks," she says of her time at *Essence*. "I was overwhelmed at *Essence*. There was really no time to work on the strip. Being the fashion and beauty writer, I was responsible for a lot of pages. Even though it's fluff copy, it was a lot. If there was a lull I didn't want to do anything. It wasn't until my father started mentioning the *Detroit Free Press* was looking for a strip that I pushed it again."

Once "Where I'm Coming From" got picked up, Barbara returned to being a cartoonist full time—which is an odd way to put it. Cartoonists don't work regular nine-to-five days. Barbara typically works one week out of the month to get about two months' material. That doesn't include the time she spends reading everything she can get her hands on and watching lots of television (she admits she's a TV junkie) to help her develop ideas for her characters.

It became time, Barbara felt, to push to get a syndicate that would sell her strip to hundreds of publications for her. "When I decided to try to get a syndicate, I put *Essence* on the back burner. I was lucky to have a father in this business because I was a little more sophisticated on how to approach it. I knew syndicates put out press kits on cartoons and sent them to papers, so I put together a press kit and sent it to the *syndicates*." A press kit is a package of information, in this case about Barbara and her cartoon strip. The kit contains everything that people who might be interested in Barbara Brandon's work

would possibly want to get their hands on.

"I'd make them up as they were needed. I just bought a black folder, and I took some characters down to the copy place, copied them on label paper, and cut them out. I made a little "Where I'm Coming From" logo, put it on label paper. I stuck that label on, put the characters on so their faces were all over the place. Inside I had a letter to the editors and some samples.

"I put my fan letters and stuff in there. I added a few articles that were written about me here and there—anything I could put into the kit. I'm not really trying to sell *myself*, I'm trying to sell the comic strip."

This simple act of self-promotion began to pay off for Barbara Brandon. Calls came in from editors at several papers, and soon she found the various newspaper syndicates were calling *her*. "I hate doing that thing where you call people and say, 'Hi, I don't want to bug you, but I was wondering if you got the stuff I sent you?' I really don't like it, but you got to do it 'cause at that point, no one else will."

Now that she's been syndicated for a few years, she has quickly grown to enjoy her success. "It's exciting. I'm the first Black female syndicated cartoonist in the mainstream press. I feel lucky, actually. There's stuff I want to stay. Somebody was comparing me to the comic strip 'Cathy.' She's just this one little neurotic character, who even looks like a little girl. She talks about her weight—I'm not saying people don't get into it, I trip the same way! I know that type of cartoon means a lot to a lot of women, but being the first Black female cartoonist, putting that point of view out there, I don't want it to be just totally neurotic women."

Then Barbara breaks into her familiar laugh. "Some of my characters *are* neurotic, 'cause some of *us* are. But, we're also concerned about gang violence, and we're concerned how we talk to one another. If I can deal with stuff like that in a strip and make the point . . ." She trails off, having made *her* point.

Her strip began as a forum about relationships, but it has evolved into much more than that. "There are some people that say, 'I don't get it.' There are some editors that just don't get it. I like the fact that my characters are adults, and I can put out some adult issues. I really don't want it on the funny pages, because it's not really that kind of strip. Hopefully people will better understand Black American women. We come in a whole array of characters."

Barbara's characters are only heads with hands and arms. Women's bodies, she says, are displayed enough in comics and videos. "It's very interesting how you can change a character's expression so much just by changing the shape of their mouth. I think my first concern was drawing characters that looked *similar* but were different. How do you keep them connected? Even after I had been published I kept working on it. The characters have evolved and the drawing has gotten more refined."

These characters often deal with issues within the Black community that, frankly, some non-Black readers may *not* get. The issue may be discrimination among Blacks of light-skinned Blacks, Black women with hair weaves, and simply fighting oppression. Barbara thinks, maybe, some readers will be enlightened by this unorthodox view into the minds of Black women.

"This is my perspective. That's why the strip is called 'Where I'm Coming From,'" she says with a laugh. "It's *my* take on our experience. I feel really fortunate, 'cause when I'm dead and gone and somebody way down the line is looking at the strip, they can get a bit of our history from reading it. They can learn more about where we're coming from. It's just a different way to record our history. I feel it's a bigger responsibility than just throwing anything out there and trying to get a quick laugh."

Darryl Roberts

The temperature was sixty degrees below zero, and Darryl Roberts was still recovering from the frostbite on his foot that he got during training the previous week. Now on the eighth day of a fifty-six-day trek to the North Pole, he had developed a *second* blister on his heel. This one was beneath the first and was four inches in diameter. A few days later both burst, leaving a half-inch-deep gash in his foot. The pain was *b-a-d!*

"It felt like my foot was on hot coals on a barbecue," Darryl remembers. "And not when the coals are red-hot, but when they're white-hot. When they're white-hot you know that steak is gonna be *gooood!*" He laughs heartily. "And you wrap those coals onto the back of your foot. Every step you take," he says, emphasizing each word with his fist hitting the open palm of his other hand, "that's what it feels like."

Over the almost-two-month adventure, Darryl wore away most of the flesh and nerves of his heel—almost down to the bone. But it

would have taken much more to keep the then-twenty-three-year-old native New Yorker from achieving his goal. As a member of the international Icewalk Expedition, in 1989 Darryl Roberts became the youngest person and the second Black man ever to stand on the North Pole. He is also the youngest person ever to travel across the Arctic Ocean (the Arctic Ocean is frozen on the surface) and the second Black man to do so.

The Icewalk Expedition marked the eightieth anniversary of Admiral Robert Peary's and Matthew Henson's pole journey. Although Peary is often given the credit as the first man to reach the North Pole, his Black colleague, Matthew Henson, is considered by many historians to be the first. Despite this, Henson died in virtual obscurity.

It was the group's British leader, Robert Swan, whose idea it was to include a Black American on this trip. Of all the people he could have chosen, he chose Darryl even though the Harlem-born adventurer lacked experience with polar expeditions. According to Darryl, there is only one reason why: He dared to dream. To understand this, we must start at the beginning.

Darryl was raised in the city housing projects of Harlem by his divorced mother. When she was twenty, he was two. "She was basically what we would call a statistic. People thought, 'Well, she's not going to do anything,'" he explains.

But she refused to be a statistic. She went back to high school and got her diploma. She continued her education, earned a law degree, and became an attorney. "It was her example I saw over twenty years. She never, ever once gave up. Once I got a little older I started to understand what that meant."

He used her example to guide him through his life. As a young boy, Darryl noticed that whenever any of his friends answered the inevitable question "What do you want to be when you grow up?" they would have the same response—a policeman, a doctor, a fireman. "I remember thinking, if we're all policemen or doctors or firemen, it's going to be a very boring place! I wanted to do something so different that people would have trouble understanding the value of what I did."

After graduating from high school, Darryl studied engineering but found it wasn't people-oriented enough. He then majored in business but became bored with it in a few months. He told a friend, "I'm tired of following other people's goals. I want to do something *really* different. Something like canoeing down the Mississippi."

A few weeks later, some friends invited Darryl to join a relay trip down the Mississippi. Each group, consisting of several kids and adult supervisors, traveled a segment of the river. At their destination another group would pick up where the previous had left off. In the middle of the trip Darryl realized this would be something he would love to do regularly. He had spoken to several people on the trip about his desire. "The next night, under the starriest sky I had ever seen, they asked me to work with them."

Darryl had been unaware that during the trip they had been teaming him up with the problem kids. "I just thought, 'Oh, great! I get a chance to make more friends,'" he says, laughing. "By the end of the day they weren't a problem!"

At nineteen, Darryl moved on to work with the Outward Bound program as an intern. Outward Bound takes people and makes them face physical challenges in the great outdoors. By being pushed to acknowledge their fears and doubts, they learn self-discipline and develop self-esteem. At seventeen and eighteen, the kids in the program were not much younger than their counselor. "It's a hard line to walk, to keep their respect *and* be playful.

"I said, 'In a year I want to be an Outward Bound *instructor.*' I became an instructor in *less* than a year. I saw that this pattern of setting goals for myself was working."

While on an Outward Bound trip in Maryland, Darryl thought, "What would be the most difficult thing I could ever do physically, mentally, and spiritually? Working with people can be extremely difficult. And working in the out-of-doors is never easy, because you can't control nature. Most of all, I want to work in the extreme cold because I cannot *stand* the cold!" His strong dark face shines as he laughs. "If I could overcome all these things in an extreme environment, then there's nothing in the world I can't do."

After eight months of talking to people about his idea, he was told that explorer Robert Swan, who had walked to the South Pole, was going to walk to the North Pole in 1989 and was looking for a Black American to include in the team. Swan inspired Darryl with stories of the efforts of Matthew Henson, a member of Peary's 1909 North Pole expedition. Swan, impressed by Darryl's accomplishments, ingenuity, maturity, and outgoing personality, invited him to join the expedition.

"On the training trip we were out on the ice for five days and the temperature went down to minus seventy-five degrees, and that's a temperature most human beings never conceive of. At minus sixty, if you took your glove off, you'd watch your skin change color as it froze. Minus seventy-five is *dastardly* cold."

Because of his inexperience in such a cold environment, Darryl was unaware of the severe frostbite on his foot, so severe that he was in danger of losing his toes and part of his foot. "The cold is a different sensation at that temperature, and I didn't recognize it."

"I don't know how deep that frostbite is," said the doctor, a Soviet member of the team, "because I've never seen frostbite on a Black man before." Darryl laughs at his recollection of that incident.

"I set this goal. I was at the last phase of what I call my Method of Success. That's daring to dream, writing it all down, talking to people about it, educating yourself about the thing you want to do, and then never giving up until you get there and get the thing done. I said, 'I can't quit.'"

The doctor told Darryl, "As your friend, I know what you're trying to do. You want to go back to New York and talk to kids where you grew up. That's important. I'm going to do everything within my medical capability to help you get through your mission if you simply *try*."

"In my mind I was so determined to get to the North Pole that I was willing to come within inches of dying. I think kids in our cities need to see someone who has their interests so deeply rooted in his heart and mind that he will give everything for them."

Six hundred miles and fifty-six days later, surviving on dried fruit, nuts, oatmeal, *mucktuck* (whale skin), and protein biscuits, Darryl Roberts completed his historic walk. Now he spends much of his time traveling to schools in different cities sharing his story. He motivates kids with his accomplishments—the accomplishments of someone not much older than their big brother or sister, or even themselves.

"In this day and age, some kids don't care. They will kill in a minute, they'll take anything in a minute. We have to have similar tactics but in a constructive nonviolent way. We have to show them an outrageously unconditional display of concern and support.

"Even if your parents are strung out on crack, even if you sometimes can't get into your house to sleep at night, the only person who's going to determine if you make it is *you*. And if *you* don't have that desire to die trying to make something out of your life, then no one else will.

"The choice is up to me to be as successful as I'd like. It just depends on how hard I'm willing to work."

221

Wallace Hill

As best as Wallace Hill can guess, there are only three people in the United States who create traditional African drums by hand, and from scratch. Wallace is one of them, the second works with him, and the third person is somewhere in the southern United States and Wallace would like to meet him.

The Minneapolis Drum Center on Lyndale Avenue South in the Lynlake area of Minneapolis, Minnesota, is a long way from the home in New York where Wallace grew up. It is also a long way from the places where the drums he makes and plays originated.

The Drum Center is a dream come true for Wallace and his wife and partner, Andy. It houses a music and dance teaching facility, a performance space, and a place for Wallace to create the drums that have been a passion of his since he was a small boy growing up in the Bronx. "As a youth, I played with African dance companies," Wallace explains.

Efram Odoc, who was one of the first Nigerian traders in the Bronx, taught me about the structure of drums, what it took to skin and make a drum. Part of learning to play in West African dance companies *was* restringing drums and making drums."

Skinning is the term used to describe attaching the head—the surface a drummer strikes—to the rest of the drum. Drums traditionally used animal skins for the head. Most quality drums like the ones Wallace creates still do, but these days, many heads are made from synthetic materials.

"I was always repairing and making drums when I was a young kid—thirteen, fourteen, fifteen years old," Wallace continues. "I was teaching at the age of sixteen in Greenwich Village at the Café Warren, the Second Step, and all these little clubs. In the afternoons we would play and pass the hat around. I'd also teach classes where people would pay me whatever they wanted because I was so young. I was only teaching what I was learning from guys like Cubano, of the Bronx, and the Cardona family. I played with the Universal Drummers of Life at the World's Fair in New York City and at the Expo in Canada some years later."

A lot of Wallace's drum-making skills resulted from doing things that were not directly related to drums. He explains, "I learned woodworking in the Carpenters Union. My first experience was furniture making with Dalton Summers at the Brooklyn Navy Yard. He was Haitian and a maker of fine furniture. He was the type of guy who would tell me, 'You American Blacks, you're so stupid!' Then he'd grab my hands and he'd push them along the wood to get me to sand the wood properly. Some days he didn't even want me to sand," Wallace says with humorous indignation. "He just wanted me to stand around and push the buttons on the machine because sometimes he thought I wasn't worthy to even *sand* the wood."

"You looked like you didn't even have any fingerprints!" says Andy from across the room as she remembers her husband's experience.

"That's how much I was sanding by hand," Wallace adds. "He wanted to teach me how to make wood shine *before* they stained it. It would look like it had a stain from the glasslike texture I created. It was furniture he would tell me, 'you will never own. You'll just *build* it!' I just asked him, 'How much does this stuff cost that we're making, like that armoire over there?' He said, 'Don't worry! You'll *never* own it!' Wallace can't help but laugh at the arrogance. "That's the kind of training I had. He gave me a raise *once*." Andy laughs, "Five cents an hour!"

"Eventually, I started assembling the furniture. One day, Dalton gave me a set of legs from a very expensive table—not the top. He just left me with the puzzle of how to put it together, and said, 'One day you'll make your own table.' I still have the legs today!

"I wasn't a young kid. I was in my thirties!" says Wallace, still chuckling a bit. "But I wanted to learn so bad how to work with wood. I knew I had to take a lot of stuff from this guy. If I was going to learn from anyone, it was going to be him. He was the best. I'll always be grateful to him for that . . . and his abuse," he says with a sarcastic laugh.

Now Wallace is the master, although he is probably too modest to admit it. He has been making drums for other musicians for years. And his clients, who are among the most notable percussionists around, come to him because of the care he takes to create a beautiful, lasting instrument with which to make the music they love.

"I hand select all the skins," he says of one aspect of the time-consuming process of building custom-made drums. "We own the machines that cut the angles on the wood, and we only choose maple or oak to make the drums. Or also, I've found a wood that is abundant out here called butternut, which is just like oak but it's half the weight of oak, so it makes the drum easier to carry." Different skins produce different sounds; thin goatskin creates a high ringing sound, whereas the thicker calf- and steer skins are flatter and deeper sounding.

"We then ship the drums to New York, and Caly does the metalwork," he continues. "Caly Rivera, of JCR Handmade Percussion Instruments, is an old traditionalist ironworker who makes the metal keys for congas and the bongos and metal timbals. He's famous for his bells—the hand bells, timbal bells, and the little cha-cha bells that are used in all the biggest bands around the world."

All that shipping, it seems, would make creating these drums a time-consuming and expensive process. And in fact it does. "Why do I still ship to Caly for the metalwork?" says Wallace in his defense. "Because, truthfully, he's the best. Some I did here on my own. I had a metal guy come in. I designed it for him and showed him what to do, but it's not the same, because of the experience Caly has."

Wallace and Andy decided to get into the business of making drums by hand not only as a money-making venture, but also to continue a cultural tradition. "The first drum was made twelve years ago. Milton Cardona, who's my longtime friend and associate—we grew up together in the same neighborhood—we got together and we made what is called the djun-djun. It's a two-headed drum, which you play using sticks. One stick hits a bell attached to the drum, and you hit the skin with the other stick. The djun-djun is traditionally strung. You will see a lot of the African dance companies use smaller versions of the djun-djun. They have other names for them.

"We decided we were going to make the djun-djun with Western trap-drum heads (trap drums are the drums rock and jazz drummers use). This way we could tune the keys easily and put plastic heads on them so we wouldn't have to rope them.

"We got Caly to do the barrel, which is the body of the drum," Wallace tells me, "because he also does woodworking. Then he put a metal brace around it. We put the keys on it and then skinned it. Some years later LP [Latin Percussion] came out with a smaller version of the djun-djun and mass-produced them. There went our idea, so we decided to go back to roping them."

Roping is a term for one of the original techniques used to tighten the skin from which the drum head is made. As you tighten or loosen the rope, the skin changes tension. This changes the pitch of the drum, making it higher or lower.

When Wallace and his wife, Andy—Andy is the business mind as well as a creative force of the Drum Center—moved to Minneapolis and started the school, Wallace found additional work repairing drums for local percussionists. As he started playing around town, people began to realize he was not only a talented repairman, but a well-rounded musician and student of the instrument. After hearing complaints and comments from other musicians about the quality of the instruments available, Wallace decided to design his own drum.

"I know what a good drum should sound like, so I took my thirty years of experience in music and used it to help design my first drum. I used one of my favorite drums as a model. But something happened when I made that first drum," he says mysteriously.

"First I went around town and found a guy who could do mechanical drawings for me. Once I gave him the rough sketches, he would do the mechanicals that I'd use to cut the staves [side pieces]. Those I used to put the drum together. He also helped me build the jigs, which are templates to cut the staves. When that was done I'd made my first conga.

"That first prototype turned out a little different from the drum that I wanted to make. It was shaped differently, but it had a nice shape—I kind of liked it." He laughs at his first reaction to his propitious mistake. That drum became the first of the Andrums, "which is a combination of *Andy* and *drums*—like *Android*, because it was a different type of drum," he says with a laugh.

"They had a higher, clearer pitch than I'd expected, with a deep, low resonating bass. The belly was supposed to be sort of in the middle, but it had dropped down lower for some reason. It's quite an art form to get the thousands of pounds of pressure that are needed around the drum to bend it and have it hold together without cracking.

"I was trying to do one thing, and something different happened, and I went with it. Like a strong tree in the wind, I wound up bending. I didn't just say, 'Well, this isn't traditionally the way they're made! I've got to throw it away and make a traditional one!'" he says, continuing to laugh. "If I'd had that attitude, I'd be out of a very nice drum."

Wallace sent the drum to New York to have Caly put the tuning keys on and immediately heard from his old friend. "Caly told me people would come into the shop and the old-timers would look at it and grumble: 'No, I don't like it.' 'No, it's not the traditional shape. It looks too futuristic.' But when they played it after it was put together, Caly said their whole attitude changed; they loved it." The Andrums have become a popular drum for Wallace, but he and Caly still make the traditional conga for their customers.

Wallace wants to work out a permanent manufacturing system that will allow him to make more than a dozen drums every six to ten months. Part of that plan is to convince his New York partner to join him and Andy in the Twin Cities.

Aside from Wallace's adventures in drum making, he and Andy spend a lot of time traveling throughout Minnesota to teach young people about the traditions of African music and dance. In their performances they often have other musicians accompany them. While Wallace and friends demonstrate the sounds and styles of the various West African cultures, which are the roots of most Black Americans, Andy sings and speaks to the audience, explaining their meanings and significance.

"I think basically what Wallace and I do," Andy goes on, "is keep our culture alive. It's up to us as individuals to do that, because they don't do it in the school system—especially in a state like Minnesota, where everything is sports oriented.

"We'll also give the students a little demonstration in various languages; for instance, we'll take certain words and we'll translate them from English to Spanish to Yoruba. Some of the songs we sing are in the Yoruba tradition. The Yoruba are a clan of people from western Nigeria. And we'll do demonstrations where we talk about the family of drums and how that relates to everyone's family, because there's a mother drum, a father drum, and a child, and we describe the certain parts that they play. And we also give them a hands-on demonstration."

"This participation helps the students learn how the parts go together and how intricate and well thought out these rhythms are," Wallace adds. "We let them know it's almost a science to be able to play music *and* be harmonious with it. We help them see where the patterns go and how they can enjoy it. We try to expose them as fully as possible to the West African culture and the tradition of the drums they're playing."

"What makes it important, too," Andy says, "is not only the exposure to the culture, but how there are various parts of the music that they hear *today* and where it comes from. We've gone out a couple of times, and once we've started playing, the kids jump up and they start dancing—it's so funny! They start doing the 'Running Man,' the Hammer, and other dances!"

"It's because they can feel the same pulse." says Wallace.

The audience learns that drumming in its traditional sense is not random banging. Andy and Wallace get across the idea of the tonality of the drum. "The rhythms were also tonalities attached to the language of Yoruba, especially when I'm talking about Nigeria," says Wallace, "because the language is like 'do re mi,' so the drum says, 'dong gong gi.' The rhythms are attached to a song, which is attached to a dance that makes it whole. So it says passages to people who can hear them and understand what's being said and sung, and it makes clear what force of nature they're praising."

And even when they have kids who don't get it and are out of line during a presentation, Wallace sees it as a way to get a simple point across. "If I see disrespect, I address that. I either ask the kids to participate or, if they don't want to participate, I ask them to leave. I don't care if they don't learn a rhythm or learn everything about a culture, the ultimate thing is to have *respect* for that culture."

Dr. Joanne Martin and Dr. Elmer Martin

Frederick Douglass and Mary McLeod Bethune are riding in the back of Joanne and Elmer Martin's car. Nat Turner is leaning against one window, and John Brown has the other. In 1980, it was a common occurrence for these historic Black figures to travel together on their way to a school or a mall to meet with Baltimore residents.

Dr. Elmer Martin, who has a doctorate in social welfare, and his wife, Dr. Joanne Martin, whose degree is in educational psychology, would take Frederick, Mary, Nat, and John all the time to see how the public would respond to them. They were all wax figures.

Both Elmer and Joanne felt they needed to do something to help give young people a strong sense of their *own* history. There seemed to them to be a cultural pride missing from our Black youth. "I realized that something had to be done in terms of passing on certain values, as well as a sense of Black identity and history. I was coaching and sponsoring a

baseball team of little kids," says Elmer. "One of my kids was upset by a picture that was taken of him for our team I.D. He said to me, 'The picture is too dark—that picture made me black.' He was kind of ashamed of it, and the kids started teasing him about it. I looked at the picture, and it was the exact likeness of him. But he wanted the photographer to lighten his picture so that it would be acceptable.

"And I thought, my God! Here we went through all of that effort in the sixties, but our kids still feel bad about themselves. What went wrong—why didn't my generation pass on that pride?"

Black community awareness is an issue of which Elmer is constantly mindful. When he and Joanne first married, Joanne was teaching French and Spanish at Grambling State University. "I think that more than any other influence," says Joanne, "it has been Elmer's emphasis on the needs of the Black community and our need to teach Black history that has shaped how I feel. I remember one day he said, 'Right now, Black kids don't need to learn to speak French; they need to learn to speak English! We can worry about teaching them French later.'

"That was really the start of my focusing on the kind of things that would satisfy our basic needs now, like teaching those kids who had to learn to speak English and learn to read. That was the impetus which lead to my working on my master's in reading."

"Well actually," says Elmer, with a mischievous smile, "I was worried about her getting a job. . . ." The two laugh like people who know each other very well.

Although the Martins have written two books that deal with issues of family and traditions in the Black community, *The Black Extended Family*, published in 1978 by the University of Chicago Press, and *The Helping Tradition in the Black Community*, published by the National Association of Social Workers, both knew that they weren't reaching the people who needed the information the most. A lot of *these* people would never see those books. There had to be a way to convey their message to these people.

"We went to France," Joanne says, "and we saw the emphasis the French put on their history. We also saw the kind of self-assurance that can come from being aware of who you are as a people and knowing that you've made your mark in history. We saw that much of the French people's history is institutionalized. When you walk down the streets of France, the country's history is apparent everywhere, in the architecture and in their monuments."

"And when we were in Spain," Elmer adds, "we visited a monument built to commemorate their civil war—a tremendous monument, it's seven hundred feet across and has all these historical figures. It was then that we started to realize that every street, every cobblestone, and every cathedral was named after a historical figure. But besides all of that, they've got a lot of imagery—statues and paintings and so on—to further commemorate their history and such. We then realized that visual imagery might be the best way to reach young people."

Joanne continues, "That was one of the things that was missing for Black people: Despite all of the talking we did in the sixties about being Black and proud, and about Black being beautiful, we hadn't institutionalized these thoughts and our history. So we had to start from scratch. We decided that institution building was going to be one of the keys to reaching these people we felt it was important to reach."

Years before, Joanne and Elmer had taken a trip to St. Augustine, Florida, where they visited a wax museum. It was an experience they always remembered because being able to stand in the same room with lifelike figures of famous people, many of whom you'd never be able to see, is hard to forget. That memory started to gel with their ideas of creating an "institution" to celebrate the contributors to Black history.

"When we returned from Spain, we started exploring the possibility of a Black history wax museum and were surprised to find out that there were none in the country," says Elmer. "But we also found out why there were none in the country. The people in the wax museum business are very secretive. They feel competitive. Even though they might be in Alabama, they feel that their wax museum should be the only wax museum in the whole United States.

"So we had a hard time, a very hard time finding information about who makes wax figures, how much they cost, everything. Eventually we did find out that they were very expensive—five thousand to eight thousand dollars apiece. But we decided that we would pursue it anyway and maybe see if we could get grant money or other assistance. We used money that we were saving to buy a house, bought four wax figures, and went around to churches, schools, and so forth to test the idea as a pilot project before we got into the larger project. You just don't go out and buy up a whole bunch of figures and find out that folks are going to be afraid of them because they think they're dead people—and we did get some of that. After all, you don't see wax figures of Black people every day!"

Joanne picks up the story here: "We started in 1980. For two years we traveled to schools and churches. We did an exhibit for Martin Luther King's birthday, before it became an official holiday, to test the idea to see just how the public would receive the idea of a wax museum. We quickly saw that we had to become a permanent display.

"The reaction was very positive. We also found that people were beginning to say, 'I saw your museum,'—these four wax figures," Joanne continues. "But the figures were being damaged because we were taking them around to so many places and because they were living with us at our two-bedroom apartment. Besides, I just got tired of going in the spare bedroom and seeing Mary McLeod Bethune's head on the dresser." She laughs.

"But we had a story that we wanted to tell—that we needed to tell—and it was time. We had done all the testing that we could do, and either we were going to push ahead or we weren't."

Elmer and Joanne opened up their museum, Great Blacks in Wax, in a little Baltimore storefront with twenty-two figures. "One newspaper called it a 'mom-and-pop wax museum,'" Elmer recalls. "The response was good. You can set a wax figure over in a corner and you can set a book in another corner, and all kinds of good paintings in another corner, and the kids will automatically gravitate toward the wax figure. And when they ask, 'Who is that?' then we tell them, and ultimately teach them.

"Folks found out that we weren't dipping people in the wax, contrary to all those Vincent Price movies. We had too many people coming down there just to see those twenty-two figures. Buses were lined up. Merchants started complaining about all the buses. We didn't have enough room to push folk in there."

Maryland Senator Clarence Blount introduced a bill into the Maryland legislature seeking a grant for the museum. The only problem was that if he was successful in getting them the $100,000 grant, the Martins would have to *match* it to get the money. "We had started our operations on a shoestring," says Joanne, "taking our own resources. So the idea that we had to raise one hundred thousand dollars in order to get this one hundred thousand dollars was a challenge, to say the least. We decided to close the museum and put all our effort into raising the money."

The Martins had to move to a larger space. Contributions and membership in the museum picked up, and they raised their $100,000. They got the grant from the city, *plus* a $200,000 loan. This allowed them to buy and renovate the old firehouse on East North Avenue in Baltimore, which is where they are now located.

When the new location opened in 1988, three years after the original closed for the fund-raiser, Great Blacks in Wax had 90 figures; by 1992 they had 115. The figures are set up in different scenes that depict each figure's role in history and tell something about the time in history in which that person lived. The clothing is handmade. Some of the authentic clothing is loaned to the museum and could possibly have been worn during the subject's life. Visitors often help out when they notice inconsistencies, as when someone noticed the Joe Louis figure was wearing Adidas sneakers.

The sculptures are lifelike and striking, from Muslim leader Malcolm X to Rosa Parks being handcuffed and escorted off the bus by police in Montgomery, Alabama, after refusing to give up her seat to a white passenger; to Matthew Henson, the first Black man (and probably the first person) to reach the North Pole; to Nat Turner, radical abolitionist and escaped slave who incited other slaves to violently demand their freedom. There is an old woman drinking from the "Colored Only" water fountain in the middle of the museum. The Martins say a line often forms behind her before people realize she is only a wax figure.

The creation of each wax figure is an involved process that takes several highly skilled people. "We have a team of sculptors who work for Great Blacks in Wax. You have to have someone who does just hair, because the hair is woven in one strand at a time," Joanne explains. "It starts out with

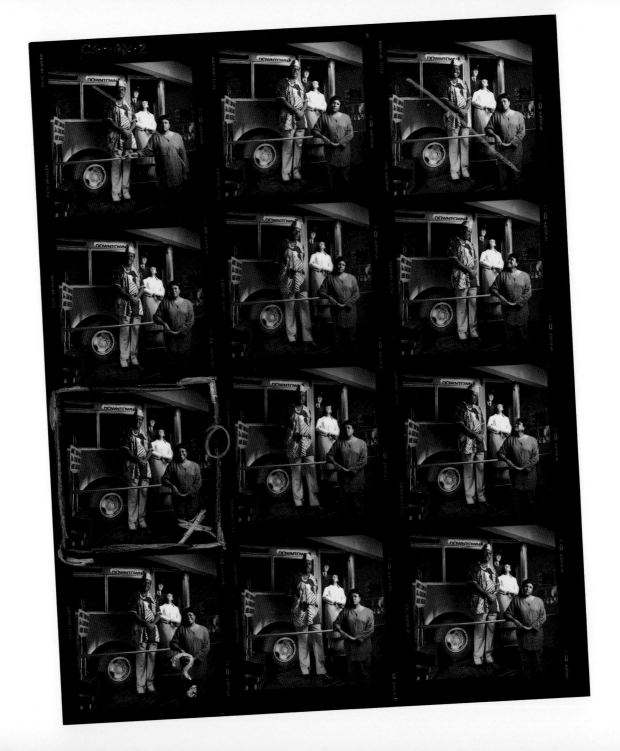

the traditional basic sculpture. Some people do just that part. The eyes have to be inserted. They are made out of glass and are the same eyes that a doctor would use if you lost your eyes. They're medical eyes and very expensive as opposed to inexpensive plastic eyes that you see in dolls."

The sculptor creates a clay model of the figure, shaping and molding the features until they are just right. Next, a mold is made of that original model. When the mold is complete, then the appropriate color wax is poured into it to form the head, hands, or other body parts that will be attached to the finished figure. Skin texture and color is touched up in the final stages.

"Getting the skin color right is a specialized art in itself," says Joanne. "In looking at some of the other wax museums where there might be one or two Blacks on display, we noticed they tended to all be the same color—very dark. And since we sometimes distinguish ourselves by saying light-skinned Black or dark-skinned Black, skin color and hair texture were very important.

"We wanted historical accuracy, but many of the photos and documents we had for the figures are not in color. Elmer got the idea, in trying to figure out what we were going to do about the skin color, to send a photographer out into the streets of Baltimore to take pictures of a lot of Black people, and then we'd match that along with the color and features that we wanted a particular figure to have.

"We tried to be as accurate as possible in our depiction of hair texture and skin color and those things that distinguish us as a people and which vary significantly from person to person. But it is a very complex process," she continues. "In a traditional museum you might just need a biography, but here we've got to get research about height and weight and whether the person had a limp or noticeable scar, that kind of thing."

The Martins hope to expand their museum. Elmer has plans to build an entire slave ship so people can walk around and experience the complete horror of the slave passage. They also expect to handle themes regarding non-African people who have made contributions to Black history.

"We want to deal with Blacks internationally," says Elmer. "I remember a teacher was in here and a kid asked her, 'Has there ever been a Black president?' And I happened to be there and said, 'Oh, there are all kinds of Black presidents of different countries. But there has yet to be one here in America.' I told the teacher to explain to the kids that Black people have been running nations for years, you just have to look out there. She said, 'You know, it never even dawned on me to tell the kids, yes, there are Black presidents all over the world.'"

233

Spike Moss

Spike Moss

234

If you picture America's Midwest, you may see farms, rural settings, and wide-open spaces. The last thing on your mind is probably troubled youth or gang violence, although in places like Minneapolis, Minnesota, and other midwestern communities, both have become a part of the fabric of life.

The Minneapolis-based The City, Inc., aside from the other valuable services it provides to the youth of the Twin Cities, has a program that counsels young people, both male and female, who find the gang lifestyle appealing. Spike Moss, who heads that program, came up through America's civil rights movement. In 1967 he "moved into the Black Power Movement and founded an agency which stayed in the forefront for twenty-some years."

The At-Risk Youth Service, of The City, Inc., works with young people who are in gangs, penitentiaries, or are involved with drugs, and

offers an alternative to what they are doing. One of those alternatives is called United for Peace, which Spike explains: "We bring the leaders of the various gangs in the city together every Tuesday at one o'clock. They discuss their differences and work out their conflicts at the table instead of out in the street. We also provide meaningful employment, educational opportunities, and economic opportunities in terms of developing a business." These businesses usually spring from the members' own ideas. Spike finds ways to channel the talents the gang members used for criminal activity into a positive and productive force.

"The main thing is teaching our brothers how to work together *as* brothers by creating unity," explains the powerfully built Spike Moss. "Showing 'em what they can do for themselves, making role models out of 'em." To show them how seriously he took them, Spike had the group incorporated. "United for Peace has a business. They do contracts of security, at first at concerts and nightclubs; now they're doing security for properties and businesses. We'll be opening up a sportswear store in a community restaurant, which we'll own and also run. By employing gang members and taking care of their educational and family needs, we're helping to rebuild their lives, and we're making them a visible model for their own soldiers to see what can be done." Instead of being torn away from the circle of other gang members and told, "Be good and don't be in a gang," each member can be much more effective by taking their newfound pride and ideas back to their homeboys. They are far more persuasive than any social workers trying to worm their way into the gang's inner circle.

The history of gangs, according to Spike, is that "most of the midwestern gangs came from Philadelphia and Chicago, then spread rapidly to Gary, Indiana; Detroit, Iowa, and most recently, Minnesota. They're mainly from the gangs called the Vice Lords and the Disciple nation. Different branches of Disciples as well as different branches of Vice Lords are here in this town. We also have different branches of Bloods here as well as a Chicago-based group called the Mad Black Souls. If you break those nations down, there's about fifty-nine different gangs here in Minneapolis alone."

Gangbangers are not only male. There are plenty of females involved in gangs, and according to Spike, they are often far more dangerous than any male banger. "A lot of the guys will tell you, 'If you see me with three of my guys and a female, don't watch the guys, watch the female.'" Spike continues, "'She's the quickest to do, and more apt to finish it if all the weapons are not pointed at her. There's something about our females that, when they get ready to throw down, they throw down. I'd rather piss off a brother and listen to his mouth runnin' where I can tell what's comin' next, than upset a sister and get surprised.'"

One incident Spike remembers involved a young lady he now counsels. While they were hanging out at a club one evening, her girlfriend got into a heated argument with another young lady. The first girl walked up to her friend and told her not to argue with the other girl—"just kill her." When the argument continued, the first girl reached around her friend and stabbed the other young woman in the chest. "And it wasn't even none of her business," Spike adds, only half-surprised. "That's why I say they're the most dangerous."

Spike's efforts have paid off in many ways, and he uses each of the group's triumphs to impress upon the community that these are valuable members of society. When a number of senior citizens were mugged as they tried to cash checks or buy groceries, the group's members put on their United for Peace T-shirts and escorted elderly people to the bank and helped them get their groceries. "We have to be visible so the community can see that we're takin' care of a very necessary job," Spike constantly tells his crew. Besides impressing the citizens of his community, Spike hopes to get a message out to gang members on the street: "When you show up we'll be there. Don't cross that line. If we're escorting them old folks, don't you try it!

"I know in my heart that most of these kids suffer from not having the right opportunities, but when given them, they become some of the best workers in this town, and they can be dedicated, committed, and loyal. The only thing being denied them is the same thing that was denied my generation, and my father's generation—opportunity. And that's based on our Black skin color. Kids sellin' drugs will stop sellin' drugs if you give them another option. It's ridiculous to think they wouldn't."

Now that many of the people Spike and his colleagues work with have had a

236

chance to speak to other young people and adults, they've begun to feel confidence. Suddenly, their ideas and words are important to other people—often the same people whose attention they thought they could get only by putting a gun in their face. Spike says that his job is to constantly challenge his group. Each time they make a step, they must be forced to look at the next step—and understand the last one they took.

"I ain't goin' to eat no pork, man; swine, that's poison." This is the kind of thing Spike hears from one of his charges. It doesn't go unnoticed. "'Well, you just went over there and smoked a joint. You're arguing about the ribs, but you just drank that beer and smoked that cigarette. Now that you done learned somethin' from the Muslims, you're actin' like the pork is the only thing on earth that's goin' to hurt you. You can smoke crack, and shoot dope—give me a break!' I can challenge them because I know I have their respect; I trust that nobody will jump on me or pull a gun," he says. "So I take advantage of my friendship, or of their love or their respect for me."

No one tries to get over on Spike. "They don't even want to because the bottom line is that I'm not here to turn 'em in. I don't care how old they are, they 'fess up anyway, just like I'm their daddy. Because they know that I'm not askin' to meddle; I'm here for them; I'm tryin' to try to save their life."

Kathleen Cross

Every day we see African-Americans, Caribbean-Americans, and other Black people whose complexion is lighter than most. For the most part, they are accepted by both Black and white people as Black. However, there are many people of African descent living in our country whose skin color seems to say otherwise.

The reasons for this can be varied; one or both of their Black parents may be fair complexioned, and that was passed on to them. More often, one parent is Black and the other is not. In these situations the offspring are frequently discriminated against by both whites *and* Blacks in our society. "Who do you think you are?" they are asked by both groups, each refusing to accept these people as their own, ready to throw them to the "other side" because, according to them, they are neither Black enough nor white enough.

It is a painful experience for the Black Americans who look white to

be treated as outcasts when they relate in every way—from parents, schooling, neighborhoods and role models—to being Black. In Portland, Oregon, Kathleen Cross has had to spend a great deal of time explaining herself to both Black and white people.

Her mother is white and her father is Black. Kathleen's skin and features look white, but she has spent her entire life in the Black community, much of that time working for issues that are of primary importance to Black Americans. Her parents both gave her a strong sense of identity. But she has felt the need to become a strong voice for Black people as well as for those who face the discrimination and pain she has experienced.

In a story she wrote for *Ebony* magazine, Kathleen recalls a party during her teens where a young Black man, singing the chorus of Wild Cherry's "Play That Funky Music White Boy," made a point of bumping into her and singing "Play that funky music *white girl!*" It took her a moment to realize his tone and cold stare were because of the color of her skin.

"I wondered how I could tell him that I was half-Black. That I lived in the Black community all my life, that I grew up on Marvin Gaye, the Temptations, Blue Magic, and Teddy Pendergrass," she said in the article. "How could I let him know I was raised on greens, neck bones, and sweet potato pie. That I was a 'mean' domino player. That my grandmother still told stories about her mother's life as a slave. I was sure he'd feel differently if he knew that the light-skinned brother with the ten-inch natural standing by the door was my big

brother, and the party which he had crashed was taking place in *my* living room."

While Kathleen was celebrating a wedding anniversary with her Black husband, two women at a nearby table lambasted them mercilessly. Why was that Black man with that white woman? Who did she think she was? There's another "white bitch" stealing our men.

Kathleen has seen people's reaction to her appearance manifested in such remarks many times, and she is far from oblivious to the feelings that are behind it. While her life experiences have not been white, she knows they have not been wholly Black either.

Her skin is white and freckled; her dark hair is curly but far from the coarse texture most Black hair possesses. Her facial features are more linear and angular than they are round and full. Kathleen sees the prejudice among Blacks toward light-skinned Blacks as something going back to the times of slavery. "I don't think we would have a problem with it if we didn't still believe the myth of white superiority. And white people are *not* the only ones who believe that. There are a lot of Black people who still are not quite convinced that Black people really aren't inferior," she says with a hint of anger in her voice. "How can we get beyond that and really believe that humanity is one? You certainly can't do it by looking. If you *look* and you base it on the American standard, obviously white people have more; obviously white people have more access to education. And if *that's* the standard you base superiority on, then we're all in trouble."

As a counselor and teacher working with Portland's Self-Enhancement program, Kathleen comes into contact with students every day whose needs range from dropout prevention to learning how to use their leadership skills so they can help other kids who could use a boost. "There's a lot of self-hatred that goes on in this community," she says. "I hear it every day in the classroom when kids are stinging on each other. Instead of calling each other 'stupid,' they call each other 'Black.' So there's still a sense of Black not being okay.

"Most Americans feel it's better to be a light-skinned Black person than it is to be a dark-skinned Black person, particularly for women. It's a part of our language. I remember growing up and kids playing with my hair and telling me that I had 'good' hair. And because it was a part of my experience, *I* used that term myself. There was never a 'bad' hair. No one ever told me, 'Carolyn has bad hair,' but they always let me know who had 'good' hair. As a result, there's a certain level of ignorance that, if we're not able to rise above it as a community and say, enough of this, it's going to continue."

Her three daughters, Khalia, Akira, and Melody, are beautiful and all "look Black," though they are various shades. One day she heard her daughter say to her lighter sister, "I wish God didn't make me brown." That tore Kathleen up. "It's not fair that I have to spend an hour explaining to my daughter why she is beautiful; that I have to show her all the things that God made brown that are beautiful and wonderful."

Working with biracial children has

become an important job for Kathleen. She helps to fortify their self-esteem, heal their wounds, toughen them up, and educate them. "When I talk to biracial kids, I tell them *they* have the responsibility. It's not fair, but it's the truth. They have the responsibility to understand what they represent, and I say that from my own experience. Because, I know what I represent. So, is it fair for me to resent someone who resents *me* for looking white when I *know* why they feel that way? I don't take it personally, or at least I *try* not to. But there are times when I'm like, 'Look, you don't know me. Get out of my face!'" She has to laugh.

Much of these issues fall back on the famous 'sellout' accusation that is made by many Blacks toward those who've become successful. The argument, says Kathleen, who laughingly admits she *sounds* more Black than she looks, is not totally without merit. Her experience has shown her that many successful Black people will move away from the Black community, rather than stay and become an example for others to follow. It is something she has seen particularly with numerous Black athletes in her own state. She and many other Black people wonder why, when these athletes visit schools and community centers, they rarely visit in the Black communities. They usually visit and live in communities like Beaverton, an affluent, predominantly white suburb of Portland.

"They don't live in the Black community, and I can't believe it's just a safety issue, because *I* live in the Black community. And if anybody would not be safe, you would think it would be me.

Appearing to be white but walking down the street and *sounding* Black makes me a 'wanna-be' *white* girl," she says through her laughter.

Black people, Kathleen contends, by being angry at successful Blacks, are still reacting to what has been a historic precedent, which she thinks dates back to the postslavery years. It was a time when any Black person who had the opportunity to become respected and treated with some sort of dignity by the Whites who had oppressed them would snatch that opportunity by the horns. "When a Black person went to college, or became so-called middle class, we lost them. It was as if there were no way to become educated and successful without losing your roots.

"I think people who are in a position to do so have to go back and say, 'Look, I worked hard to do this. It wasn't easy, and now I want to come back and do something for the people who were not as fortunate as I was.'"

If anyone has set an example by their actions, certainly Kathleen Cross has. She's devoted a lot of her time working for an outreach program called Outside-In. As a counselor with that organization, she spent countless hours helping kids who lived on the streets, kids ranging in age from twelve to twenty years old. She calls her time there "working in hell." Outside-In did not intervene; they simply tried to help youth survive on the streets until they began to realize they could have a better life. "I had a twelve-year-old girl who told me she was going to stay on the streets and prostitute long enough to turn fourteen and get a

work permit so she could work at McDonald's. That was her life's goal," she says, relating this heartbreaking experience.

"Coming into contact with this little girl was what really made me leave there. I realized I couldn't work there any longer, because I have three daughters of my own. It just crushed me. When I first met her, she was in our drop-in center, teaching a fourteen-year-old how to shoot up without getting air bubbles in her veins.

"Now I work for an organization where, if I had to, I would do this job for nothing," she says. A warm smile spreads across her face. "I'm fortunate to be able to feed my children and do something that I love; that gives me hope. And at the same time I'm looking at teachers and recognizing that teachers are the most valuable people on the planet. I cannot believe basketball players and musicians make as much as they do, and these teachers . . ." Her voice trails off, and she shakes her head.

For a woman who is not immediately recognized by her own people, who has faced the daily arrows of sharp words and malevolent looks, Kathleen Cross loves her people and her heritage very much. She has made an effort to further the interests of those who sometimes push her away as a half-breed or "not really black." No matter what anyone else says, she knows who she is.

"There's a statement," continues Kathleen "that comes from the Bahai writings that says, 'Black people are compared to the pupil of the eye, which is surrounded by white. But it is the *pupil* which contains the vision.'"

241

Willy T. Ribbs

did not fit in with the image most people have of Florida. What might have given away the location that mid-February day was that very few people were wearing anything over their short-sleeved shirts. The grass at Daytona International Speedway was drenched, as were my shoes. Hopscotching over muddy puddles rainbowed with streaks of motor oil was the only way to get around.

The noise in the speedway seems almost as big as the event that is about to take place. As you walk through the sea of motor homes and "monster" trucks, the sound of cars gunning around the track is not unlike that produced by a swarm of giant mosquitoes.

Big, sleek, close to the ground, and vibrantly painted—some of the automobiles are just shells while their internal organs are being worked on with surgical precision by racing crews in the many small, open

garages that are lined up row after row.

Wearing a bright red sweater, Willy T. Ribbs is standing at the top of the steps in the trailer of what, a few days before, was a truck. Now it's a combination office, workshop, and conference room. It's big, but so is Willy's presence. As part of Dan Gurney's All-American Racers team, he is preparing for the speedway endurance race, the 24 Hours of Daytona. As Willy explains it, it's not a race, it's survival.

Racing cars is just about the only thing Willy T. can remember ever wanting to do when he was growing up in northern California. Willy wasn't a wild kid or a troublemaker, but his parents felt he needed some discipline and a chance to work off some youthful energy. So when he was thirteen, Willy went to live with his grandfather on his ranch.

"I was a lucky kid. My family had a very successful business, and my dad was racing as a hobby. We had pretty much everything we wanted as kids: motorcycles, go-carts, you name it. So naturally when I grew up, I started driving at an early age. As soon as I could see over the steering wheel, I was racing around in my grandpa's Jeepster."

One of his grandfather's methods of discipline still stays with him to this day, and according to Willy it is the reason for his success. "Work! After school I had to work around the ranch. He had a hired ranch foreman who I worked with. It was a great experience, and it was very important in my life." During school, Willy's grandfather also made sure he did his homework—academics were important to him. When school was out, "I was up at six-thirty in the morning and worked during the day. We were doing things like cutting logs and trees, I mean *hard work*. We'd take a lunch break, then go back and work until sundown."

Willy's grandfather was a good example. He came to California in 1921 and worked for his room and board while he learned the plumbing business. By 1927 he had his license and was doing well for himself. As he started making money, he began to buy and sell land and build houses and apartment complexes. Even though Willy's grandfather came from a well-off family, his father never gave his sons money because he wanted them to learn the value of hard work. "It was very important when we were children to listen to Grandpa relate his father's experiences in becoming successful," says Willy T. "And if he could do it then, there is no excuse for us now. And there *is* no excuse."

Willy T. Ribbs is the first Black American Indy-car driver. There are other racers of color, one of the most noted from Brazil, but Willy T. has set a precedent among American race-car drivers.

Willy decided to go to England to race when he turned twenty-one, and he became a very successful sports-car driver there. He first established himself by winning the Star of Tomorrow formula-car championship. By the time Willy returned to the States, he'd earned the respect of his colleagues. Now he began to take advantage of his familial connection to the business. "A lot of people in the business knew my daddy. He had some help, getting suppliers to give him spark plugs or half off on tires or something like that when he raced, but he had no major money behind him. Because I was around the tracks as a kid, people knew me.

"Because I won the sports-car championship in Europe, a lot of people knew of my success. A gentleman by the name of Jim Truman—who was a big patron of the sport—sponsored me, and I in turn did well. Ford Motor Company signed me and I raced for them and did well, and then from there I went on to racing for Dan Gurney's All-American Racers GTP team."

In the Indy-car division, Willy T. is one of the top drivers; his skills and winning record attracted Bill Cosby, who became Willy's sponsor. "I've been lucky in a lot of ways. Bill called and asked me what I wanted to do in the future and I told him. As the years went by, Bill and I became very good friends—we think a lot alike. We approach life in almost the same way.

"Bill is a no-nonsense individual; he likes to work hard, strives to be successful, and is very confident. And he is very intelligent. So when Bill and I talk, we talk about many different things, not only auto racing. We talk about other sports, and politics. It was the perfect marriage.

"Bill and I started looking for a team that we could merge with," Willy continues. "I knew that Raynor Manufacturing was also interested in merging. They were already in Indy-Car racing."

Race-car driving is not just a sport of endurance, coordination and fast speeds. It is a business, and that's something Willy feels people need to understand. "What I've learned to do in my career—and in my life—is to be a good wheeler-dealer. And you've gotta be able to put deals together, and that's what we did with Raynor.

"My whole approach is that I will deliver what you need, and you deliver to me what *I* need. 'This is what we want, and this is how we can do it.' Very positive. *No* stuttering. No bull. If you're honest with people, it will happen. That's what I've found. Be straight and when the word gets around that you operate that way, the doors will open."

One of the admirable characteristics of Willy T. Ribbs is that he is not afraid to address an issue head-on. Many of the things he has spoken out about in numerous interviews surprise people because they are "sensitive" issues that others prefer to dance around. For example, when asked about the future of Black Americans in auto racing, Willy T. is anxious to make some points.

"It's sad that African-Americans in this country segregate themselves. And I don't want to hear anybody tell me, 'We're *being* segregated!' No. You're segregating *yourselves*. It doesn't make me feel good to make statements like that, but the reason I'm saying it is because . . . Get with it, man. It can be done. I'm using auto racing as an example.

"Anybody can race in this sport. But there's a saying in this business: 'If you want to *play* with the big boys, you got to *pay* with the big boys.' You can come here like the rest of these people, just show up with your team and your crew, file your entry forms, and you can compete. Just *come!* Get a group of people together. But don't come looking like some shabby-back-of-the bus group. Get a group of people with some money together, get good team management, and form a team. Form a marketing group. Create your own publicity, and you can be here, too.

"A lot of African-American media people have said, 'Well, not many Black people follow auto racing because we're not in it.' Well, *get* in it! The door's not *locked* here. I'm doing it!

"Will we see more Blacks in racing?" Willy asks. "Well, we'll see more when we decide to show up! It's pretty simple. This is a tremendous business to be in. It's great! And I have had very little opposition, and the reason is, a person's reputation can get around fast. When you have a reputation for not dealing with any garbage, and you're also *good*, then you are respected. I'm friends with the biggest names in the business. The Andrettis, the Unsers—we're friends, and we've known each other for a long time.

"You can't wait for someone to bring it to you on a silver platter," Willy tells me. "You gotta go get it."

There are many who think Willy's approach is hard. "Sometimes I don't say things in the most gentle manner and that comes from a racing psychology and philosophy. You've got to be very sure of what you're doing when you're driving at two hundred miles per hour. A pure one hundred-percent feel—no wavering. No second thoughts or subconscious apprehensions. Sure, you're going to make a mistake. You *did* it though. Now, if it didn't work, do it a different way."

Willy shifts forward on the big red semi-circular leather couch in the crew's office. He leans on the Formica-topped table in front of him with his hands clasped. "It's important that you're here to document reality, because there are a lot of kids out there with nowhere to go. I mean they have no *idea*. 'What do I want to do in life? Maybe I can't play football. Maybe I can't play basketball. Maybe I don't want to be a lawyer or doctor.' It's good to have a goal and know that you can achieve it, and there are people out there who can help direct you, even if it's only by example.

"I would say to parents, give your children discipline. Make them become responsible by having them do things around the house. And help direct them in the areas that they might want to go in life. Be good examples. My grandpa used to tell me this all the time: 'Kids don't raise themselves.' It starts with the parents. Be responsible."

Willy's message to kids: "Do what's right. Be respectful—it starts with respect. The first laws you learn in life are in your own home. Right and wrong. Challenge yourself to be *good* at something instead of being a screwup. *We* did. We didn't run the streets in gangs. Me and my friends, we challenged ourselves to be good at driving. We'd be out at the track and we'd race each other in go-carts and in cars, because we wanted to be good at it.

"Especially if it's schoolwork, challenge yourself to be good at it. Don't look at the teacher as the opposition, even if you feel that person doesn't treat you with respect. Challenge yourself to be smarter than they are."

Bob Minor

It's not like when he was a little kid growing up in Birmingham, Alabama, or later in Southern California when Bob Minor's mother would tell him to go play in traffic. So what would make a grown man want to jump in front of cars, roll off their hoods, and engage in other dangerous activities?

Bob was always a good athlete and in school he excelled in track and field. He set a record for the 120-yard high hurdles while attending L.A. Trade-Tech Junior College. Within two years he broke his own record five times.

Bob spent a lot of time in the gym working out. He eventually got into bodybuilding and began to compete. After about five years of training he saw himself win the titles Mr. Baldwin Hills, Mr. Val Verde, Mr. Venice Beach, and Mr. Junior Los Angeles. The gym was the place he found his next challenge.

·"I was working out at the gym," Bob recalls. "I was preparing to go on to further contests. There was a guy working out, a stuntman who worked on the TV show 'Hawaii Five-0,' and I overheard his conversation. He was talking about stunts, which kind of made my ear lean that way. I approached him and started asking questions about the stunt profession. At that time I realized there was maybe one major Black actor who was really doing any type of dramatic action, and that was Bill Cosby on 'I Spy.'

"At that time Blacks were used to being stereotyped on TV and in films, playing chauffeurs, butlers, and things like that. You never really saw a Black actor in a dramatic or action role, where he's actually shooting someone, especially a white guy"—he laughs—"and isn't *penalized* for it! On 'I Spy' Bill was with Robert Culp, and they were two traveling detectives. They were working together, so if Bill's character shot somebody, everything was okay," he says, laughing again.

Bob was hoping more Black actors would be cast in dramatic and action roles, and fewer characters would be stereotypes. If this happened, he was certain he could be successful doing stunts. The stuntman he spoke with in the gym told him the requirements for the stunt profession were athletic versatility, mental alertness, and determination—all of which Bob felt he had.

"So I looked into it. This guy sent me to a school that was actually a health club in Santa Monica called the Santa Monica Athletic Club, run by a veteran stuntman, Paul Stader. Paul thought I had the right frame of mind, and with my athletic background and my size, he felt I could probably make a name for myself if I worked hard, which is the same thing I had thought.

"I began training at his school. I started training with high-falls, fight scenes, tumbles, rolls, boxing, some fencing. I started jumping off ladders in front of the building, and then I practiced falling off billboards. I worked my way up to one-story, two-story, three-story buildings. *Now*, I've gone as far as doing a high-fall off a ten-story building."

Jumping off buildings is not something most people consider normal, and even for a stuntman, it helps to have a measure of fear involved, because it keeps you sharp.

Aside from all the physical aspects of his training, Bob realized he was going to have to understand the technical aspects, the tools he would be using for stunt work. "I wanted to be the best that I could be," Bob emphasizes, "so I worked real hard in the gym and I went to Bondurant School of Driving at Ontario Motor Speedway, Ontario, California. I took some classes at a hundred and fifty dollars a day to study American and European car performance. I practiced on regular asphalt and also a skid track. I studied diagrams, I looked at movies. I did stuff in a car that I *never* would have thought I'd be able to do! One eighties, three sixties, reverse spins, ninety-degree turns, and a lot of little tricky things got me ready. But all in all, you still have to go out and practice. You've got to perfect these things."

There finally came a point where Bob knew he was ready to go out and get his first stunt job. This can be a difficult stunt itself. You must be a member of the Screen Actors Guild to be *hired* for most motion pictures, *but* to become a member of SAG you must have worked in a film. Bob's other goal was to join the Stuntmen's Association of Motion Pictures. There was, and still is, a group called the Black Stuntmen's Association, which has an all-Black membership. Bob felt it was important to break into the at-that-time all-white SAMP. "To me it was like breaking the color barrier of anything else, like we always have to do in history to make it. I knew some of the guys in the BSA, and I worked with them. All of us were kind of new at the time, but my goal was to break into this all-white elite group." Part of the qualifications included getting five members of SAMP to sponsor his membership. Bob also had to join the Screen Actors Guild and get a job!

Bob heard about a spot in a film called *Beyond the Valley of the Dolls*. "I went in for the interview. I expressed myself well, and I ended up getting the job doubling one of the actors. That enabled me to get into the Screen Actors Guild.

"My first stunt was a fight scene and also driving a car, hitting a guy with the car as he jumped on top of the hood. The guy's head busted the windshield right in front of my face. It kind of blew my mind!" Bob laughs as he remembers his reaction. "Then I circled around the studio lot two or three times, put on the brakes, stopped, jumped out of the car, grabbed the guy, threw him off the hood, jumped back in the car, and sped off. Then I was supposed to hit a curb as I turned the corner. Unexpectedly, the car tilted up on two wheels as it was turning. Thank God it didn't flip over. That was pure luck! If I had to do that again, I would never do it that way. I would never hit a curb and turn at the same time, because it's too dangerous. But being a rookie, I did what I was told. I didn't know to tell them it was not safe." Bob pauses for a second. "But it *was* a dramatic shot," he then says with a big smile. "They loved it! That was my first movie. That got me on my way."

His next film, *Come Back Charleston Blue*, saw him working on location in New York for three months. One of the other stuntmen on the job got called away for another production, which meant Bob had to double for *nine* actors. "That really gave me a big reputation. I ended up with plenty of letters and qualifications to get into the Stuntmen's Association. So I became the first Black stuntman in the association. That was about 1972."

With the increasing number of dramatic roles for Black actors, Bob began to see that if he worked on his acting skills, he would probably be able to expand his opportunities. That plan began paying off big.

"From 1980 to 1982 there was a white stunt coordinator on the television show 'Magnum, P.I.' The stunt coordinator works with the director to plan and choreograph the stunts. There had been an interview for a coordinator, and I was chosen for the job, but when they called me for it, I had just signed a contract to star with Chuck Norris in a movie called *Forced*

Vengeance in Hong Kong," Bob explains.

"When I got back," he continues, "the person who took the job had other projects in mind, so I replaced him. I stayed on the job from 1982 to 1988. I was the stunt double for the costar Roger Mosely, who played T.C. During the last two years on the show, I earned my Directors' Guild card, because I was directing second unit on *Magnum*. This meant I was directing all of the action sequences.

As a stuntman, Bob Minor has done everything from being set on fire to making a dramatic nineteen-foot leap across two buildings, thirteen stories high, without a safety net. "I've been in situations where I've gotten banged around. I've been sent to the hospital, but nothing devastating. I've taken a few squib hits inside of a car. [Squibs are small explosive charges used as a special effect.] I've had some nice bruises, but I just go home, soak in the tub, get up the next morning, and do it again if I have to. I've been very fortunate. Our percentages are with us more than against us. That's because everything is planned *exactly*. It's a science."

As an actor he has been featured in films like *Norma Rae*, with Sally Field, and *Unlawful Entry*, starring Kurt Russell and Ray Liota. He has been the stunt coordinator for the films *Glory*, *Boyz 'N the Hood*, *Poetic Justice*, *Posse*, and Michael Jackson's music video *Remember the Time*.

"I want to be recognized for my work, not because I'm Black and they say, 'This is a Black show so let's get a Black stunt coordinator.' In no way am I ashamed of my people, but what I'm saying is, it's good

to know that you can be called upon because of your *ability*. And *because* of your ability, you will be considered to coordinate shows with quality talent, regardless of race. I do think that Black actors should remember us as they come up through the ranks. And when they have the opportunity to suggest hiring us, *if* we're qualified.

"Because we have had more successful Black movies now, people like Mario Van Peebles and Kevin Hooks are getting a chance to direct. They seem to know we have Black brothers and sisters that are good behind the camera. They have some of the top Black stunt coordinators and second-unit directors and different department heads available to them, so why not give these people an opportunity to get the job?

"In order for us to make it as a Black race, we have to try to remember each other and pass that baton. And as that baton goes on, it gives us all an opportunity to educate ourselves, and the opportunity to be successful in this business."

He's put in a lot of work to have the privilege of working in movies and the trust of the men and women whose lives he puts in potentially dangerous situations. But having done his homework, Bob Minor is among the top of his profession. "It's like a gunfighter who works his way up and develops a reputation," he says. "I'm thankful that I was able to succeed, I was at the right place at the right time. When I had the opportunity I made the most of it. I am a developed gunfighter. Now I don't have to look for them; they usually come looking for me."

Dolores Sheen

The little flecks of peach-colored paint on Dolores Sheen's ever- present sunglasses were distracting. I was hearing everything she was saying, but I kept looking at those bits of paint.

She was two hours late to our meeting, but she was squeezing me into her already-tight schedule. Dolores Sheen was about to hold one of two press conferences about a new endeavor Sheenway School was embarking on. Yet she managed to make me feel as if I was the most important person she was going to see that day. And just a few hours before, Dolores was painting a classroom. Hey, somebody had to do it.

"Aunt Dolores," as she is known to her 120 students, is head-mistress, publicist, spokesperson, fund-raiser, executive director, part-time cook, and coordinator of Sheenway School and Cultural Center in Watts, which is located in south central Los Angeles, California.

In 1970, the Black community in Watts finally lost its patience and its temper. People were tired of feeling as if they were second-class citizens.

The community was deprived of the same opportunities white people had every day in neighborhoods that were just a stone's throw away. After the police arrested a Black man for a traffic violation, the combination of the arrest, a very hot summer day, and people at the end of their rope caused an explosion of anger. Stores, homes, and businesses were looted and burned to the ground. Police fought with people in the streets. Many on both sides were injured and killed. When the riots ended days later, Watts was practically destroyed. This was the original Los Angeles riot.

Dolores's father, Dr. Herbert Sheen, had an office in Watts, and for some reason it was not touched by the madness. "He built the office from scratch," remembers Dolores, "and I think that was the rationale behind the rioters not destroying it. Because if you had enough money to build something, you certainly didn't have to build it in Watts."

Dr. Sheen decided the only way to prevent such a horrible incident from happening again was through education. By educating the community, you'd give them the skills they needed to go out into the world and make their own opportunities. He decided to start a school. "I asked, 'What kind of school?'" Dolores recalls. "He said preschool, because we had to start early. He talked to everyone in the family, and the members wanted to know how much they were going to get paid. He told them there was not going to be any money, so no one thought it was a good idea. I thought it was great!"

Dr. Sheen wanted to expose children to things they might not hear or see in their own community. Dolores developed her ideas from observing a woman who was the first director they hired for the school. In typical Dolores fashion, they met because Dolores needed to get involved.

"There was this family huddled together in front of their house while these Black children were throwing garbage and stuff at them and at the building. I passed by and said, 'What is going on?' The kids pointed at the family and said, 'These white people are moving into our neighborhood.'"

Dolores calmed the group down and went to talk with the woman protecting her family. "The woman told me she was from Africa and owned a Montessori school. She was East Indian and was born and raised in Africa." Her family had fled her homeland in Africa because the government there had been overthrown.

"I came out and said to the kids, 'Look, these people are African. These people are blacker than *you* are.' The kids looked at this light-skinned family in disbelief. I said, '*Yes!* These are *real* Africans.' They didn't have any trouble after that."

The woman invited Dolores to visit her school, which Dolores did. She learned a lot from those visits. "The Montessori technique is amazing. It is such a relaxed way of teaching. I was very impressed. I took the Montessori course and got my teaching credentials. My Montessori teaching skills and my medical background produced a very different kind of educational technique. That is what created the Sheen Experience. It's like my father always said, he didn't care what kind of method we used, as long as we taught the children how to think."

After their children spent a couple of years in preschool at Sheenway, parents didn't want to send them to public schools to continue their education, so Dolores and her father added first and second grades. Every year it would be the same thing; they constantly added grade levels, until finally they got to grade eight.

Dolores has also brought the world outside the classroom closer to her students. Teaching and learning at Sheenway is not only ABCs and math. There is a small barnyard with farm animals—pigs, goats, chickens, dogs, and rabbits. The animals are not just pets—the children are responsible for the feeding and everyday care of the animals. All of the instructors are volunteers from various fields. "We have a Chinese studies teacher, a French chef, architects, a wonderful artist, a violin teacher, and various computer specialists. All of these people come willing to teach the children. They have a feeling of being able to share what they have accomplished in life, and want to watch the learning experience firsthand. They eventually become attached to the children and to the experience."

The classes are small at Sheenway, typically ten to fifteen students, so there is plenty of time for individual attention. Dolores's goal is to treat each child as an individual with special needs. Most of the kids attending Sheenway are from low-income families. Several of them are former gang members Dolores has personally rescued from the streets.

All the students at Sheenway must pay a nominal tuition to attend. Those who can't pay are usually sponsored by local businesses or private citizens. All students' parents are required to give some time to Sheenway to offset the expense of keeping the school running, because keeping the doors open is always tough. Dolores Sheen has already mortgaged her home to pay off debts to keep the school operational.

The classes that make up the Sheenway program reflect the idea of incorporating the unusual with the usual. Classes like karate. "From the very beginning we had the karate school, because martial arts emphasize many disciplines that are lacking in today's fractured family. Practicing martial arts teaches you to respect everything and to *be* respected. It also teaches you to use your *mind* more than your body, because without using your mind you can't use your body effectively. You learn how to concentrate and how to finish a task. All these are very important disciplines."

Dolores's introduction to martial arts came after her divorce. When her youngest son complained of being picked on constantly, she knew she needed to teach him how to defend himself. Dolores began taking karate, deciding she could learn martial arts while teaching her son at the same time.

"It was horrible. They beat me up every day. They were big dudes." Even so, Dolores earned a black belt and in the process realized how the discipline of karate could benefit her students. "Karate is required here. I've found that the discipline will last forever. I am very strict, but I am also very loving.

And somehow, Sheenway keeps growing.

"These two girls begged me to open a high school at Sheenway. I told them we sim-ply didn't have the money to do it. I thought you needed to have a big football field and all the rest! 'Aunt Dolores, please! We're not learning anything at our school. I want to go to college, please! *Please!*' I said, 'Okay, I'll call and find out what to do,' but I just knew they were going to say it was impossible.

"I called the superintendent of private schools. I'll never forget his name: Mr. Milner. I said, 'This is Dolores of Sheenway School. What do you have to do to open a high school?' He said, 'Sheenway School?' I said, 'Yes.' He told me, 'If Sheenway puts a high school sign on the roof, we will okay it, because we know what you're trying to do.'

"I said, 'Oh my God.'"

She has many success stories. Two are Chunga and Miracle, two young men who, at fifteen and fourteen years of age, got out of the street gangs, thanks to Aunt Dolores.

When someone painted graffiti on a wall of the Sheenway School, a building gangs had never touched, Dolores got mad. It was the first time this had ever happened, and she was determined to find out who had done it. Walking through the housing project near the school, she confronted a group of gang members in a stairwell. "You better get out of here, old lady," someone told her. "You're gonna get hurt!"

"Young man," she said to the one who stepped up, "I know you wouldn't talk to your mother that way. I am easily old enough to be your mother. Now, somebody damaged my property. The colors represent your gang, so I know it was one of your homeboys. I want to find out who it was and if you don't watch your attitude with me you'll wish you mother *was* here."

Dolores remembers the incident. "I was scared. I knew the young man had a gun, but I just couldn't let him think he was in charge. I wanted to run out of there so fast. I kept asking myself, what did I think I was doing?" When she left, one of the boys who had been standing there watching quietly followed her. Dolores knew he was one of the leaders and she was nervous. The boy, fifteen and the size of a man—a big man—stopped her and told her the problem would be taken care of.

A few days later that young man, named Chunga, became one of Sheenway's students. He was so impressed with Dolores's commitment and courage that he was sure she'd have something to offer him. A few weeks later Chunga convinced a younger friend, Miracle, to join him at Sheenway. They have become two of the school's best examples of how the Sheen program can find and shape the potential inside anyone.

At her press conferences, Dolores will explain the upcoming venture—a camping trip with members of rival gangs. She has already convinced a few summer camps to volunteer their facilities. Dolores wants the gang members to realize that in the long run they have to depend on one another. That someone wearing colors different from yours could help you when no one else is available. And what goes around, comes around.

The mural on the side of Sheenway's main building, painted by a former student, depicts the face of Herbert Sheen. It seems a contented face, especially when surrounded by the children he has made a place for, children who play in the neighborhood and learn in the school he left his daughter to run.

Richard

Not every story is about helping others, having a special skill, climbing mountains, or even about helping the community; sometimes it's just about helping yourself.

Fifteen-year-old Richard lives in Imperial Courts, a housing project in the Watts section of Los Angeles. While most kids were in school, Richard was out on the streets getting into trouble with gangs. Trouble with gangs means trouble with the police. He was fortunate enough to meet up with Fred Williams from Common Ground's outreach program in Compton. "He really helped me out," says Richard.

"Make me look good now," says his buddy, nicknamed Mr. Fred, standing beside Richard with a big arm draped over his shoulder.

Fights and absenteeism would put Richard in bad standing everywhere he went. At each school it was the same thing: With so many gang-related incidents, he was constantly being tossed out. Often trying

to stay out of trouble just brought on more. If you don't play along, the gangs make life difficult. You had to either be a part or be a target. His situation was not unlike that of many others, but he knew it wasn't what he wanted, and he decided to do something about it.

"We were running around," he says of Mr. Fred and himself, "to all these different schools trying to get my paperwork so I could get into another school.

"Then when I would have a problem in school, I would talk to Fred about the problems and he would help me work it out. He would talk to the schools and get them to trust me and give me another chance."

"So what's the difference between then and now?" I ask.

"When I wasn't in school it really wasn't fun, 'cause you'd just be runnin' around on the street getting jacked up by the police—you get tired of that. Police searchin' all on you, feelin' all on your personal parts. . . ." The group that has assembled on the street grumbles sympathetically. "But then, when you go to school, you see all your friends . . ." He pauses. "You learn. You learn somethin'

you didn't know about. That's fun."

Richard's classes are only half-days because he does not attend a regular school. The school he goes to was set up to help kids like him who have had numerous problems with regular school. Instead of accumulating suspensions, they are given a chance to learn. The school shares a small building with an adult-education program, and although "The School" has no formal name, everyone in the area is familiar with it. "You need a regular full day of classes," Jim Goins, also of Common Ground, emphasizes to his protégé. "You gotta get those credits." Richard nods in agreement.

He looks down the street to the small school just behind us. "If you don't go to school, when you grow up, you're short on the education." Richard looks down the road again. Something serious is going through his mind.

Someone asks, so then what do you do? "You get a woman with a job." With that, Richard and the whole group on the street break into laughter. "No! No!" he interrupts the laughter, still laughing himself. "For real! That's how they be doin' it, though. There's a whole lot of guys with no job. They didn't go to school. They got

a woman with a good job to take care of them."

Mr. Fred interrupts: "Yeah, but you can't rely on one person to take care of you. What if you've got kids? As expensive as things are around here—a two-pound pack of ground beef is over three dollars."

"Four thirty-four," Richard informs him.

"So," continues Fred, "two is better than one. If only one takes care of you, y'all will stay in the same place and you might fall. But with two you might graduate."

Richard looks at Fred. "Yeah. If you've got a job, your woman and your kids will be proud of you." So Richard is looking forward to this summer, to his summer job.

I say. "You make some money and stay out of trouble."

"That's what I really want to do," he says with conviction. "I want to stay out of trouble. I want to drive trucks," Richard says of his future.

"Big diesel rigs?" Jim asks.

"Yeah, or work on a car lot. Selling or mechanical work. Doesn't matter. As long as it's got four wheels and a motor." Fred says: "He's really good with his hands."

It's nice to have a future.